Special Education

A Reference Book For Policy and Curriculum Development

Special Education

A Reference Book For Policy and Curriculum Development

Arlene Sacks

Grey House Publishing

PUBLISHER: Leslie Mackenzie
EDITORIAL DIRECTOR: Laura Mars-Proietti
EDITORIAL ASSISTANT: Kristen Thatcher
MARKETING DIRECTOR: Jessica Moody

AUTHOR: Arlene Sacks

COMPOSITION & DESIGN: ATLIS Systems

Grey House Publishing, Inc.
185 Millerton Road
Millerton, NY 12546
518.789.8700
FAX 518.789.0545
www.greyhouse.com
e-mail: books @greyhouse.com

Publisher's Cataloging-In-Publication Data
(Prepared by The Donohue Group, Inc.)

Sacks, Arlene.
Special education : a reference handbook / Arlene Sacks. – [2nd ed.]

p. ; cm.

Previous ed. published: Santa Barbara, Calif. : ABC-CLIO, c2001.
Includes bibliographical references and index.
ISBN: 978-1-59237-292-8

1. Special education–United States–Handbooks, manuals, etc. I. Title.

LC3981 .S33 2009
371.9/0973

Contents

Preface

"Special education," frequently viewed solely as an outgrowth of regular education, actually developed from several disciplines. Historical accounts describe special education as a product of superstition, abandonment, and elimination of such persons identified as mentally or physically disabled, whereas religious influences, primarily Christianity, gave rise to a more humane treatment of the disabled. Philosophers presenting early views of the differences between nature and nurture offered alternative theories regarding potential growth of persons with disabilities. Physicians who initially advocated treatment continued to develop supportive theories, which grew to include brain research. Artists eventually began to present a more humane picture of children and adults with physical disabilities, frequently placing them in paintings with aristocrats in order to attain a new view of these individuals. Through a combination of these developments, society slowly became both aware of and sensitive to the needs of persons with disabilities.

Understanding how special education developed as an outgrowth of regular education is necessary if one is to realize the current challenges and controversies of special education. In addition, knowing the special education success stories of John Lennon, Winston Churchill, and others can provide readers with a useful reality base.

In the United States, the Fourteenth Amendment and the civil rights movement of the 1960s laid the groundwork for the many special education laws set in place by federal and state legislatures as well as for the court cases decided in its favor. Head Start, a federal program developed in the 1960s, outlined provisions for young handicapped children. Over time, the rights of special needs students slowly but surely have been secured. Testing and assessment became specifically designed to make referral and eligibility to special programs more scientifically appropriate and less subjective.

Each law described, each program developed, and funding for each special situation has almost always been achieved through an adversarial situation, often taking years or decades before ultimately being resolved in the political world. Senators, presidents, and teacher labor unions have come to understand that they need to actively participate in the challenges facing special education.

Popular culture in the form of television, movies, and theater has—possibly without realizing it—become a vehicle for advocacy. Actors such as Tom Cruise, Dustin Hoffman, Cher, Ann Bancroft, Patty Duke, William Hurt, and Marlee Matlen have brought attention to issues of special education whether through theatrical roles or personal advocacy.

Now, many special-needs children who used to be isolated are included in normal classrooms. This new position comes with challenges for professions in all related fields of education. Curricula are being rewritten, and inclusive situations are being provided. The ultimate outgrowth of this is the greater acceptance of all children.

This second edition is published as there continues to be ongoing research and development in the field of special education. Each chapter contains new information, including: new laws and court decisions impacting special education after 2001; innovations in curricula such as response to intervention, universal design learning, recognition and response, service learning, and inclusion through technology; new policy issues since the passage of No Child Left Behind, reauthorization of IDEA 2004, relationships of IDEA, NCLB and Section 504 of the Rehabilitation Act; as well as additional web, print and non-print resources impacting advocates, parents and others related to this field. In addition, Chapter Six, "Primary Documents and Quotations," is brand new to this edition. It includes quotations and excerpts that summarize the latest trends in the field. This chapter also includes complete reprints of several articles on autism and inclusion. References for further reading appear at the end of all chapters.

My intent in this book is to present readers with all the information they need to obtain full understanding of how special education can serve as a model for all education.

Arlene Sacks

Introduction

This second edition of *Special Education: A Reference Book for Policy and Curriculum Development* is the first published by Grey House Publishing. The previous edition was published by ABC-CLIO in 2001. This new edition includes all the latest legal news, advocacy research, technical innovations and medical advancements that affect students, parents, teachers and health professionals in the special education community.

You will find up-to-the-minute information on:

- Laws and court decisions;
- Innovations in curricula, such as response to intervention (RTI) and universal design for learning (UDL);
- New policy issues since No Child Left Behind;
- Impact of the Reauthorization of Individuals with Disabilities Education Act;
- New relationships brought about by the Rehabilitation Act.

You will find that Chapter 6 is now a brand new feature—**Primary Documents & Quotations.** This includes quotes, speeches, and article excerpts, as well as several full text articles, from a spectrum of sources, including W.E.B. DuBois in 1939, Senator Hubert Humphrey in 1972, and 2008 articles from *Education Week, The New York Times* and *The Washington Post.* This thoughtful collection of documents provides readers with valuable insights, trends, and opposing opinions, usually not included in such an edition.

In addition, *Special Education: A Reference Book for Policy and Curriculum Development* includes more **Print and Non-print Resources**, more **References** for further reading, a current, revised **Glossary**, and a detailed, multi-leveled **Index**, all designed to offer a comprehensive reference that will help professionals and non-professionals alike in their search to advance the cause of special education students in our educational system.

Las Meninas by Diego Rodriguez Velazquez, 1656. Photo Credit: Scala/Art Resource, NY

Las Meninas, After Velazquez by Pablo Picasso, 1957. © 2009 Estate of Pablo Picasso/Artists Rights Society (ARS), New York. Photo Credit: Bridgeman-Giraudon/Art Resource, NY.

Chapter One

Overview

In today's research, terms related to the field of special education are frequently used interchangeably. *Children with special needs, disabled,* and *exceptional* historically have been used throughout the literature. For purposes of this reference text, the terms are used synonymously because all indicate services and education for children that fall outside of the regular education classroom. To develop insight into the vital issues and challenges concerning special education in the United States, one needs first to understand *special education* as it relates to *regular education.*

THE DEVELOPMENT OF REGULAR EDUCATION IN THE UNITED STATES

The desire to educate young citizens equally in the interest of a developing society became a cornerstone philosophy of America's forefathers. Though the Tenth Amendment of the U.S. Constitution gave states jurisdiction over education matters, no state required school attendance until 1840, when Rhode Island passed a compulsory school attendance law. By the mid-1880s, public schools throughout the country had adapted an age–grade level system, categorizing students into grade levels according to chronological age. Differences between students placed in this system became very obvious; strong students graduated to the next grade level while poor students were retained in the same level, or "flunked." In the early 1900s the National Education Association, a national organization for teachers, endorsed the Stanford-Binet Scale of Intelligence Tests as being a useful predictor of school success or failure. The tests introduced the concept of intelligence quotient (IQ), which became a significant factor in student stability placement. Through the 1940s and 1950s educational concerns emphasized nutrition (subsidized school cafeteria facilities were enacted in 1946) and proficiency in math and science. Not until 1965, with the passage of the Elementary and Secondary Education Act, were any federal educational programs in place to address the needs of children from low socioeconomic backgrounds. The Head Start program was one result of this act; it was developed in the belief that early educational intervention would increase the likelihood of later school success.

THE DEVELOPMENT OF SPECIAL EDUCATION

For most of our nation's history, schools were allowed to exclude certain children, especially those with disabilities. How the process of exclusion developed and where it began is quite a narrative.

Prior to the 1800s, superstition drove the treatment of persons with obvious disabilities, such as the severely retarded, mentally ill, deaf, blind, and physically disabled. Many children with disabilities were abandoned and left to die. Witch hunts, burnings, and exorcisms also were common means to an end for such "problem" children. Advocates of humane treatment for the disabled were few and far between. They include a Spanish monk named Ponce de Leon, who during the sixteenth century successfully taught deaf students to communicate; Juan Pablo Bonet of Spain, who developed a method of finger spelling for the blind during the seventeenth century; and Jacob Rodriguez Pereire, who simplified sign language and invented an arithmetical machine to teach students how to calculate. The English philosopher John Locke distinguished between idiocy (mental retardation) and insanity (mental illness) in 1690 by advocating the idea that there is no basic human nature, that our minds at birth could be opened to all kinds of stimuli.

In 1799, Jean Marc Itard, a French physician and educator, expressed his belief that idiocy could be treated through educational intervention. He went so far as to begin describing the concept of individualized intervention, sensory stimulation, and systematic instruction. He did so by taking responsibility for Victor, a 12-year-old "wild" boy found in the woods by hunters near Aveyron, France. The boy had developed no language, exhibited uncontrollable behavior, and was described as savage or animal-like. Hoping to cure his condition, Itard put Victor through a program of sensory stimulation. After 5 years, Victor had developed some verbal language and had become reasonably socialized to his new environment. This demonstrated two things: (1) learning could take place, even for individuals determined by professionals to be hopeless; and (2) appropriate treatment could be continued and expanded on by others (Hardman, Drew, Egan and Wolf, 1990).

The Spanish artist Diego Velazquez in several of his most famous paintings exhibited another example of a more humane attitude toward the disabled. Dating from the 1630s through the 1650s are Velazquez's famous depictions of court dwarfs. Unlike court jester portraits of earlier artists, these dwarfs are treated with respect and sometimes appear in the same painting as the royal family. An example of this is Velazquez's masterpiece "Las Meninas,"* or "The Family of Philip IV," completed in about 1656. In this enigmatic painting of Spain's royal family appear the child Infanta Margarita, two maids of honor, the king and queen of Spain, and most important to this issue, two attendant dwarfs.

Velazquez created other paintings depicting these members of the court. "El Nino de Vallecas" (1636) shows a dwarf named Francisco Lezcano, with additional characteristics of the mentally handicapped, seated on an outcropping of rock; the painting of a jester entitled "Calabacillas" (mid-1640s) depicts a dull-faced, crossed-

---

* See images preceding this Overview.

eyed subject without mocking or exaggeration; and "El Primo" (1644) shows a jester who was in charge of the king's royal stamp. These paintings demonstrated that the dwarf—a disabled person—was capable of maintaining an esteemed role in royal society. Another painting by Velazquez, "Sebastian de Morra" (1643/4), shows how "Despite being deformed and a dwarf, his face and his straightforward and penetrating gaze show no hint of mental weakness whatsoever, though they do express a rather melancholy, introspective air" (Seraller, 1999, p. 55–57).

Velazquez's paintings demonstrate a specific effort on the part of the artist—as well as the Spanish court, since it approved the portraits—to give respect and dignity to individuals with special needs. This is both ironic for a society functioning on a class system and courageous for its time.

As though parallel to the gradual chronological development of caring and respect for people with special needs, Velazquez's work in "Las Meninas" inspired generations of artists to follow. What is significant to special education is that although in the 1600's the Spanish Court kept "dwarfs" as playthings perhaps because they were [considered] ugly and deformed (Benseeson, n.d.) Velazquez kept them included, as part of this painting. Many painters to follow for example: Degas, Manet, Scottish artist John Phillip, and most profoundly the 1957 work of Pablo Picasso who provided a series of 45 variations of the paintings based on "Las Meninas" (Stratton-Preutt, 2003) continued this inclusion. "There is no doubt that Picasso achieved his goal with the series ... into his own repertoire of styles." Picasso, though in his own style replicated the piece of Velazquez and retained all the characters, to include the dwarfs. Picasso painted one dwarf, Maribarbola, as macroencephalic and the other as kicking the dog with his foot (Claustre Rafort i Planes, 2001). In Picasso's version, the dwarfs actually are exaggerated and have more prominence; this is supported by other paintings in Picasso's series of 45, which focuses on the individual dwarfs which are studied, one particularly paired with the princess. This emphasis continues to support the high level of acceptance and respect of these figures as part of normal society.

Salvado Dali followed Picasso in 1958 as did English artist, Richard Hamilton in 1973 with continued inclusion of the dwarfs in their art. These artists, like Velazquez, included these special people, in order to level the subject matter, Alberto Gironell paints the dwarf Francisco Lezcano (also known as Nino de Vallecas) alone, wearing Velazquez's decoration, the cross of the Order of Santiago. The dwarf has now commandeered Velazquez's position. American photographer Joel-Peter Witkin dedicated his work "Las Meninas," New Mexico (1987), to Velazquez to include the maimed and disabled.

Special Institutions and Schools

From 1800 to 1900 the first institutions for persons with special needs were developed in both the United States and Europe. Two conflicting objectives prevailed: (1) to offer humane treatment; and (2) to remove these people from general society. In 1817 Thomas Hopkins Gallaudet, an American minister and educator, established the first American residential school for the deaf. In 1832 Samuel Gridley Howe, an American physician and educator of the blind and deaf, founded the Perkins Institute for the blind. Additionally, Howe advocated public financial support for education and treatment of exceptional populations. In 1834, Louis Braille, a French educator, developed a system of reading and writing for the blind that is still used today. In 1837, Eduoard Seguin, a French physician and educator, developed the first school for the intellectually retarded in Paris using the sensory motor method of application. In 1854, Sequin helped establish the first residential facility for the retarded in the United States.

In the mid-1880s, Dorothea Dix, an American educator and social reformer, secured reforms for mental institutions. She helped the American public view those institutions as hospitals for the "sick" rather than as prisons for the criminally insane.

Toward the end of the 1880s, Maria Montessori, an Italian physician and educator, developed theory, curricula, and instruction for early childhood education of normal and exceptional populations. This developed out of her experiences with the mentally retarded and the poor.

Also at the century's end, Alfred Binet developed the Binet-Simon Intelligence Test, the first scale for measuring intelligence and for determining mental age. Lewis Terman revised the Binet-Simon Intelligence Test for use with English-speaking children, which became known as the Stanford Binet Intelligence Scale. Terman also produced the first longitudinal study of gifted children.

As the twentieth century dawned, Alexander Graham Bell, while speaking to members of the National Education Association (NEA), suggested the establishment of public school annexes for the education of the deaf, blind, and mentally challenged. In 1902, Bell urged that public "special education" be provided for children with disabilities so they could remain in their homes and communities. Work with Helen Keller, her teacher Anne Sullivan, and Captain Keller, Helen Keller's father, influenced Bell's philosophy of education. He grew to oppose segregated schools for students with learning handicaps.

Nationwide compulsory school attendance in the early 1900s flooded schools with thousands of new students, and policymakers had to find ways to deal with children who did not fit the mold. Many stayed in school until they could legally withdraw. In an agrarian society, there were plenty of jobs for unskilled and uneducated workers, so the social or economic ramifications of dropping out of school were few. But as the world changed, so did the issue.

Gradually, more public schools promoted special classes for children with learning handicaps. With the increased use of intelligence tests, it became easier for educators to diagnose children with potential academic difficulties.

In the first half of the 1900s, Alfred Strauss described the learning-disabled child, (identified by the term "Strauss Syndrome") thereby marking the beginning of the field of learning-disabilities research. Slowly, more regular classrooms began to accept mildly handicapped students, and school achievement for the disabled proved greater; however, it wasn't until the 1960s that the federal government took major legislative action to support special students in the educational process.

Growing Awareness of Special Needs

Since the 1960s there has been an avalanche of development concerning special education in the United States. Numerous court decisions and legislative acts now protect those with disabilities and guarantee that children receive a free and appropriate, publicly supported education.

It is important to remember that parents and families are often the heroes in this effort. Politicians such as President John Kennedy publicly shared information about his mentally retarded sister with the country, as did Hubert Humphrey regarding his grandchild with Down's Syndrome. As a result of this sharing, individuals with handicaps have become part of our public awareness.

Buehler and Dugas (1979) in their *Directory of Learning Resources for Learning Disabilities* give examples of famous people with learning difficulties, including the following:

Hans Christian Andersen (1805–1875), author of children's books: Wild variations of spelling and word formation in the handwritten manuscripts of this young man have led clinicians to conclude that he had a language disability—a fact that one might logically suppose would bar him from a literary career. It did not.

Thomas Edison (1847–1931), inventor: As a boy Edison was unable to learn in the public schools of Port Huron, Michigan. His parents withdrew him from school, and his mother undertook the slow, painstaking job of teaching the "three Rs" and other basic curriculum at home.

Woodrow Wilson (1856–1924), twenty-eighth president of the United States: Wilson did not learn his letters until the age of eight or learn to read until he was eleven. Letters from relatives consoled the parents because they believed the boy was so "dull and backward." At school, he excelled only when the subject had to do with speech. But then, wrote a biographer, "it has been noted that dyslexics not infrequently become fluent speakers, perhaps, in part, as a compensation for poor facility in reading and writing."

Winston Churchill (1874–1965), prime minister of England: This Englishman had considerable learning difficulties as a child. Recently, a "dummy" application was sent to his old boarding school, it was a duplicate of the application his family had actually submitted many years before, with only the name and personal data disguised. The school rejected the application out of hand, saying that the boy clearly would be unable to meet the school's standards.

George S. Patton (1885–1945), general and commander of the U.S. Third Army, World War II: Severely learning disabled, Patton could neither read nor write at the age of twelve. He overcame his difficulties to a sufficient extent to win appointment to the U.S. Military Academy at West Point, but even there, he had to hire a "reader" to help him get through his studies.

F. Scott Fitzgerald (1896–1940), one of America's leading novelists: As a boy Fitzgerald exhibited dreaminess, poor concentration, and a seeming inability to learn anything that did not present immediate, vivid interest. These characteristics caused his parents to doubt his ability to progress in school or in the world.

Nelson A. Rockefeller (1908–1979), governor of the State of New York, vice president of the United States: After watching a program on learning disabled children, this public figure wrote the following in *TV Guide* magazine: "I was one of the 'puzzle children' myself—a dyslexic or 'reverse reader'—and I still have a hard time reading today. But after coping with this problem for more than 60 years, I have a message of encouragement for children with learning disabilities. ... Don't accept anyone's verdict that you are lazy, stupid, or retarded. You may very well be smarter than most other children your age. You can learn to cope with your problem. ... Face the challenge. ... Never quit."

John Lennon (1940–1980), songwriter, The Beatles: This young man from an English industrial city had persistent difficulties in school. Lennon's autobiographical writing at times sounds like the product of the language problems that he actually experienced (although it is comically intentional): "I attended to varicous schools in Liddypol. And still didn't pass—much to my Aunties supplies."

Many other renowned individuals throughout history were born with disabilities that did not stop them from achieving great goals. To wit:

- Jane Addams, Nobel Prize winner, social worker—physically impaired
- Ludwig van Beethoven, composer—gifted/handicapped
- Alexander Graham Bell, inventor—hearing impaired
- Terry Bradshaw, former NFL quarterback—AD/HD
- Louis Braille, teacher, creator of Braille writing system—blind
- James Carville, political consultant—AD/HD
- Ray Charles, singer—blind
- Whoopi Goldberg, actress, comedian—dyslexia
- Leonardo de Vinci, artist, inventor—gifted/handicapped
- Robert Graham, sculptor—dyslexia
- Sir Isaac Newton, scientist—speech and language impaired
- Franklin D. Roosevelt, president, USA—physically impaired
- Philip Schultz, poet and winner of Pulitzer Prize—dyslexia
- Charles Schwab, founder, chairperson and CEO of Charles Schwab Corp.—dyslexia
- Stevie Wonder, singer, composer—blind

Additional attention was brought to those with special needs with the passing of the Fourteenth Amendment, which aimed at securing rights for all persons regardless of creed, color, or condition. Professional and parent organizations, listed in Chapters 5 and 7 of this text, advocated educational equality for all students. The concept of "learning disabilities" emerged as an explanation of school failure as opposed to mental retardation. As a result, "special education" became a subsystem of "regular education." As this concept and more sophisticated learning strategies developed, the controversy of leaving some "special education" students in the "regular education" classroom with some additional aid has developed.

LEGAL IMPLICATIONS AND FUNDING

As evidence of the strength of the recent laws and funding allocated to special needs children, over 4 million children and youth (infants and toddlers) now receive special education and related services. Understanding the language and intentions of the laws empowers families to advocate more effectively for their children and strengthens their ability to participate as partners in their children's educational teams. This knowledge also assists professionals in understanding the intent of service delivery system, ensures protection of civil rights, and improves collaboration with other agencies and families. Because federal laws are often changed or amended regularly, keeping up to date on them is in the best interest of both the families of children receiving special education and the professionals who provide services to them.

Whenever Congress passes an act, it is given a number such as P.L. 94–142. P.L. stands for Public Law. The first set of numbers means the session of Congress during which the law was passed. For example, the 94 means the 94th session of the U.S. Congress. The second set of numbers identifies what number the law was in the sequence of passage and enactment during that session. Thus, the 142 means that this was the 142nd law that Congress passed and the president signed during the 94th session of Congress.

Laws passed by Congress reflect a general policy. Once the law is passed Congress delegates to an administrative agency within the executive branch the task of developing detailed regulations to guide the law's implementation. Federal regulations are detailed in the Code of Federal Regulations (CFR), which is available in most public libraries. The CFR interprets the law and discusses each point of it. States and state agencies must comply with federal laws and regulations. In many instances states may go beyond what is required in the regulations (the federal minimum standards) so long as they do not conflict with federal regulations; for example, they may include gifted children in their special education programming. However, special education has elaborate sets of regulations regarding programming and procedures that must be provided in order for states to receive federal funding.

It is important to remember that there is no constitutional provision requiring that the federal government provide education—under the Tenth Amendment, regulation of education is reserved to the states. However, states are required under the due process and equal protection clauses of the Fourteenth Amendment to provide education on an equal basis and to provide due process before denying equal educational programming. Most laws providing for public education are generally state and local laws rather than federal laws. Although some educational programs, notably Head Start, are highly regulated by the federal government, education is still predominantly a state function.

You can become familiar with state laws and regulations by writing to your state's Department of Education for a copy of its State Special Education Law, regulations, recent amendments, policy, or court decisions related to children and youth with disabilities. For example, in order to receive federal funds for special education and related services under the Individuals with Disabilities Education Act (IDEA), every three years a state must have approved state plans to show that it intends to provide a free, appropriate education for all children and youth with disabilities. These plans must be made available to the public for review and comment before they are adopted and sent to Washington, D.C. Dates for review must be announced far enough in advance for parents and other interested persons to appear at hearings and express their views. Each citizen has a right to see a copy of state and local plans for educating children and youth with disabilities. Chapter 2 lists the laws, court cases, and significant acts that apply to special education.

ASSESSMENT AND EVALUATION

Whether dealing with regular education students or special education students, assessment and evaluation generally focus on a student's: (1) ability to learn, (2) achievement, (3) specific learning problems, (4) giftedness, (5) creativity, and, (6) socioemotional adjustment. Any individual assessment is part of the greater whole, the total picture. Testing is only a small part of any assessment process. Data is also collected through student observations and interviews.

In the normal process, a student is placed in the regular school classroom, where he or she is screened to determine appropriate placement or curriculum. If during the basic screening process something in the child's behavior (academic, physical, or social) seems unusual or problematic, an appropriate screening may be implemented to see if there may be cause for special planning and special placement.

Formal, Informal, Norm-Referenced, and Criterion-Referenced Assessment

To better understand how assessments are undertaken, one should understand the difference between *formal* and *informal* testing as well as *norm referenced* or *criterion referenced.* Formal assessment involves tests of intellectual ability (sometimes referred to as learning aptitude); achievement tests; measures of specific abilities such as motor and language skills, auditory discrimination, and adaptive behavior; and social adjustment. Informal assessment includes systematic observation, work sample analysis, task and error analysis, interviews, and questionnaires (Gearheart and Gearheart, 1990, p. 4).

Norm referencing and criterion referencing refer to categories of tests. Norm-referenced tests are standardized at the time they are developed; that is, they are given to a large number of students in order to provide an index of "average" performance. An individual's performance on a test is compared to that of a national or local sample of students of the same age or grade level. Students who earn significantly higher or lower scores than their age mates or grade mates are said to perform "abnormally," hence the term "norm referenced." Criterion-referenced tests provide a measure of the extent to which individuals or groups have mastered specific curriculum content. Such tests are developed "by specifying the objectives or criteria to be mastered, usually in basic skill areas like reading and math, then writing items to assess mastery of those objectives or criteria. The results indicate the degree to which the content or skill representing a particular instructional objective has been mastered; they are used to describe what each pupil has learned and needs to learn in a specific content area" (Ysseldyke and Algozzine, 1990).

Functional Behavioral Assessment (FBA)

A different type of assessment known as functional behavioral assessment (FBA) was developed from the field of educational psychology. It is the process of determining the cause of behavior before developing an intervention. By basing intervention on a specific cause, the application of assessment becomes more functional. To assess the causes (function) of behavior before analyzing and interviewing an individual, one uses functional assessments such as interviews and observations; in order to implement a functional analysis one manipulates different environmental events in order to produce specific behavioral changes.

Observing a person in his or her natural environment and analyzing what preceded the behavior, as well as what consequences followed the behavior, is basic to FBA. Trained behavioral analysts can help a multidisciplinary team create appropriate interventions that meet the needs the child's inappropriate behavior is providing. When devising an intervention program, realistic goals for students and management are important. Setting interventions focusing on positive behavior in small increments is most desirable.

Learning Potential Assessment

The purpose of conventional intelligence tests is to provide a measure representing stable characteristics of the individual they may serve within reasonable limits, as a reliable predictor of future performance. Viola (1997) believes this to be of little value for any educational endeavor "where the prescription of intervention procedures is to modify instructional procedures to enhance learning" (p. 65). In contrast, he suggests the *learning potential assessment framework,* which examines the process of learning and employs strategies facilitating the acquisition of new information and skills. It provides a student's response to intervention by using a test-teach-test format. Both Lev Vygotsky and Reuven Fuerstein have developed learning potential assessment devices. Vygotsky believed social influences are crucial to the learning process and that learning occurs due to a transfer of responsibility based on an interpersonal relationship between instructor and student; therefore, learning and cognitive development are enhanced by cooperative and collaborative experiences. Fuerstein similarly emphasized the importance of the social role between teacher and student in the cognitive potential for learning. Fuerstein assessed human potential and remediated cognitive deficits of all stages and ages of children through adolescence (Lerner, 1993).

The significance of a trained special education teacher is essential in this type of assessment due to the fact that the teacher provides the learning experiences, selects specific concepts to be taught, and interrelates them into the pupil's learning experiences. This learning strategy, or learning potential assessment, is an important part of experiential and cognitive assessment in that it provides detailed description of the student's response to intervention. The focus is not assessment for identification of *who is eligible* for special education services but rather *who is in need, how to meet those needs, and if this can be done in the regular or special education classroom.*

REFERRALS, ELIGIBILITY, AND PLACEMENT

Decisions regarding referrals, eligibility, and placement are specified by each school district. Several factors should be considered when placing a student in a particular setting: (1) the benefits to the student of being placed in a least restrictive setting, (2) the ability of the student to function in the setting, and (3) the intensity of services needed by the particular student. As a student progresses in a setting, a change of placement may be important in order to maximize that child's potential. A change of placement may also be necessary should a child be unable to function in a less restrictive setting. In addition, if the parents disagree with the evaluation of their child and so bring the case to a mediator, a decision in favor of the parents may necessitate a change of placement.

The referral process leads to screening. Referrals for young children are very different from referrals for older children because young children are often not referred from specific situations with professionals observing their success or failures in an educational setting. Often a young child will be referred through a program called "Child Find," which disseminates information dissemination in the form of pamphlets, newspaper articles, and local presentations that promote screening procedures for all incoming students. The purpose of this early screening is to identify children with potential learning problems before they identify themselves. Screening involves various measures to help identify children who may be "at risk" for special education services. Such screenings have been effective in identifying children with developmental delays and speech and language disorders, and it is believed that early identification may actually decrease the amount of (or even eliminate)—special education services needed for many students in the future. There is no labeling of a child at this early stage, and the children, usually referred by parents, pediatricians, and others interacting with the children frequently, generally have positive experiences in special education settings.

Most referrals of older children, already in educational settings, come from teachers recognizing some learning problems. Teachers can refer a child for evaluation without the need for parental consent, though parents must be notified that a referral has been made. The parents must then give consent before any individual assessment of that child can be administered. Although referral timelines are not consistent in all states, ninety days is usually given to complete an evaluation based on a formal referral. Referrals have been criticized as sometimes being biased or disproportionate from certain groups. For this reason, the knowledge base and educational experience of the referring teacher should be considered, and all avenues to keep the child in the educational mainstream should be attempted first. Once a child has been assessed, if placement in a special education environment is determined to be a more positive experience, a detailed, individualized educational plan is developed.

Very different assessment techniques are used for young children, elementary school children, and middle and secondary school children. Additionally, each area of academics has developed specific tests and techniques to evaluate appropriate placement once any sign of abnormal learning is discovered. Within each age category there are not only specific tests for specific disciplines but also observational charts and checklists to make the experience more subjective.

Along with age and stage differences are concerns of language and cultural diversity. As McAfee and Leong (1997) point out, "Fair, impartial, and objective classroom assessment of all children must take into account the diversity found in most schools and centers. Of particular concern in contemporary society are sociocultural differences and individual differences" (p. 219).

Appropriate assessment is essential to the development of schools and communities that regard language, culture, and ethnic diversity as an opportunity rather than a problem. Teachers must be sensitive to the ways children and families from different cultures and backgrounds respond to the assessment approaches used and make adjustments as necessary. The wide variety of classroom assessment methods and contexts now available makes this possible (McAfee and Leong, 1997).

Assessment techniques for very young children (ages 0–5) usually involve not only the child but the parent(s) and other family members and are often required for purposes of family intervention services. Formalized testing for remedial or therapeutic purposes, as is used with older children, is not applicable to this age group. This presents many challenges and requires excellent communications skills on the part of educators.

Assessment of elementary, middle, and secondary school-age children is a complicated task involving formalized tests; informal assessments; cognitive and adaptive behavior scales; appropriate reading, math, and language instruments; assessments of sensory, perceptual, and motor skills; career, vocational, and transition-related assessments; and gifted, talented, and creativity assessments. It is important to remember that all these assessments must take into consideration the laws and regulations that apply to placement and special services. Additionally, effective instruction, setting specific objectives, and managing and evaluating such instruction are all part of appropriate assessment.

As there is no nationwide special education classification system, it is possible to diagnose a child as disabled in one state and not in another. Often, placement based on assessment and evaluation needs to consider the number of deficits, severity of disability, and the complexity and intensity of intervention. Assessment may be the emphasis, but multiple factors are considered before placement.

ASSESSMENT ISSUES WHEN PROVIDING FOR DUAL EXCEPTIONALITIES FOR THE GIFTED

Gifted students with disabling conditions, remain a major group of underserved and underestimated youth (Cline and Schwartz, 1999). Often times, greater consideration must be given to the disability than to the superior intellectual ability; in such cases, appropriate assessment is a particular challenge.

To begin with, assessment processes such as standardized tests and observational checklists, which are necessary for appropriate curriculum development, require major modification when applied to children with so-called dual exceptionalities. Two examples are the hearing-impaired gifted child who cannot respond to oral directions and may lack vocabulary that truly reflects his or her complex thought processes; and the speech- and language-impaired gifted child who cannot respond to tests requiring verbal responses. Other examples include visually impaired gifted children who are unable to respond to specific performance measures—although their vocabulary may be advanced, they may not understand the meaning of words they use (e.g., color words); and learning-disabled gifted children who may use high-level vocabulary but cannot express themselves in writing.

INDIVIDUALIZED EDUCATIONAL PLAN AND ASSESSMENT

The Individuals with Disabilities Education Act requires that each special education student receive a full individualized educational plan (IEP). This plan is the key to planning services for all children and youth with disabilities. The IEP team documents which parts of the general curriculum are relevant to each special education student. With regard to state assessments, if the student's current curriculum and program address areas parallel to part of the assessment, then only that part should be maintained. If the curriculum goals are unique to that student and not evaluated in a general assessment, the student cannot be assessed by that portion, and a modified assessment plan can be developed. Examples of modifications include deleting certain test items or sections, or substituting items and/or assessment tasks. Alternate assessments designed to reflect the individual circumstances of the student are intended to level the playing field for students with disabilities. These accommodations are intended to provide access to tests, not to alter the essential elements of the test.

Specific areas to be included in the IEP are present levels of educational performance, noted by test scores; and measurable annual goals, including benchmark and short-term objectives specific to the disability. Included with the objectives are ways to measure the child's progress or lack of it in the special education program. Objective testing to indicate real progress is the way to be certain the IEP goals are being achieved. If a child is not making progress as outlined in the goals, the IEP needs to be revised.

Special education programs rely on assessment procedures developed from the laws concerning persons with disabilities. Section 504 of the Rehabilitation Act and the Americans with Disability Act of 1990 require entities receiving federal funds to make accommodations for the handicapped in order to protect the individual's rights for being discriminated upon on the basis of a disability. If students are excluded from assessments that lead to special programs, their opportunity for postsecondary education and employment ultimately will be limited, thereby resulting in a form of illegal discrimination. IEPs must therefore be very specific so that there is a clear link between what the student was taught and what the assessments measured (Shriner, 2000).

TYPES OF ASSESSMENTS FOR EXCEPTIONAL EDUCATION STUDENTS

Individual Tests of Intellectual Functioning

Kaufman Assessment Battery for Children (K-ABC)

- Kaufman Infant and Preschool Scale
- McCarthy Scales of Children's Abilities
- Stanford-Binet Intelligence Scale–Fourth Edition
- Wechsler Adult Intelligence Scale–III (WAIS-R)
- Wechsler Intelligence Scale for Children–Revised (WISC-III)
- Wechsler Preschool and Primary Scale of Intelligence–Revised (WPPSI-R)

Tests of Academic Achievement

- Basic School Skills Inventory (diagnostic version)
- Brigance Diagnostic Inventory of Early Development
- Kaufman Test of Educational Achievement (K-TEA)
- Key Math
- Test of Early Mathematical Abilities (TEMA)–2
- Test of Early Reading Ability (TERA)–2
- Test of Early Written Language (TEWL)
- Test of Written Language 2 (TOWL-2)
- Test of Written Spelling (TWS)
- Woodcock-Johnson Psycho-Educational Battery–Revised (achievement)
- Woodcock Reading Mastery Test–Revised

Assessment of Social/Emotional Behavior

- Behavior Evaluation Scale
- Behavior Problem Checklist (Quay and Peterson)
- Burke's Behavior Rating Scale
- Child Behavior Checklist (Achenbach)
- Children's Personality Questionnaire (CPQ)
- Devereaux Adolescent Behavior Rating Scale
- Devereaux Child Behavior Rating Scale
- Devereaux Elementary School Behavior Rating Scale
- Goodenough-Haris Drawing Test
- High School Personality Questionnaire (HSPQ)
- Minnesota Multiphasic Personality Inventory (MMPI)
- Piers-Harris Children's Self-Concept Scale
- Thematic Apperception Test
- Walker Problem Behavior Identification Checklist

Assessment of Adaptive Behavior

- Comprehensive Test of Adaptive Behavior (CTAB)
- Scales of Independent Behavior (SIB)
- Vineland Adaptive Behavior Scales (VABS)

Assessment of Psychological Processes

- Bender Visual Motor Gestalt Test
- Detroit Tests of Learning Aptitude (DTLA-2 and DTLA-P)
- Developmental Test of Visual-Motor Integration–Revised
- Test of Adolescent Language (TOAL-2)
- Test of Language Development–2 (Primary or Intermediate)
- Woodcock-Johnson Psycho-Educational Battery–Revised (cognitive)
- Woodcock Language Proficiency Battery

FULL-SERVICE SCHOOLS

The *full-service school* is a term that was coined in 1991 when the Florida state legislature passed statute 402.3026. This legislation supports the establishment of partnerships between the State Board of Education and the Department of Health and Rehabilitative Services for the purpose of identifying and meeting the needs of at-risk students (Dryfoos, 1994).

Coordination is the foundation of the full-service concept; diverse agencies are required to work together to provide integrated education, health, and social services to eligible families. The full-service school is an umbrella term that encompasses a variety of models, including family resource centers, school-based health centers, and community or neighborhood schools. Regardless of the label, its mission is to eliminate barriers to student achievement through programs designed to involve children and parents on the school grounds. The full-service school seeks to create a "one-stop" shop that will meet the needs of the diverse population it serves, with an expanded curriculum appropriate to both regular- and special education children. Programs at full-service schools often include parent education, life skills, adult basic education, teen pregnancy groups, dropout prevention, and substance abuse programs (Burnett, 1994).

As every community has its own characteristics, there is as yet no district or state-mandated blueprint for building full-service schools. They are, rather, ongoing projects that evolve as the needs of the community change. The foundation of the design is poured when specific questions are answered:

- Who will be the stakeholders in the community's school?
- What are the unique needs of the community?
- What special services need to be provided to respond to those needs?
- Where will these services be housed?
- When will they be delivered?
- How can the program ensure that services are delivered in a cohesive and effective manner?

A full-service school should reflect the best practices in community partnerships. This community involvement offers specific benefits for children with special needs if health services, transition facilities, and social services are involved in the education plan. Where collaboration is real, you are likely to find principals who are willing to lead and take some risks. They understand that the school alone cannot do the job of helping all children succeed and that sharing this responsibility means forging partnerships built on reciprocity, in which the school exchanges information, services, support, and benefits with its families and communities (Davies, 1996).

Key to the success of these cooperative relationships is the establishment of common goals and desired outcomes. Special education children require specific outcomes, goals, and objectives that must be reviewed annually. Their needs can be met more easily in a school community union that closely monitors the extent and integrity of its collaborations so as to avoid fragmentation and duplication of services. Ongoing communication between community participants and defined interagency agreements can minimize barriers to an effective service delivery plan. Sharing a facility allows for more practical use of space and increases opportunities for sharing information among educators and with families.

By linking schools with support services, families begin to view their neighborhood school as a hub for "inclusion" rather than "exclusion." In far too many communities across the country there are few interactions between family and schools. A change in the education and social service paradigm calls for a "whole family" philosophy. The creation of a full-service school partnership program that collaborates with community agencies can contribute to the elimination of basic barriers to family empowerment. In this way, schools and communities can work together to mitigate environmental conditions that place our children at-risk of school failure.

MAINSTREAMING

Mainstreaming refers to placing special-needs children in the least restrictive educational environment, the regular classroom. It is not to be confused with *inclusion,* which will be discussed later in this chapter. The concept of mainstreaming developed after federal laws were passed requiring students to learn within the "least restrictive environment" (LRE). Prior to that, special education was considered a separate situation with separate classes and, sometimes, separate schools. Mainstreaming was typically done on a voluntary basis when special education teachers received permission from general education colleagues for their students to spend time in the others' classroom (Brantlinger, 1997).

Under the new laws, although students could be categorized with separate learning difficulties, they still needed to be integrated into as normal an educational placement as possible. Because various educators, judges, parents, and advocates interpreted the laws' intent differently, several interpretations of mainstreaming developed. According to the National Association of State Boards of Education (1992), "mainstreaming refers to assigning a student with disabilities to a general education classroom for part or all of the school day" (p. 187). This means that a child with learning challenges in reading, for example, could be put in a special class for reading, but for the rest of the school day, the least restrictive environment might be the regular classroom. Similarly, if a child had reading and math challenges, he or she could still be placed with regular-education children for physical education, art, music, social studies, and science.

A myriad of situations developed with the hope of mainstreaming the special education student into the "mainstream" of society. The reasons for this were socialization, peer interaction, and movement out of special education classes as soon as possible. To assume (1) that physically placing students in regular classrooms would increase social interaction between the two groups, (2) that mainstreaming would increase the social acceptance of exceptional students by nonhandicapped peers, (3) and that special education students would imitate appropriate behaviors of regular class peers was taking a concept and making it a process based on hope—and a misinterpretation of public laws regarding appropriate environments and placements. Additionally, those most responsible for the act of mainstreaming a special education student into the regular classroom—the teachers—were the least prepared for this challenge. Regular education teachers had little training in dealing with individual differences and specific instructional processes developed for special-needs students. Preparing instruction for groups is very different from preparing an individualized plan. The roles and responsibilities of regular education teachers were never clearly defined in this process. In most cases, regular education teachers and their regular education students were not prepared for the mainstreaming process.

In 1992 the National Association of State Boards of Education (NASBE) completed a study group on special education and found poor outcomes with regard to the unnecessary segregation and labeling of children for special services, and the "ineffective practice of mainstreaming, which has splintered the school life of many students—both academically and socially." The study identified a vast bureaucracy that has developed to educate students labeled as disabled. "This bureaucracy is characterized by separate and parallel policies for special education students and staff; separate funding mechanisms; separate administrative branches and divisions at the federal, state, intermediate, and local levels; a system of classification for labeling children that is considered by many to be demeaning and nonfunctional for instructional purposes; and a separate cadre of personnel, trained in separate pre-service programs, who serve only students with diagnosed disabilities" (NASBE, 1992, p. 187).

Choate's 1993 research indicates that there are no definitive answers regarding the most appropriate placement options for students with disabilities, and decades of studies have failed to produce a specific alternative for the most appropriate placement; some studies suggest gains due to regular rather than special education placement, while others do not. Important in Choate's findings are simple explanations influencing mainstreaming, such as: Schools and school systems vary in their mainstreaming practices; there are very few uniform process guidelines for mainstreaming; no two schools use the same assessment placement decisions or options; and instruments used to measure the effects of effective placement vary. These findings affect how one views the success or failure of mainstreaming and how well it compares, theoretically and in practice, with inclusion.

INCLUSION

From these discussions on mainstreaming and guided by the concept of the least restrictive environment, the concept of inclusion was created. For example, placing children within the least restrictive environment was interpreted to mean that to the maximum extent appropriate, children with disabilities are to be educated with nondisabled children. Special classes, separate schools, and removing disabled children from the regular educational environment can occur only if the nature of the disability is such that a regular education class with the use of supplementary aids and services cannot be achieved satisfactorily. According to the concept of inclusion, special education students should attend their home school with their age and grade peers, all day, in the regular education classroom rather than being pulled out of regular classrooms to receive special services. This is in accordance with the regular education initiative (REI), a position held by some special educators that students with disabilities should be served exclusively in regular education classrooms and should not be "pulled out" to attend special classes.

The inclusion system posits that support services should be brought to the child and presumes that the child will benefit from being in that class. Full inclusion connotes full-day placement for all students, regardless of handicapping condition.

Because the IDEA never uses the term *inclusion,* there is debate surrounding what is legally enforceable by the courts. Recent legal action, cited in Chapter 2, such as *Greer vs. Rome City School District,* 11th Circuit Court, 1992; *Sacramento City Unified School District vs. Holland,* 9th Circuit Court, 1994; and *Oberti vs. Board of Education of the Borough of Clementon School District,* 3rd Circuit Court, 1993, indicate that an inclusive setting appears to be the interpretation of the original law.

The initial targeted special populations were for students who were in the range of mild disability and had some academic proficiency. No longer will they be in special sections of the school building in general education classrooms with in-classroom support. Learning is no longer viewed in terms of all students completing all tasks at the same time; rather, a more fluid classroom environment and a lessening of the role of the regular classroom teacher in directing and controlling all activity has made inclusion possible. If students are encouraged to gain a deeper understanding of material as opposed to memorizing facts, and if regular education teachers are encouraged to work in collaboration with special education teachers, support personnel such as occupational and instructional therapists, and parents, an inclusive classroom offers the opportunity for team success. According to Galis and Tanner (1995), "a more moderate view of inclusion is that placement committees should use inclusion as one delivery model for providing the least restrictive environment in continuance of service deliver models" (p.2).

The effects of inclusion are being felt not only in elementary, middle, and secondary schools but also in early childhood settings. In Malmskog and McDonnell's 1999 article *Teacher-Mediated Facilitation of Engagement by Children with Developmental Delays in Inclusive Preschools*, the authors state, "With normalized peer interactions identified as an important goal of inclusion, significant levels of adult-child interaction patterns may have a negative effect on overall development and social relationships" (p. 213). Their study's teacher-mediated intervention procedures provide an appropriate balance by providing high levels of modeling in an inclusive setting.

In India the Union Ministry of Welfare began in the 1970s to recommend integrating special education children into the common schools once their communication and daily living skills were at a functional level. This focus from special education to integrated education has developed in the 1990s toward inclusion similar to that in the United States. Anupreza Chadha (1999) points out several obstacles she believes prevalent in India:

- Does the country have the resources for equipping teachers with specialized skills/competencies, or making curricula disability sensitive, or addressing prejudices of children?
- Even in highly educational socioeconomic schools, only partial integration has been achieved. Most disabled children are integrated only for social activities, not in academic areas.

- Disability is described as a problem, not a priority. Building access and accommodations for the handicapped are not prevalent.
- Not all regular education teachers have the attitude that they are responsible for all children assigned to them, regardless of the handicap. (pp. 32, 33)Chadha's comments regarding inclusion as it exists in India are similar to experiences encountered internationally. Her advocacy for inclusion is based on the belief that schools isolating special education students deprive those children of opportunities for social interaction with their peers. Additionally, urban areas can provide necessary money and equipment for children with special needs whereas rural schools cannot. She believes inclusion in India needs to change in three directions: (1) movement toward school diversity, (2) movement from a teacher-centered approach to a student-centered approach, and (3) movement toward changing the view of a school as a provider of educational services to that of educational support.

Additionally, Baum and Wells (1990) in their article *Promoting Handicap Awareness in Preschool Children* write that "research suggests that the most opportune time to initiate planned instruction concerning handicapping conditions, particularly those that are more highly visible is during the preschool and primary years" (p. 45).

Technology's Role in Classroom Inclusion

Adding to the success of inclusion is the use of technology, which can be integrated into the curriculum to facilitate learning objectives through a range of activities. Appropriate technology in the regular school classroom for special education students keeps those students involved in that classroom. Using technology in the form of adaptive input and output devices assists students with disabilities while keeping them in the least restrictive environment.

Students with mild mental handicaps, learning disabilities, or behavioral disorders such as hyperactivity or attention deficits are frequently instructionally integrated for academic subjects, especially at the middle or high school level. Sequential presentations, along with special organizational strategies, help these students succeed. Technology can aid both the regular education and special education student to stay on a task longer since it is visually more stimulating as well as motivating.

Especially effective with students with disabilities are software tools such as word processing, databases, and spreadsheets. For student with emotional disabilities, the computer offers a personalized learning environment without complications of adult interactions or even peer interaction. Students with attention difficulties often appear to attend longer and more consistently to tasks presented on the computer (Center for Special Education Technology, 1990).

Initially, computer-assisted instruction (CAI) programs were developed for all students and were predominantly limited to drill and practice programs, tutorials, and simulations. As time went on, research focused on how technology could be applied to the "low-incident" populations of the hearing, visually, mentally, and physically disabled. Beginning in the early 1980s, the U.S. Department of Education's Office of Special Education Program funded work research in the use of technology for students with disabilities. The potential for CAI to raise academic achievement for children with mild and moderate disabilities is now viewed as positive (Woodward and Rieth, 1997).

Provenzo, Brett, and McCloskey (1999) explain how computers, adaptive computer interfaces, and specialized software are especially important to children with disabilities. They believe output devices such as monitors, printers, and speakers can be adapted for children with disabilities in order to encourage access. Adaptive input devices enable children with special needs to activate and send information: Keyboards can be modified, and alternative keyboards (usually larger in size) can provide access. Touch Windows, a touch-sensitive screen, is a direct way for students with disabilities to interact with the computer. Output devices such as monitors with enlarged text and graphics, printers producing large print or Braille, tactile devices produced using Braille, output hardware, and speakers are important for children with disabilities and also help meet the criteria mandated by the IDEA.

Assistive technology may appear in three places in the IEP: (1) in the annual goals and short-term objectives, (2) in the listing of supplementary aids and services necessary to maintain the student in the least restrictive setting, and (3) in the list of related services necessary for the student to benefit from his or her education.

When using assistive technology as part of the annual goals and short-term objectives of an IEP, the goal must be specific as to the role of assistance the technology will provide and how and why the technology will be used to accomplish this particular goal. It also must include which academic or social skill will be acquired.

As part of supplementary aids and services, assistive technology may be used to facilitate a student's ability to remain in the least restrictive environment by helping the student perform specific educational and social tasks. If assistive technology is necessary as a supplementary aid, its presence must support the student sufficiently to maintain the placement, and its absence would require the student's removal to a more restrictive setting. An example of this would be a student with multiple physical disabilities who could only make independent educational progress on his or her IEP goals in the regular classroom with the use of a computer and an augmentative communication device but could not make such progress in that setting without the devices.

Related services are mandated by the IDEA. Examples of these include transportation, speech pathology and audiology, psychological services, physical and occupational therapy, recreation, and social work. The federal law provides for almost all necessary developmental, corrective, or support services as may be required to assist a child with a disability to benefit from special education. The individual states have legislated additional related service requirements to include mobility training, training necessary for successful use of augmentative communication devices, and occupational therapy to include positioning in order to take advantage of assistive technology, computer keyboards, and communication boards (RESNA, 1999). Specific information with regard to technology for special education and how to access such technology is presented in Chapter 4.

Realities of Inclusion for Regular and Special Education Teachers

Despite the trend to meet the goals of the regular education initiative (REI) as well as full inclusion, one recent study found that regular education teachers generally do not support inclusion, nor do they believe they possess the competencies necessary to effectively instruct children with disabilities (Minke, Bear, Deemer, and Griffin, 1996). Furthermore, the study identified that many regular education teachers do not believe the regular classroom is the setting in which these students' needs can be adequately met. The attempts of regular education teachers to make adaptations in instruction were indicated as being few. They tended to be hesitant unless they were provided sufficient protected resources (instructional resources tagged solely to serve low-achieving students). Regular education teachers outside of a collaborative situation were most negative regarding inclusion. This study shows the importance of continued collaboration, protected resources, and careful selection of teachers in inclusive schools.

Teachers' Experiences with Inclusive Classrooms

Additional realities regarding inclusion for students with mild disabilities include:

- Continued inadequate allocation of resources, even when the role of special educators has been revised from one of direct service to one in which they provide assistance to the general educators; it is now the general educator who has the instructional responsibility for students with disabilities;
- The general education classroom is now confronted with the reality of teaching to the lowest achieving student; and
- How do educators make the idea of "inclusion" result in successful intended academic outcomes for students with mild disabilities as well as regular education students? (Deno, Foegen, Robinson, and Espin, 1996)

A variety of tools is now available to help educators and families make inclusive classrooms a success. Following are some specific techniques and tools useful in the planning of inclusion:

- Circle of Friends (also called Circle of Support) is a technique used to enlist the involvement and commitment of peers in developing and supporting effective inclusion.
- Coach is an assessment and planning tool designed to help educators identify family-centered priorities for their students, define the educational program components, and address these components in an inclusive setting.
- Maps (Making Action Plans) is a creative tool that inclusion facilitators can use to help individuals, organizations, and families move into the future.
- Path (Planning Alternative Tomorrows with Hope) is a creative tool used by inclusion facilitators to develop long- and short-range planning by encouraging people to think "backwards."

The two sides of inclusion are definite. Civil rights activists advocate for inclusion in order to decrease discriminatory treatment and segregated schooling. Others believe that inclusion can never meet the special needs of *all* students with disabilities. One thing is certain: Inclusion will continue to be an ongoing conversation involving students, teachers, related school personnel, families, and community leaders.

BRAIN RESEARCH

Our understanding of the brain's development and processes offers significant insight into approaches to early childhood education (ECE) and especially to early childhood special education (ECSE).

In the past, medical and educational professionals could only speculate about the functioning of the living human brain. However, in the early 1990s technologies were developed that now enable researchers to view brain circuitry in detail and monitor how, and where, the brain processes information. Magnetic Resonance Imaging (MRI) and the Positron Emission Tomography (PET) scans record and measure the activity levels within the brain and have been used to monitor how the normal brain develops. These technologies have initiated an explosion in the field of brain research.

Three decades of research in child development corroborate brain research findings regarding the earliest years. We now have a better understanding of how nature and nurture impact the architectural shaping of the brain. Educational initiatives focusing on early intervention have developed and intensified in response to this new wealth of information.

Even before birth, brain cells make connections that plant the foundation for who we become as adults. These connections, or synapses, are created as a result of stimuli within that baby's environment. We are each born with 100 billion brain cells (neurons) that communicate with each other through synapses. Although the number of brain cells cannot later increase, it can decrease. Brain cells that go unused just wither away.

A key piece of the brain development puzzle is the fact that there are critical periods in brain plasticity when environment plays a major role working in tandem with biological factors. Synapses formed as a direct result of environmental stimuli cause the brain to develop rapidly. Repeated influences and experiences "hard wire" the neurocircuitry.

A child's earliest experiences are now believed to be extremely significant to brain development. Preterm infants are especially vulnerable to the environment because they enter the world with brains that have had less time to mature in the protected intrauterine environment. (Shore, 1997).

Knowing what we now know about preterm development, nursing practices in neonatal intensive care units throughout the nation have been modified (Gilkerson and Als, 1995). By moving from "protocol and procedure-driven to relationship-based developmental care," researchers have found there to be a substantial improvement in preterm infants' potential for mental and physical well being. An additional positive outcome is the decrease in duration of hospital stays and financial expense.

Scientific advances in the field of neuroscience with respect to a child's first years have crucial implications for the development of policies and practices concerning early childhood. Current research supports redirecting our attention to provide more services to children from birth through the age of four. The education of children must begin long before they arrive at the doors of the kindergarten classroom. Florida's late governor Lawton Chiles informed participants at the Brain-Mind Connections Conference at the University of Florida that "education must start at gestation" (January 30, 1998).

In more recent studies regarding brain research and its application to learning in a classroom setting, understanding neurological differences as it impacts reading new words is being studied with expectations that learning more about brain research may help to produce greater results in the classroom.

Laurie E. Cutting, Director of the Education and Brain Research Program at the Kennedy Krieger Institute in Baltimore, is studying neurological differences among students who are skilled readers, those who have difficulties and those with diagnosed learning disabilities (as cited by Hernandez, 2008). "If neuroscientists can pinpoint which parts of the brain are activated when a reader puzzles over an unknown word, they may eventually help teachers tailor reading instruction for individuals" (Cutting as cited in Hernandez, 2008, p.1).

Additionally, this scientific data supports research based evidence mandated by NCLB. It also supports teaching strategies such as Response to Intervention (RTI) with regard to targeted interventions and Recognition & Response (R&R) (see Chapter 3). These areas focus on diagnoses and interventions for both students with disabilities as well as children with instructional disabilities.

"One of the most startling recent revelations in neuroscience has been that the brain's structure is more flexible (a concept called neuroplasticity) than was previously thought; this understanding may help teachers find ways to train the brain to better solve math problems or understand a book" (Hernandez, 2008, p. 2).

Other educators are applying concepts based on neuroscience and neuroplasticity to help deal with prescriptive information, phonemic awareness to include linking letters to sounds for students with reading disorders and education of autistic children.

"At-Risk" Children

The process of getting children ready for school begins long before they begin preschool. The 1992 report "Heart Start" dealt with the emotional foundations of school readiness and looked at the characteristics children develop in their first three years of life in preparation for school success. The report stated that too many preschools find themselves providing remedial support to three- and four-year-olds who are already delayed in their development. Heart Start cited seven characteristics a child needs to have in order to successfully learn once in school: confidence, intentionality, curiosity, communication, age-appropriate self-control, cooperativeness, and relatedness. For children lacking some, or all, of these characteristics, school becomes an "at-risk" situation. These children "tend to fall behind, become discouraged, resentful, perhaps disruptive, and, often, drop out" (Beatty, 1992).

Because toxins present within the mother move through the placenta, the exceptionally vulnerable fetal brain can be exposed to risks it may not be able to withstand. Prenatal cocaine exposure has been the subject of several research studies. Dixon and Bejar (1988) found that 41 percent of thirty-two infants prenatally exposed to cocaine suffered brain hemorrhage, cerebral infarction, and/or atrophy. Some prenatally exposed babies are born with a small head circumference that continues to chart small, which is "a significant predictor of poor development" (Griffith, 1992, pp. 30–34).

Alcohol use by the pregnant mother also creates an "at-risk" in utero environment for the baby. Fetal alcohol syndrome causes the child to develop a smaller brain as well as negatively impacting a child's motor coordination. Hyperactivity can also develop as a result of this syndrome (Healy, 1994).

Substance abuse by a parent places the unborn child at risk for a variety of negative outcomes. However, the environment the baby comes home to after leaving the hospital cannot be overlooked in the equation of the rapidly forming brain. Neonates become "caretaking victims" when parents lack the necessary skills and mental and emotional health to nurture them appropriately. If a parent is more concerned about nurturing a drug habit than nurturing the baby, serious implications exist for that baby. A chaotic and unpredictable environment can leave a permanent mark on the developing brain. Fear, anxiety, and neglect in young children can cause lifelong brain impairment. Impairment can take the form of emotional disturbances or learning problems. It is now known that "unpredictable, chaotic or traumatic experiences over-activate the neural pathways that control the fear response, causing children's brains to be organized for survival in a persistently threatening and violent world" (Perry, Pollard, Blakley and Baker, 1995, pp. 271–291).

In *Ghosts from the Nursery,* Karr-Morse and Wiley (1997) state that "the majority of youthful offenders' records indicate that consistent patterns of antisocial behaviors are apparent by the time a child reaches four years of age. Toxic experiences such as neglect, abuse, family violence and substance abuse are being physically and emotionally absorbed by large numbers of our youngest babies."

Researchers now believe that children come into the world capable of learning any language. In essence, they are citizens of the world. Neurons from the ear form vital connections in the auditory cortex as a result of the child hearing repeated sounds. By the time a baby reaches three months of age, the brain can decipher hundreds of spoken sounds. The auditory map is uniquely wired for the language spoken in the baby's environment by the time he or she is six months of age. "The critical period for mastering sound discrimination occurs early; even by six months the infant's brain is already pruning out sensitivity to sounds that are not heard in its environment. If the brain doesn't get good quality input and interactive practice with real people during these years, the child may have later difficulty with reading, spelling, and speaking clearly" (Healy, 1994, p. 75).

Dr. Stanley Greenspan has conducted extensive research in the area of autism as it relates to language. "Diagnosed between eighteen months and four years of age, these youngsters display a variety of bizarre and disturbing behavior—wandering aimlessly, compulsively flapping their arms, continually rubbing a spot on the carpet, repeatedly opening and closing a door, painstakingly marshaling small objects into rigidly straight lines—but almost no ability to respond to even the most basic attempts at communication" (Greenspan and Benderly, 1997).

Greenspan and his colleagues worked with over 200 children diagnosed with autistic spectrum disorder. It was found that by providing an intensive program that includes occupational and speech therapy as well as an interactive play component involving family members, early intervention could make a positive impact. "Working with these children, we found that the basic unit of intelligence is the connection between a feeling or desire and an action or symbol. When a gesture or bit of language is related in some way to the child's feelings or desires—even something as simple as the wish to go outside or to be given a ball—she can learn to use it appropriately and effectively" (Greenspan and Benderly, 1997). Greenspan and Benderly (1997) further report that out of approximately 200 of these students, they found that "between 58 percent and 73 percent have become warm, loving and communicative" (p. 310).

Research is rich with studies on the effects of quality early childhood programs on "at-risk" populations. The Carolina Abecedarian Project, the Yale Child Welfare Research Program, and the Perry Preschool Project all found that early intervention produced positive outcomes for children and families (Hamburg, 1994). Of these, the Abecedarian Project was found to have the greatest positive effect on young children who received child-focused, center-based services fifty weeks each year. In a recent article, Campbell and Ramey (1995) note additional evidence of the Abecedarian Project's merit.

Advocates of early childhood education have seized the opportunity neuroscience findings have provided and mobilized to disseminate this information to as wide an audience as possible. The Carnegie Corporation funded a project in fourteen states called the Starting Points Initiative, designed to train professionals to visit to their communities and communicate the importance quality caregiving and parenting during the first three years of life.

Sacks and Watnick (1998) share the Carnegie Corporation's 1194 findings that there is a "quiet crisis" in this country for children under three years old. Their study supports that many children in this age group have disabilities due to low birth weight, abuse, neglect, and difficulties encountered by teenage mothers. These children are at-risk for developmental delays additionally based on poverty and parent undereducation. Disturbing statistics brought forth in their report include:

- One in four infants and toddlers under the age of three (nearly three million) live with families who have incomes below the federal poverty level;
- From 1987 to 1991, the number of children living in foster homes escalated by more than 50 percent—300,000 in 1987 to 460,000 in 1991;
- With growing economic pressures on both parents to join the work force, more than five million babies and toddlers are being taken care of by other adults;
- One in three victims of physical abuse are children under the age of one year;
- During 1990, approximately 90 percent of the children who died from neglect and abuse were less than five years old; 53 percent of these children were under one year of age;
- The major cause of death among babies and toddlers is accidental injury. (pp. 29–43)

Among the goals of early intervention services are to identify children who have disabilities or are at-risk for disabilities and meet criteria to have specialized services to maximize their potential for success, to include the family in order to ensure greater success of the child both in school and in the home, and to develop an individualized approach. Because parents of young children with special needs often require help themselves as well as help with other siblings, the services and support of organizations and community agencies (including clinics and transportation providers) has added to the overall success of early intervention. In a "normal" family, the child models much of what is going on around him. In families with young special needs children, frequently, the opposite is true—the child drives the family. The needs of such children can be so intense, as well as linked to sources outside the home, that the family finds itself operating around the needs of the special child. The interrelated structures outside the home must be coordinated in order to bring some type of normalcy to families with special-needs children. Strong communication and positive links between the intervening professionals and integrated service providers make the advocacy process more likely to succeed.

Controversy over Critical Learning Periods

The concept that parents have a window of opportunity regarding critical learning periods is disputed by John T. Bruer (1999) in *The Myth of the First Three Years,* who writes that "apart from eliminating gross neglect, neuroscience cannot currently tell us much about whether we can, let alone how to influence brain development during the early stage of exuberant synapse formation. If so, we should not be surprised that brain-based parenting advice is vague and contradictory" (p. 22).

Studies by Nelson and Bloom (as cited in Bruer, 1999) suggest that brain continues to "reorganize itself in response to experience or injury throughout life" and that the one window of opportunity, as described by brain research advocates, is not accurate (pp. 649–657).

Advances in brain research have produced what has been called "brain-based education," which favors an active learning model engaging students in their own learning and instruction. According to Bruer (1999), support for this idea is based on a cognitive and constructionist model, rooted in thirty years of psychological research, easily found in any text on educational psychology but not developed from the biological sciences or pure sciences.

> For nearly a century, the science of the mind (psychology) developed independently from the science of the brain (neuroscience). Psychologists were interested in our mental functions . . . neuroscientists were interested in how the brain develops and functions. . . . Psychologists were interested in our mental software and neuroscientists were interested in our neural hardware. . . . In the past 15 years these theoretical barriers have fallen. Now scientists called cognitive neuroscientists are beginning to study how our neural hardware might run our mental software, how brain structures support mental functions. (Bruer, 1999, pp. 649–657)Bruer and others believe this to be a very dangerous combination, as so much of the perceived "connection" is based on limited brain science research and is speculation.
>
> The work of Dr. Harry Chugani is frequently quoted as a basis for brain research, brain-based studies, and education. According to Bruer's 1999 article, *In Search of . . .*

Brain Based Education, "Chugani believes, along with some educators and early childhood advocates, that there is a biological window of opportunity when learning is easy, efficient, and easily retained. But there is no neuroscientific evidence to support this belief. And when there is no scientific evidence, there is no scientific fact" (pp. 649–657).

Obviously, scientific research on brain development needs to continue before we can conclude with conviction either way.

EARLY CHILDHOOD SPECIAL EDUCATION (ECSE)

ECSE can be defined as an education setting in which specific interventions are set forth for young children at-risk for abnormal school development.

As Bowe (1995) explains, ECSE provides services for children under 6 years of age and their families, in response to disabilities or developmental delays in the children. ECSE joins Part H and Section 619 of Part B of the Individuals with Disabilities Act (p. 6).To assure all young children an equal opportunity for success in school legislation, Public Law-99–457 was added through a federal amendment to already existing special education legislation (PL-94–142). The intent of this legislation was to provide states with specific funds to plan, develop and implement early intervention policies and programs for infants and toddlers who were handicapped, developmentally delayed, or at risk of handicaps or developmental delays and their families. A complete discussion of these laws follows in Chapter 2.

Numerous research studies have indicated the effectiveness of intervening on behalf of children during their early years. Conditions that may seriously impair a child's optimal development may be significantly reduced or improved if the right combinations of services are experienced as a form of intervention. A significant part of ECSE is the active participation of the family in decisionmaking, participation, and recipient services.

In a twenty-five-year longitudinal study of preschoolers, researchers followed forty families who had sought help from the Regional Intervention Program (RIP), a federally funded program, in Nashville, Tennessee, and twenty-seven other areas (Regional Intervention Program, 2000). Each of these families looked for guidance due to displays of extreme behavior problems from their preschoolers. The researchers found that both the schools and the families had little chance of correcting antisocial behavior in their children after the age of nine. These antisocial behaviors often led to problems with the law, social rejection, and academic failure.

Through RIP, parents were trained in behavior modification skills such as monitoring their child's behavior, stating expectations and choices, rewarding appropriate behavior, and working with others to teach the child self-control and appropriate interaction behaviors. The study found that by the time the children reached elementary school, they were equal to their peers in responding positively to teacher requests, being appropriately engaged in structured and nonstructured activities, and reacting positively to teacher requests. A major finding of this study was that the earlier a child enrolled in RIP, the better the results. Because teacher surveys continuously point out that teachers believe they need more management and behavior management skills, this study has significant applications for early childhood special education. In addition, it supports the research supporting the need for early childhood intervention and the emphasis on early childhood special education programs as well as funding.

HEAD START

The Head Start programs of the 1960s gave regular educators their first opportunity to observe mass screening programs that had the potential for identifying and remedying behavioral and learning problems at an early age. The program's initial goals for early childhood education were to compensate for deficits in children's education and living environments. Disadvantaged children were to be provided with educational and environmental experiences to give them a "head start" for school. A subgroup of these children were the special needs children; to better serve their needs, Head Start developed an infrastructure and program that continues to support children with disabilities (Gearheart, Mullen, and Gearheart, 1993). It has created new opportunities through funding for Early Head Start programs to work with pregnant women and at-risk infants and toddlers. Another original Head Start principle that has continued is an emphasis on the central role of parents in the program; this has since become a significant element in preschool programs for children with disabilities.

The Division of Early Childhood (DEC) of the Council of Exceptional Children has urged Head Start to include in its agenda the following seven goals concerning special-needs individuals and special education (National Head Start Association, 2000):

1. Assure that all families of Head Start children, including those with disabilities, have the opportunity for full-day, full-year service;
2. Identify and publicize programs that have been effective in increasing access to and maintenance of comprehensive services for Head Start families of children with special needs;
3. Continue to encourage collaboration with community partners, including Early Intervention (IDEA, Part C), and ECSE (IDEA, Part B), and provide incentives to Head Start grantees for doing so;
4. Prepare every staff member to observe individual differences and support children with special needs, and follow up training with appropriate supervision and assistance;
5. Increase support of research tied to community-based practice, as well as dissemination of findings in language(s) from which staff and families can benefit;
6. Explore, as part of Head Start's increasing use of technology in the new century, the importance of and mechanisms for accessing assistive technology for Head Start children and families, to allow them full participation in learning opportunities;
7. Encourage employment of persons with disabilities in diverse roles in Early Head Start and Head Start services at all levels.

WHY SPECIAL EDUCATION TEACHERS?

According to the statutory requirements of IDEA 1997, the IEP decisionmaking team *must* include a regular education teacher if the special education child is participating in the regular education environment. That teacher must participate in the IEP process by assisting in the determination of positive behavioral interventions, supplementary aids, program modifications, and supports for school personnel to be provided for the child. If the regular education teacher is not comfortable with or adequately knowledgeable about these tasks, the leader of the multidisciplinary IEP team is required to assist the teacher so that he or she can be appropriately included.

Many teachers continually search for ways to bring information to various levels of comprehension and are constantly aware that the goal of language communication is the same for a child with special needs as for the normal child. Although the training of teachers focuses on academic or functional life skills, management skills and behavior modification skills must be woven into lessons in order to facilitate progress with special-needs students. Though individual lessons concern specific academic areas, hours of planning on how to get the material into small sequences, increasing frequently limited attention spans, and reinforcing the act of repetition for these children are a necessity.

The special-needs teacher, then, has to make the whole school receptive to the special-needs child. All the work done within the class to prepare that child to go into the mainstream of normal classes and activities can be undone by the normal classroom teacher's frown or body language or by another child's ridicule. Like any child, the special-needs child may experience the sting of pain each time he or she is ridiculed or criticized. Because the special-needs teacher is trained to help students develop their self-esteem, he or she can often help the student get beyond the pain to a place of happiness.

Children with special needs take time, individualized instruction, and specific instructional strategies set within annual goals based on their specific disability often using individualized remediation techniques. The regular classroom teacher has neither been trained nor prepared for these special educational structures. Due to the differing emphasis, unique curricula commonly used only in special education additionally need to be coordinated with special services provided along the way. All curricula must be adjusted and modified to match learner needs and abilities by the special education teacher (Meier, 1992). As stated before, general education teachers and special education teachers have very different professional knowledge structures and foundations. They identify strengths and weaknesses differently. "Special educators emphasize student strengths and needs that relate to curriculum and instruction, and general educators emphasize student strengths and needs related to social skills and behaviors. Traditionally special education teacher preparation programs have been grounded in behavioral theory whereas general education teacher preparation is grounded in cognitive or constructivist theory—a process orientation" (King-Sears and Carpenter, 1996, pp. 226–236).

The role of the special education teacher involves bearing the instructional responsibility similar to that of the regular education teacher; however, determining eligibility for services, which involves diagnosis; following IEP progress; and facilitating the participation in general education settings, when appropriate, are additional responsibilities. Along with collaboration with regular education teachers, the special education teacher works with the school psychologist in order to collaborate on prereferral observations and screening for possible special education placement.

In response to a survey in 1998 given by the Council of Exceptional Children(CEC) to its membership on special education teaching conditions, the greatest challenges facing effective teaching were: (1) paperwork, (2) class size, (3) conflicting role expectations (additional certifications added to special education courses already completed, by some states), (4) lack of collaboration with general education teachers, including lack of problem-solving opportunities with general education teachers, (5) lack of access to technology, (6) poorly trained paraeducators, and (7) lack of opportunity for professional development. The CEC is now holding regional meetings throughout the nation on special education teacher conditions and is working with other professional associations and parents to explore solutions.

According to Deiner (1993) the special education teacher and often the general education teacher in an inclusive setting must be able to specifically (1) program both for children with and without disabilities in one classroom, (2) hold individual conferences with parents about their children and cooperate with them to design an individual program, (3) conduct parent meetings to include the parents of all the children in their class, (4) participate in the early diagnosis of children with disabilities and be able to interpret the assessment and diagnostic reports coming from educational as well as noneducational sources, (5) write (with input from parents and other professionals) and implement IEPs for children over three years of age and IFSPs for children below three years of age, (6) evaluate the child and the program itself to make changes and determine its effectiveness, (7) become the child's advocate when that child's needs are not being adequately met, and (8) be aware of legislation and litigation pertaining to teaching.

Welch, Judge, Anderson, Bray, Child, and Franke (1990) describe prereferral consultation as a form of collaborative consultation. Prereferral consultation is a process that occurs before prescreening, an attempt to do very basic screening by communication of observations in order to identify children who are eligible for special services and placement. In the prereferral process, educators mutually identify a problem, consider a variety of possible interventions, and attempt and monitor such. This process is neither the regular or special education teacher advising the other. It can be two regular classroom teachers, two special education teachers, or a special and regular classroom teacher. One educator seeks support from a colleague in order to clarify and facilitate a situation.

Collaborative consultation is a method used to generate creative alternatives to traditional educational approaches for individual students. The educator develops a plan for selecting among resource and instructional alternatives to traditional pullout services. There are times during the day when the least intrusive form of assistance can be employed without taking the mildly disabled student out of the class. Through collaborative consultation, it is hoped that one of two things will occur: by collaboratively assessing current techniques and the effects on the student, a referral process might no longer be necessary; or this model might serve as additional verification that services different from those available in the regular education classroom are necessary (Donaldson and Christiansen, 1990).

The University of South Florida has responded to the need for reform, which can be applied to the regular and special education teacher roles. Its concept of change is based on five contextual phenomena: "(a) school reform which requires a rethinking of the system of which special education is a part; (b) the promotion of an inclusion policy at the national level; (c) the emergence of serious debate regarding the paradigms guiding traditional educational research; (d) decreasing resources available to support teacher education programs; and (e) increasing demands for well-educated and appropriately certified teachers" (Paul, Epanchin, Rosselli and Duchnowski, 1996, pp. 310–322).

PARENTAL INVOLVEMENT AND THE NEED FOR PARENT EDUCATION

More attention is now being paid to *parental involvement* as a fundamental element in the academic success of all children. The field of early childhood now recognizes the important role parents play as the child's first and most important teacher. The National Education Goals Panel in 1998 established a set of goals that all persons involved in education and related health and social services were asked to achieve. Goal 8, "parental participation," states, "every school will promote partnerships that will increase parental involvement and participation in promoting the social, emotional, and academic growth of children" (The National Education Goals Panel, 1998, p. 36).

Building bridges between home and school becomes especially important in the case of exceptional student education. A parent of a child with a disability not only serves as caregiver but also takes a key role in the education, assessment, and advocacy of and for their child. This role thrusts a parent into a collaborative process that has potential to alienate rather than help. By providing this parent with the tools necessary to comprehend the legal and educational ramifications of professional collaboration and service delivery models, children will be the beneficiaries. Empowering parents can minimize family stress and provide critical resources for support. All members of a family are affected by a child with disabilities, and a full range of services and support is often needed. Parent education is a critical piece in helping a child with disabilities reach his or her full potential.

Today's statistics serve as a strong indication that families are faced with risk factors that can directly impact their children's academic success. The Children's Defense Fund (1999) published the following key facts about American children:

- 1 in 2 live in a single-parent family at some point in childhood;
- 1 in 3 will be poor at some point in his or her childhood;
- 1 in 3 is born to unmarried parents;
- 1 in 3 is behind a year or more in school;
- 1 in 4 is born poor;
- 1 in 4 lives with only one parent;
- 1 in 5 is born to a mother who did not graduate from high school;

- 1 in 8 never graduates from high school;
- 1 in 8 is born to a teenage mother;
- 1 in 12 has a disability;
- 1 in 25 is born to a mother who received late or no prenatal care.

For a significant segment of today's culturally diverse population, the stresses of disadvantage can place children in jeopardy. When multiple risk factors are compounded by the additional responsibility of caring for, and educating, a child with a disability, a family becomes exceptionally vulnerable. "The challenges faced by families exert a primary influence on their ability and desire to access services, and their resources for maintaining an active role with formal education and service delivery systems" (Hanson and Carta, 1996, p. 201).

Because of the intricacies of service delivery of exceptional education programs, the parents' role as advocate becomes particularly dynamic. Public Law 105–17, the Individuals with Disabilities Education Act (IDEA) Amendments of 1997, builds upon Public Law 94–142 and Public Law 101–476 by further strengthening the rights of children with disabilities and their parents. These laws recognize and validate the key role parents play in the educational process of their children. This role is one that incorporates every aspect of a child's education including the process of evaluation, placement, monitoring of records, and management of behavioral issues.

IDEA 1997 also acknowledges parents' need to know to be significant. In order to empower parents, the following changes were implemented:

1. "Parent counseling and training" means that parents will receive support to help them acquire those skills necessary to implement their child's IEP or IFSP;
2. A new section has been added with regard to children with disabilities in public charter schools; their parents retain all rights under IDEA, and compliance with Part B of IDEA is required regardless of whether a public charter school receives Part B funds;
3. Parents may invite any individual "with knowledge or special expertise" to be on the IEP team;
4. Public agencies must inform parents relating to the participation of other individuals on the IEP team who have knowledge or special expertise about the child; and
5. Parents must be given a copy of their child's IEP without cost or having to request it.

Since IDEA 1997, PL94-142 has once again been amended to become IDEA 2004. This reauthorization is explained in detail in Chapter 2 as well as how it relates to the 2001 NCLB legislation, PL107-110 (see Chapter 4). Both these significant steps include children with special needs in regular education while still meeting their legal rights as outlined in IDEA, as well as Section 504 of the Rehabilitation Act.

We live in a nation of great diversity, and families' expectations for their children are sometimes deeply rooted in the value systems within their own cultures. Because of this, professionals cannot prescribe generic educational plans for individual children. There is a need for those practicing in the field of special education to "personalize" their professional relationships with their families. This requires those working with families to understand the family based on a *family systems theory,* which considers a family to be its own social system with its own particular needs and attributes (Turnbull and Turnbull, 1990). The underlying premise of this theory is that each family member's school experiences have an impact on the other members of the family because members are so closely interrelated.

Parents who are informed about early intervention can positively influence development in their young children. For older students, parents can serve as "the primary determinant of success in transition programs" (McNair and Rusch as cited in Turnbull and Turnbull, 1996, p. 3).

Whereas parent involvement in the educational planning process of children with disabilities dates back to 1975, the involvement of adolescents in their own planning is relatively new. "Research has shown that student involvement in educational planning is for the most part either nonexistent or passive" (Van Reusen and Bos as cited in Turnbull and Turnbull, 1996, p. 3). By educating adolescents so that they understand their own potential and capabilities, exceptional education professionals and parents are empowering their children to enter adulthood with self-determination.

The unique characteristics of family make it imperative that parents and children understand the legislation, requirements and educational services available concerning special education. This is the only way to ensure that their children will have full access to a free and appropriate education.

REFERENCES

Baum, D. and C. Wells, 1990. "Promoting Handicap Awareness in Preschool Children. In *Annual Editions, Educating Exceptional Children.* 5th ed. Guilford, CT: Dushkin Publishing.

Beatty, N., ed. 1992. *Heart Start: The Emotional Foundations of School Readiness.* Executive Summary, Zero to Three. Arlington, VA: National Center for Clinical Infant Programs.

Benseeson, S. L. (n.d.) *Velazquez.* T.C. & E. C. Jack, London, England.

Bowe, F. G., 1995. *Birth to Five: Early Childhood Special Education.* New York: Delmar Publishers.

Brantlinger, E., 1997. "Using Ideology: Cases of Nonrecognition of the Politics of Research and Practice in Special Education." *Review of Educational Research* 67, no. 4: 425–459.

Bruer, J.T. 1999. In Search of . . . Brain-Based Education. *Kappan* (May): 649–657.

———, 1999. *The Myth of the First Three Years.* New York: Free Press.

Buehler, C., and D. Dugas, . 1979. *Directory of Learning Resources for Learning Disabilities.* Waterford, CT: Bureau of Business Practice.

Burnett, G., 1994. *Urban Teachers and Collaborative School-Linked Services.* ERIC Clearinghouse on Urban Education, New York: National Education Association, Washington, DC.

Campbell, T. A., and C. T. Ramey, 1995. "Cognitive and School Outcomes for High Risk African American Students at Middle Adolescence: Positive Effects of Early Intervention." *American Educational Research Journal* 32: 743–772.

Center for Special Education Technology, July 1990. *Tech Use Guide.* Reston, VA: Office of Special Education Programs, U.S. Department of Education.

Chadha, A., 1999. "The Inclusive Initiative in India." *Journal of the International Association of Special Education* 3, no. 1: 31–34.

Children's Defense Fund, 1999. *The State of America's Children.* Boston: Beacon Press.

Chiles, L., January 1998. Brain–Mind Connections Conference. Gainesville, FL: University of Florida.

Choate, J. S., 1993. *Successful Mainstreaming: Proven Ways to Detect and Correct Special Needs.* Boston: Allyn and Bacon.

Cline, S., and D. Schwartz, 1999. *Diverse Populations of Gifted Children.* Upper Saddle River, NJ: Merrill Publishers.

Davies, S., 1996. "The Tenth School." *Principal* 76, no. 2 (Nov.): 13–16.

Deiner, P. L., 1993. *Resources for Teaching Children with Disabilities.* Fort Worth, TX: Harcourt Brace Jovanich College Publishers.

Deno, S. L., A. Foegen, S. Robinson, and C. Espin, 1996. "Commentary: Facing the Realities of Inclusion for Students with Mild Disabilities." *The Journal of Special Education* 30, no. 3: 345–357.

Dixon, S. D. and R. Bejar, 1988. "Brain Lesions in Cocaine and Methampetamine Exposed Neonates." *Pediatric Research* 23: 405.

Donaldson, R., and J. Christiansen,. 1990. "Consultation and Collaboration: A Decision-Making Model." Pp. 225–228 in *Teaching Exceptional Children.* Reston, VA: CEC.

Dryfoos, J. G., 1994. *Full-Service Schools: A Revolution in Health and Social Services for Children, Youth, and Families.* San Francisco: Jossey-Bass.

Galis, S. A., and C. K. Tanner, 1995. *Inclusion in Elementary Schools.* Education Policy Analysis Archives, available on-line: http://olam.ed.asu.edu/epaa/v3n15.htm.

Gearheart, B., R. C. Mullen, and C. J. Gearheart, 1993. *Exceptional Individuals: An Introduction.* Pacific Grove, CA: Brooks/Cole Publishing.

Gearheart, C., and B. Gearheart, 1990. *Introduction to Special Education Assessment: Principles and Practices.* Denver: Love Publishing.

Gilkerson, L., and H. Als, 1995. "Developmentally Supportive Care in the Neonatal Intensive Care Unit." *Zero to Three* 15, no. 6: 34–35.

Greenspan, S., and B. Benderly, 1997. *The Growth of the Mind and the Endangered Origins of Intelligence.* Boston: Addison-Wesley.

Griffith, D., 1992. "Prenatal Exposure to Cocaine and Other Drugs: Developmental and Educational Prognoses." *Kappan* 74, no. 1: 30–34.

Hamburg, D. A., 1994. *Today's Children: Creating a future for a Generation in Crisis.* New York: Time Books.

Hardman, M. L., C. J. Drew, M. W. Egan, and B. Wolf, 1990. *Human Exceptionality.* 3rd ed.. Boston: Allyn and Bacon.

Healy, J., 1994. *Your Child's Growing Mind.* New York: Doubleday.

Hernandez, N. (2008). Learning About Learning. Brain Research May Produce Results in the Classroom. *Washington Post.* Retrieved October 30, 2008 from http://www.washingtonpost.com/wp-dyn/content/article/2008/10/24/AR2008102402987

Karr-Morse, R., and M. Wiley, 1997. *Ghosts from the Nursery.* New York: Atlantic Monthly Press.

King-Sears, M., and S. L. Carpenter, 1996. "Empowering Teachers and Students with Instructional Choices in Inclusive Settings." *Remedial and Special Education* 17, no. 4: 226–236.

Lerner, J., 1993. *Learning Disabilities.* 6th ed. Boston: Houghton Mifflin.

Malmskog, S., and A. P. McDonnell, 1999. "Teacher-Mediated Facilitation of Engagement by Children with Developmental Delays in Inclusive Preschools." *Topics in Early Childhood Special Education* 19, no. 4: 213.

McAfee, O., and D. Leong, 1997. *Assessing and Guiding Young Children's Development and Learning.* 2nd ed. Boston: Allyn and Bacon.

Meier, F. E., 1992. *Competency-Based Instruction for Teachers of Students with Special Learning Needs.* Needham Heights, MA: Allyn and Bacon.

Minke, K. M., G. G. Bear, S. A. Deemer, and S. M. Griffin, 1996. "Teachers' Experiences with Inclusive Classrooms: Implications for Special Education Reform." *Journal of Special Education* 30, no. 2: 152–186.

National Association of State Boards of Education, 1992. "A Brief History of Special Education." *Winners All: A Call for Inclusive Schools.* Report of the National Association of State Board of Education, Alexandria, VA.

National Education Goals Panel, 1998. *Promising Practices: Progress Toward the Goals, Lessons from the States.* Washington, DC: National Education Goals Panel.

National Head Start Association, 2000. "Report of the Head Start 2010 Advisory Panel." Alexandria, VA: National Head Start Association.

Paul, J., B. Epanchin, H. Rosselli, and A. Duchnowski, 1996. "The Transformation of Teacher Education and Special Education." *Remedial and Special Education* 17, no. 5: 310–322.

Perry, B. D., R. A. Pollard, T. L. Blakley, and W. L. Baker, 1995. "Childhood Trauma, the Neurobiology of Adaptation, and Use-Dependent Development of the Brain: How States Become Traits." *Infant Mental Health Journal* 16, no. 4: 271–291.

Provenzo, E. F., A. Brett, and G. N. McCloskey, 1999. *Computers, Curriculum, and Cultural Change.* Mahwah, NJ: Lawrence Erlbaum Associates.

Rafort i Planes, C. (2001). *Picasso's Las Meninas.* Editorial Meteora.

Regional Intervention Program, 2000. *Twenty-five Year Study Finds Parents Can Deter Destructive Behavior.* Nashville, TN: Regional Intervention Program.

RESNA, 1999. *Spotlight on Technology.* Arlington, VA: Rehabilitation Engineering and Assistive Technology Society of North America (RESNA).

Sacks, A., and B. Watnick, 1999. "Brain Research: Implications for Early Intervention Theory, Research and Application." *Journal of the International Association of Special Education* 2, no. 1: 29–43.

Serraller, F. C., 1999. *Velazquez.* 2nd ed. Fundacion Amigos del Museo del Prado, Alianza Editorial, S.A. Madrid: Calle Juan Ignacio Luca de Lena.

Shore, R., 1997. *Rethinking the Brain: New Insights into Early Development.* New York: Families and Work Institute.

Shriner, J. G., 2000. "Legal Perspectives on School Outcomes for Students with Disabilities." *Journal of Special Education* 4, no. 33: 232–239.

Stratton-Preutt, S. T. (Editor) (2003). *Velazquez's Las Meninas.* Cambridge, University Press.

Turnbull, A. P., and H. R. Turnbull, 1990. *Families, Professionals, and Exceptionality: A Special Partnership.* New York: Merrill/Macmillan.

———, 1996. "Helping Students Communicate in Planning Conferences: What Do Students with Disabilities Tell Us about the Importance of Family Involvement in the Transition from School to Adult Life?" *Exceptional Children* 62: 3.

Viola, S., 1997. "Redefining Assessment: Obtaining Information that Is Relevant to Curricular Interventions." *Journal of the International Association of Special Education* 1, no. 1: 61–67.

Welch, M., T. Judge, J. Anderson, J. Bray, B. Child, and L. Franke, 1990. "A Tool for Implementing Prereferral Consultation." *Teaching Exceptional Children* 22, no. 2 (Winter): 223–224.

Wolf, N., 1999. *Diego Velazquez, 1599–1660: The Face of Spain.* Cologne, Germany: Taschen Publishers.

Woodward, J., and H. Rieth, 1997. "A Historical Review of Technology Research in Special Education." *Review of Educational Research* 67, no. 4: 503–536.

Ysseldyke, J. E., and B. Algozzine, 1990. *Introduction to Special Education.* 2nd ed. Boston: Houghton Mifflin.

Chapter Two
Chronology

The following chronology presents in timeline fashion a review of the laws, court decisions, and related developments pertinent to the recognition and support of special education in the United States.

For all individuals who are non-lawyers and involved with special education, it is significant to review and stay abreast of rulings regarding the U.S. courts of Appeals. Although state rulings from a circuit court may not be binding for a particular state circuit, they may rely upon a decision as "persuasive authority." However, when the Circuits have "split" rulings on the same issue, and different legal outcomes from similar issues of fact and or law, these cases have a higher probability of being accepted for review by the U.S. Supreme Court (Wrightslaw, 2008).

1791 The Tenth Amendment of the U.S. Constitution gives states jurisdiction over educational matters.

1840 Rhode Island becomes the first state to pass legislation for compulsory school attendance.

1855 The first kindergarten is established, in Watertown, Wisconsin.

1880s Public concern regarding educational matters inspires the creation of the National Education Association (NEA) and the U.S. Office of Education. Public schools adapt an age-grade level system, categorizing students into grade levels according to chronological age. Differences between students placed in this system thus become very obvious.

1900s The NEA endorses the revised Binet test of intelligence as being useful for predicting school achievement.

1916 Lewis Terman completes the design of the Stanford-Binet Scale of Intelligence Tests, which introduce the concept of intelligence quotient (IQ). This leads to the assumption that intelligence tests can predict school success or failure, which quickly becomes a significant factor in student stability placement.

1919 All states require compulsory school attendance.

The White House Conference on Child Youth and Protection stresses that "healthful school living is the most important aspect of education."

1946 The National School Lunch Act subsidizes school cafeteria facilities, placing emphasis on diet-related health of the school-age population.

1954 The U.S. Supreme Court's ruling on *Brown vs. the Board of Education* puts an end to "separate but equal" schools. This emphasis on the rights of a diverse population will serve as a basis for future rulings that children with handicaps cannot be excluded from school.

The Cooperative Research Act, one of the first federal laws relating to education, initiates cooperative research between the federal government and universities through funding of studies in critical issues in education. This serves as a beginning for professionals to recognize the need to study the education of handicapped students.

1958 The Education of the Mentally Retarded Children Act, P.L. 85–926, an amendment to the National Defense Education Act, becomes the first federal law addressing special education. It authorizes funding to train teachers and leadership personnel in the education of children who are considered mentally retarded. Overall, the National Defense Education Act serves to shift public attention from "healthful living" toward improved instruction in math, science, and foreign languages.

1961 The Special Education Act, P.L. 87–276, authorizes funds for training professionals to train teachers of the deaf.

1965 The Elementary and Secondary Education Act (ESEA), P.L. 89–10, provides a plan for rectifying the inequality of educational opportunity for economically underprivileged children by authorizing federal aid to improve the education of disadvantage children, including students with disabilities. It results in the creation of the Head Start program for disadvantaged children and their families and will become the basis for future special education legislation.

1966 An amendment to Title VI of ESEA, P.L. 89–750, establishes the first federal grant program for children and youth with disabilities at the local school level. Additionally, it creates the Bureau of Education for the Handicapped and what later will become the National Council on Disabilities. Most important, it establishes equal status for programs for children with disabilities with the Bureau of Elementary and Secondary Education, the Bureau of Vocational Education, and the Bureau of Higher Education.

1967 *Hobson vs. Hansen* declares the tracking system, which uses standardized tests as a basis for special education placement, unconstitutional because it discriminates against black and poor children.

1968 Another ESEA amendment, P.L. 90–247, becomes the first special education legislation enacted at the federal level establishing a set of "discretionary programs" that provide support for special education services. Examples of this include regional resource centers, services for the deaf-blind, instructional media programs, and research in special education.

1970 The ruling in *Diana vs. State Board of Education of California* declares that children cannot be placed in special education on the basis of culturally biased tests or tests given in a language other than the child's native language.

The Education of the Handicapped Act (EHA) of 1970, P.L. 91–230, amends Title VI of P.L. 89–750, consolidating a number of separate federal grant programs into one authorization that becomes known as Part B, EHA.

1971 In *Wyatt vs. Stickney/Wyatt vs. Aderholt, Alabama,* the Court rules that individuals in state institutions have the right to appropriate treatment in those institutions.

1972 *Pennsylvania Association for Retarded Citizens (PARC) vs. Commonwealth* is a precedent setting case. PARC and thirteen children bring a class action suit against the Commonwealth of Pennsylvania for failure to provide its mentally retarded children with publicly supported education. The result is an agreement on the part of the Commonwealth of Pennsylvania to (1) not apply any law that would postpone, end, or deny mentally retarded children access to publicly supported education; and (2) to identify all school age children with mental retardation and place them in a free public program of education and training appropriate to their disability.

In *Mills vs. Board of Education,* parents and guardians of seven District of Columbia children are awarded a court judgment against the district school board whereby all children with a disability, regardless of the severity, are entitled to receive a publicly supported education. Just as *Brown vs. the Board of Education* applied to race, the federal district court interprets the equal protection clause of the Fourteenth Amendment to apply to discrimination of students on the basis of disability. The impact of *Mills* is to reinforce legislation passed by forty-five states mandating the funding of special education.

1973 Section 504 of the Rehabilitation Act, P.L. 93–112, bars discrimination against the disabled in any federally funded program and specifically requires appropriate education services for disabled children. This is the first civil rights law specifically protecting the right of handicapped children; originally dealing with employment, it will be amended in 1974 (P.L. 93–516) to cover a broader array of services for the handicapped. It establishes nondiscrimination in employment, admission into institutions of higher learning, and access to public facilities.

1974 Education amendments passed this year contain two significant laws. The first makes provisions for education to all children with disabilities and reauthorizes all discretionary programs; the second is the Family Education Rights and Privacy Act (the Buckley amendment) giving parents and children under the age of eighteen, and students eighteen and over, the right to examine records in their personal files.

1975 The Education of All Handicapped Children Act, P.L. 94–142, mandates for all children with disabilities (1) a free and appropriate public education; (2) the right of due process; (3) education in the least restrictive environment; and (4) individualized educational programs. These four areas will serve as the nucleus of special education philosophy, documentation, and program development. Nowhere does this law state exactly how costs are to be considered. Whenever a service is necessary, cost consideration cannot allow a school district to escape its obligation to that child. Decisions concerning instructional matters remain at the discretion of state and local authorities.

1978 In *Howard S. vs. Friendswood Independent School District*, the court found that Douglas, an emotionally disturbed teenager, had enjoyed reasonable scholastic and personal successes when enrolled in special education in junior high school. However, when he entered high school and began to manifest behavioral problems, the school chose to treat Douglas's behavioral problems as a disciplinary matter and refused the parents' requests for evaluation of Douglas's special needs. The court was persuaded by testimony that, without appropriate behavioral programming, Douglas would probably develop a worsening behavioral pattern, likely ending in incarceration. The court ordered the school district to provide behavioral programming and to reimburse Douglas's parents for the cost of a private school with a therapeutic program recommended by Douglas's psychiatrist (Martin, Martin & Terman, 1996).

1979 In *Central York District vs. Commonwealth of Pennsylvania Department of Education* the court rules that school districts must provide services for gifted and talented children whether or not advance guarantee of reimbursement from the state has been received.

The decision in *Larry P. vs. Riles,* a California case first brought to court in 1972, establishes that IQ test scores cannot be the sole basis for placing children in special classes.

1980 The ruling in *Armstrong vs. Kline, Pennsylvania,* establishes that some severely handicapped children have the right to schooling for twelve months instead of only the nine-month school year, if proof can be given that they will regress during the summer recess. The court also ruled that a state law requiring a nine-month school year violates P.L. 94–142 and Section 504 of the Vocational Rehabilitation Act.

1981 In regard to *Debra P. vs. Turlington,* the U.S. Court of Appeals for the Fifth Circuit Court holds that a diploma is a protected property right under the Fourteenth Amendment. If a state wishes to substantially change the requirements to earn a diploma, procedural due process requires that adequate notice of the change(s) be provided to students.

1982 In *Rowley vs. Hendrick Hudson School*, the issue of a free, appropriate public education (FAPE) reinforces school districts' provision of services permitting students with disabilities to benefit from instruction. Handed down by the U. S. Court of Appeals for the Second Circuit, this decision supports the philosophy behind IDEA, setting the standard for FAPE as more than simple access to education; instead, FAPE is viewed to consist of educational instruction assigned to meet the unique needs of a student with disabilities, supported by such services as needed to benefit from instruction. This law provides guidance for courts to use in deciding on a case-by-case basis, whether a school has offered a FAPE to a student with disabilities.

1983 *Hall vs. Vance County Board of Education*—involves James Hall, a student with dyslexia who had been in the public schools for six years with no real grade improvement in his primary area of deficiency despite being consistently promoted. His parents enrolled James in a private school for the 1980–1981 school year and realized significant improvement in reading scores. Having determined that the IEP developed by Vance County, North Carolina, did not provide Hall with an appropriate education citing standardized education scores of sufficient gain, the presiding judge ruled to reward Hall's parents with reimbursement for the private school tuition.

In *Brookhart vs. Illinois State Board of Education,* a case involving a student receiving special education services, the circuit court rules that students with disabilities can be held to the same graduation standards as other students, but that their programs of instruction are not developed to meet the goal of passing the minimum competency test. The court also finds that students are entitled to sufficient time to prepare for a test (in this case the minimum competency test) and that accommodations are required as long as they do not modify the test to the point of altering its validity characteristics.

The Carl Perkins Vocational Act, P.L. 98–524, has as its focus the authorization of federal funds to support vocational education programs and offer access of those underserved in the past and who are special needs students, to include persons with a disability or who are disadvantaged or have limited English proficiency. Each of these groups is to henceforth receive equal access to recruitment, enrollment, and placement activities in vocational education, including specific courses of study, cooperative education, apprenticeship programs, and guidance and counseling services. Services have to be coordinated between public agencies, vocational education, special education, and state vocational rehabilitation services. These must all be consistent with objectives specified in the IEP.

1984 The case *Burlington School Committee vs. Department of Education* again affirms the meaning of IDEA whereby public schools may be required to pay for private school placements when an appropriate education is not provided by the school district.

In *Cleburne vs. Cleburne Living Center, Texas,* the U.S. Supreme Court rules unanimously that communities cannot use a discriminatory zoning ordinance to prevent establishment of group homes for persons with mental retardation.

1985 In *Burlington vs. Department of Education for the Commonwealth of Massachusetts,* the Supreme Court addresses IEPs and what they should include. The Court rules that the free appropriate public education (FAPE) mandated by IDEA is designed for the specific needs of the child through the IEP, which is a "comprehensive statement of the educational needs of a handicapped child and the specially designed instruction and related services to be employed to meet those needs."

An EHA amendment, P.L. 94–457, mandates services for preschoolers with disabilities and establishes the Part H program to help states develop and provide systems for early intervention to include infants and toddlers from birth through age three. This is a landmark success for proponents of early intervention. The law provides for an individualized family service plan for each qualifying family.

1986 The Handicapped Children's Protection Act, P.L. 99–372, provides for reasonable attorney's fees and costs to parents and guardians who prevail in administrative hearings or court where there is a dispute with the school system concerning their child's right to a free and appropriate education.

1988 *Honig vs. Doe* again reaffirms IDEA with regard to excluding a student from school in that if a student's behavior is related to his or her disability, that student cannot be denied education.

The case *Lachman vs. State Board of Education* (852 F2d 290, Seventh Circuit) concerns parents who want their deaf child mainstreamed in a neighborhood school in contrast to the opinion of their school district, which believes that half days in a self-contained hearing-impaired classroom are appropriate. The court applies the Rowley rule to determine if the state has met federal standards in providing a free, appropriate education. The court rules in support of mainstreaming but determines that educational methods are the responsibility of the state and local education agencies and that parents have no right to dictate specific program or methodology to the school.

Martinez vs. School Board of Hillsboro County, Florida (861 F2d 1502 Eleventh Circuit) concerns a trainable mentally handicapped (TMH) AIDS-infected child who is not toilet trained, whose saliva contained blood, and who had skin lesions and was thus excluded from classroom placement. Whereas the trial court found "a remote theoretical possibility" of disease transmission, the district court finds the child presented no significant risk to exclude her from the TMH classroom. The court determines that "reasonable medical judgments" are required to determine the level of risk for children with a communicable disease. The parents win their case—AIDS cases cannot be excluded from public school.

1989 In *Daniel R. R. vs. State Board of Education*, Daniel was an elementary school student with Down's syndrome. The school district claimed that, because Daniel could not perform at the same academic level as his classmates, he would obtain no benefit from inclusion in the regular classroom. The Fifth Circuit Court created a two-part inquiry to determine whether placement in the regular classroom, with supplementary services, could be achieved satisfactorily. Second, if the decision is made to remove the child from the regular classroom for all or part of the day, then the school must also ask whether the child has been mainstreamed (spending some time in the regular classroom) to the maximum extent possible. As the court stated, "The [IDEA] and its regulations do not contemplate an all-or-nothing educational system in which children with disabilities attend either regular or special education. Rather, the Act and its regulations require schools to offer a continuum of services" (Martin, Martin, & Terman, 1996).

In *Timothy W. vs. Rochester School District,* a case from New Hampshire that is taken to the U.S. Appeals Court, a literal interpretation of P.L. 94–142 is upheld, requiring that all handicapped children be provided with a free, appropriate public education. The three-judge appeals court overturns the decision of the district court judge who had ruled that the local school district was not obligated to educate a thirteen-year-old boy with multiple and severe disabilities because he could not "benefit" from special education.

U.S. governors meet in Charlottesville, Virginia, and commit themselves to a nationwide effort to reform education around a core set of six goals for improving the education system. These goals, with the addition of two more, will be formalized into law in 1994 in the Goals 2000: Educate America Act.

The ruling in *Lascari vs. Board of Education of the Ramapo Indian Hills Regional High School District* (New Jersey) states that the required public-school IEP is intended to guide teachers and to insure that the child receives the necessary education; without an adequately drafted IEP it would basically be impossible to measure a child's progress, which is necessary to determine changes to be made to the next IEP. The court rules that the IEP in this case is incapable of review because it is based on teacher subjectivity, thereby denying the child's parents the opportunity to help shape their child's education and hindering the child's ability to receive the education to which he is entitled.

1990 The Individuals with Disabilities Education Act (IDEA), P.L. 101–476, originally realized as an amendment to the Education of the Handicapped Act, reauthorizes and expands discretionary programs and mandates transition services and assistive technology services to be included in the IEP, adding autism and traumatic brain injury to those categories for special education programs and services.

The Americans with Disabilities Act (ADA), P.L. 101–336, is passed. ADA is based on the Rehabilitation Act of 1973, which guarantees equal opportunities for individuals with disabilities in employment, public accommodation, and transportation. Included in this act are persons with HIV infection, diabetics who without insulin would lapse into a coma, former cancer patients, persons erroneously classified as having a disability (for example, a psychiatric disorder), recovering alcoholics and drug addicts, and those with a back condition. Accessibility requirements for employers with over twenty-five employees will begin in 1992 and for employers with over fifteen employees will begin in 1994. Public services affected by the ADA include public transportation and telecommunications, which must make changes to telephones services offered to the general public with respect to interstate and intrastate as well as TT/TDD users. As defined by the act, public accommodations include private entities that affect commerce, among them restaurants, theaters, hotels, shopping malls, retail stores, museums, libraries, parks, private schools, day care centers, and similar places of accommodation, all of which may not discriminate on the basis of disability. Physical barriers must be removed, new construction must all be made accessible, alterations to existing facilities must be made for travel paths and such, and new buses and similar vehicles must be accessible. ADA does not require modifications that would alter the nature of the service provided by the public accommodation; for example, a physician who does not treat that disability on a regular basis will not be required to add that service.

1991 In *French vs. Omaha Public Schools,* the court determines that the IEP at a Nebraska public school was appropriate when it analyzed the goals and objectives and the inclusion of very specific test data, including percentile ranks and grade equivalent scores used to describe the child's present levels of performance.

1992 In *Greer vs. Rome City School District* (Georgia), the Eleventh Circuit Court rules in favor of parents who objected to the placement of their daughter in a self-contained special education classroom. Administrators at the child's school had determined that the services needed to keep the child in the regular education classroom were too costly. The court's opinion states that all options must be considered before removing a child from the regular classroom.

1993 *Florence County School District Four vs. Shannon Carter, 510 U.S. 7* In a unanimous 9-0 decision, the Supreme Court found that if the public school fails to provide an appropriate education and the child receives an appropriate education in a private placement, the parents are entitled to be reimbursed for the child's education, even if the private school does not comply with state standards. This ruling opened the door to children with autism who receive ABA/Lovaas therapy (Wrightslaw, 2008).

The Third District Court rules in *Oberti vs. Board of Education of the Borough of Clementon School District* (California) in favor of a placement for a special-needs child that was more inclusive than that provided by a self-contained placement. The court bases its decision on the fact that the whole range of supplemental aids and services must be considered to make a regular education setting successful.

1994 The Improving America's Schools Act (IASA) extends for five years the authorization of appropriations for programs under the Elementary and Secondary Education Act of 1965 and requires that districts and schools receiving federal Title I funds implement a standards-based accountability system to include multiple sources of assessment data. All children, including students with disabilities, are to be included in assessment from which achievement results can be disaggregated for several groups including "special education status."

The Safe and Drug-Free Schools and Communities Act (SDFSCA), Title IV of the Improving America's Schools Act of 1994, authorizes the U.S. Secretary of Education to make grants to states to prevent school violence and to deter the use of illegal drugs and alcohol. This affects special education in terms of early intervention and rehabilitation in that the SDFSCA provides federal assistance to governors, state and local educational agencies, institutions of higher education, and nonprofit entities for (1) grants to LEAs and educational service agencies to establish, operate, and improve local programs of school drug and violence prevention, early intervention, rehabilitation referral, and education in elementary and secondary schools; (2) grants to public and private community based agencies and organizations for programs of drug and violence prevention, early intervention, rehabilitation referral, and education; and (3) development, training, technical assistance, and coordination activities.

The Gun-Free Schools Act (GFSA) requires every state receiving federal aid for elementary and secondary education to enact a law requiring a local educational agency (LEA) to expel from school for at least one year any students who brings a gun to school. Educational services must continue for students with disabilities who are properly expelled, although services may be continued in another setting. If the student's action in bringing a firearm to school is related to his or her disability, the student may not be expelled but may instead be suspended for up to ten days. The local education agency (LEA) may also seek a court order to remove a student who is considered dangerous.

In *Sacramento City Unified School District vs. Holland,* the Ninth Circuit Court upholds the decision of the lower court, which decided in favor of the parents of a California child who had been placed half-time in a special education classroom and half-time in a regular education classroom; considering the nonacademic benefits of the regular classroom to be significant, the circuit court rules that the child should be placed in the regular classroom full-time.

1996 The Ninth Circuit Court affirms in *County of San Diego vs. California Special Education Hearing Office* that a county cannot challenge a student's classification as seriously emotionally disturbed on the ground that state law gives school districts the sole authority to make such eligibility decisions.

Wall vs. Mattituck-Cutchogue School District concerns parents of an elementary student with learning disabilities who bring action against a school district in New York requesting their child be taught reading using the Orton-Gillingham instructional procedure. The student, who was educated in a public school's self-contained special education classroom, was unilaterally placed in a private school that used the reading procedure. At an earlier hearing, the parents did not challenge the appropriateness of the IEP; rather, they contested the school district's failure to offer the Orton-Gillingham program. The hearing officer found that the school district's program was appropriate, and the parents appealed to federal district court. The court, finding that the student has made progress in the school district's program, affirms the ruling for the school district.

The judge for *Evans vs. Board of Education of Rhinebeck Central School District* (New York) overturns earlier administrative rulings and awards the Evans family reimbursement for tuition at a private school because the IEP failed to identify deficit areas, was based on outdated information, and did not adequately set forth strategies for evaluating progress.

1997 In *Logue vs. Shawnee Mission Public School Unified School District,* the federal district court that hears the case determines that Kansas does not have a higher standard of appropriateness than the IDEA. The court indicates that since the measure in question parallels the Supreme Court's standard in *Rowley,* there is no evidence to indicate that the state legislature intended to bind itself to a higher duty.

Another IDEA amendment, P.L. 105–17, applies to the nation's 5.8 million children with disabilities and enhances what children with disabilities learn versus what is expected in the regular classroom, in short decreeing that children with disabilities have the right to be educated, or included, in the regular classroom. It differs from the previous IDEA amendment, P.L.101–476, in that it protects the rights of students and families by having them become more involved in general curriculum, eligibility, and placement, and requires on the part of the schools more accountability for results. Additionally, this amendment guarantees that general education teachers will be included in teams that develop mandated IEPs for disabled students when the student is in a general classroom. Students in special education were being excluded from many state and district assessments, which leads to exclusion from curriculum planning. Eligibility for alternate assessments are to be made with students with significant support needs. For example, per the 1997 IDEA amendment, if the child's disability has not changed over a three-year period, that child should not be forced into unnecessary reassessment. Participation in the regular program is to be promoted as much as possible with modifications and adaptations to include adaptive and assistive technology. Disciplinary rules and instructions in terms of behaviors are to be part of the individualized education program if the child's behavior impedes learning. It is a requirement of the IEP to include a behavioral management plan and information on a child's past violent behavior. Parental responsibility in working with the school is emphasized; parents are to be involved in eligibility and placement decisions, and the new emphasis is to be able to attain high-quality education rather than just access to education. The significance of early intervention is reiterated, and the funding formula for federal assistance under IDEA is changed to include poverty factors.

The following definitions and explanations of terms are included in the 1997 IDEA amendment in order to make explicit and clear for parents and educators the legal rights added under this amendment:

"Attention deficit disorder" and "attention deficit hyperactivity disorder" have been added as conditions that could render a child eligible under the "other health impairment" category. (See 300.7(c)(9).)

The statement "helping parents to acquire the necessary skills that will allow them to support the implementation of their child's IEP or IFSP" has been added to the definition of "parent counseling and training." (See 300.24(b)(7).)

"Travel training" has been added to the definition of "special education" and defined to mean "Providing instruction, as appropriate, to children with significant cognitive disabilities and any other children who require this instruction, to enable them to (i) develop an awareness of the environment in which they live; and (ii) learn the skills necessary to move effectively and safely from place to place within that environment (e.g., in school, in the home, at work, and in the community)." (See 300.26(b)(4).)

A new section 300.312, Developmental Delay, has been added, which makes it clear that children with disabilities in public charter schools and their parents retain all rights under this part, and that compliance with Part B is required regardless of whether a public charter school receives Part B funds.

A new section 300.313, Children Experiencing Developmental Delays, has been added to: (1) specify the conditions that states and LEAs must follow in using the term, and (2) clarify that a state or LEA that elects to use "developmental delay" also may use one or more of the disability categories for any child who has been determined (through the IDEA evaluation procedures) to have a disability and need special education. Thus, if a child has an identified disability (e.g., deafness), it would be appropriate to use the term with that child even if the state or LEA is using "developmental delay" for other children aged three through nine. The regulations also make clear that a state may adopt a common definition of "developmental delay" under Parts B and C of the act.

1998 The Assistive Technology Act offers block grants to states for public education and advocacy related to assistive technology products and services. In addition, the law authorizes a new micro loan program to encourage the development and purchase of accessible technology-related products and services.

1999 The proposed Gifted and Talented Students Education Act, also called the Educational Excellence for All Children's Act, would provide funding to states based on population. It reauthorizes ESEA (1994) and Goals 2000: Educate America Act. The funds could be used at state discretion for any of four activities: personnel preparation, technical assistance, innovative programs and services, and emerging technologies including distance learning. This proposed education bill is presently in committee.

Cedar Rapids Community School District vs. Garret F. and Charlene F. Garrett F., a minor and student in Cedar Rapids Community School District, is wheelchair-bound and ventilator dependent. He requires assistance in attending to his physical needs during the school day. The school district declined to accept financial responsibility for Garret's services in order for him to be able to attend school. The school district believed it was not legally obligated to provide one-on-one care. An Administrative Law judge concluded that the Individuals with Disabilities Education Act (IDEA) required the school district to provide "school health services", which are provided by a "qualified school nurse or other qualified person," but not medical services, which are limited to services provided by a physician. The District Court and the Court of Appeals affirmed, despite arguments from the school district, that such one-on-one care is too costly and too involved to be considered anything but medical in nature. In a 7-to-2 decision, the Court held that if the services in question are "related" to keeping the disabled child in school and able to access educational opportunities available to others IDEA funded school districts must provide such services. The Court added that although the nature and cost of providing certain IDEA "related services" is not determinative of whether their financial burdens must be met, potential financial burdens shall inform any decision governing their provision. In the present case, the benefits of providing Garret with his needed care outweighed the burdens (The OYEZ Project, U.S. Supreme Court Media, 2008).

2000 The Goals 2000: Educate America Act, P.L. 103–227, based on eight goals formulated by U.S. governors for improving the national education system, is signed into law. The eight goals are:

Goal 1: Ready To Learn—By the year 2000, all children in the United States will start school ready to learn.

Goal 2: School Completion—By the year 2000, the high school graduation rate will increase to at least 90 percent.

Goal 3: Student Achievement and Citizenship—By the year 2000, all students will leave grades 4, 8, and 12 having demonstrated competency over challenging subject matter, including English, mathematics, science, foreign languages, civics and government, economics, arts, history, and geography. Every school in the United States will ensure that all students learn to use their minds well, so they may be prepared for responsible citizenship, further learning, and productive employment in the economy.

Goal 4: Teacher Education and Professional Development—By the year 2000, the nation's teaching force will have access to programs for the continued improvement of their professional skills and the opportunity to acquire the knowledge and skills needed to instruct and prepare all students in the United States for the next century.

Goal 5: Mathematics and Science—By the year 2000, students in the United States will be first in the world in mathematics and science achievement.

Goal 6: Adult Literacy and Lifelong Learning—By the year 2000, every adult in the United States will be literate and will possess the knowledge and skills necessary to compete in a global economy and exercise the rights and responsibilities of citizenship.

Goal 7: Safe, Disciplined, and Alcohol- and Drug-Free Schools—By the year 2000, every school in the United States will be free of drugs, violence, and the unauthorized presence of firearms and alcohol and will offer a disciplined environment conducive to learning.

Goal 8: Parental participation—By the year 2000, every school in the United States will promote partnerships that will increase parental involvement and participation in promoting the social, emotional, and academic growth of children.

Goals 2000: Educate America Act. The funds could be used at state discretion for any of four activities: personnel preparation, technical assistance, innovative programs and services, and emerging technologies including distance learning. This proposed education bill is presently in committee.

The Class Size Reduction Act, P.L.106–113, Section 310, is a government initiative to help schools improve student learning by hiring additional qualified teachers so that children, especially those in early elementary grades, can attend smaller classes. Beginning July 3, 2000, the Department of Education sends class-size reduction funds to all states, the District of Columbia, Puerto Rico, the outlying areas, and the Bureau of Indian Affairs. The amount of each allocation is based on Title I or Title II of the ESEA, whichever would result in the larger amount for the state or entity.

2001 *Amanda C. vs. Clark County School District & Nevada Department of Education (9*th *Circuit)* This strongly written decision cites research about ABA/Lovaas treatment; describes purposes of the IDEA; IEPs and procedural safeguards. District's failure to provide parents with evaluations adversely affected parents' ability to make decisions and damaged child; district failed to provide FAPE; standard of review in two-tier system; credibility of witnesses (Wrightslaw, 2008).

Burriola vs. Greater Toledo YMCA (W. D. OH) In ADA case, federal Judge issue injunction, orders day care center to readmit child with autism; staff must be trained; discussion of reasonable accommodations, exhaustion, training (Wrightslaw, 2008).

*Fales vs. Garst (8*th *Circuit)* Three special education teachers filed suit against principal who tried to block them from advocating for students; free speech vs. employers rights (Wrightslaw, 2008).

*Jaynes vs. Newport News Public Schools District (4*th *Circuit)* Case on behalf of child with autism whose parents provided intensive homebound ABA/Lovaas program; statutes of limitations, procedural safeguards, notice requirements, and reimbursement. (Wrightslaw, 2008).

No Child Left Behind (NCLB) Act (PL 107-110) is a US federal law (Act of Congress) that reauthorized and consolidated a number of earlier programs and laws in order to improve the performance of U.S. primary and secondary schools by the standards of accountability for states, school districts, and schools and provide parents more flexibility in order to make choices as to which schools their children will attend. *ft
NCLB reauthorized the Elementary Special Education Act (ESEA) of 1965, promoted an increased focus on reading, was passed in the House of Representatives on May 23, 2001, US Senate on June 14, 2001, and signed into law on January 8, 2002.

NCLB is based on the belief that standard based education reform, setting high expectations, and establishing measurable goals will improve individual outcomes in education. Standards are set by each state and each state must develop assessments in basic skills to be given to all students in certain grades. Giving the state control of this complies with the 10th Amendment of the US Constitution specifying powers not given to the federal government are reserved for the states. Supporting NCLB emphases on assessment is the belief that systematic testing provides data that sheds light on which schools are not teaching basic skills effectively, so that interventions can be made to improve outcomes for all students while reducing the achievement gap for disadvantaged and disabled students.

2002 *Polera vs. Board of Education Newburgh City School District (2nd Circuit)* In damages case under Section 504 and ADA, court rules that disabled child must first exhaust administrative remedies under IDEA. Decision includes extensive discussion of relief under statutes, compensatory and punitive damages, exhaustion requirement, and futility exception (Wrightslaw, 2008).

2003 *Maroni vs. Pemi-Baker Regional School District (1st Circuit)* Decision breaks new ground, Court rules that parents can pursue IDEA claims in federal court without an attorney (Wrightslaw, 2008).

2004 *Reauthorization of IDEA* On December 3, 2004, President Bush signed the Individuals with Disabilities Education Improvement Act (P.L. 108-446), a major reauthorization and revision of IDEA. The new law preserves the basic structure and civil rights guarantees of IDEA, but also makes significant changes in the law, including new provisions regarding how schools can determine whether a child has a specific learning disability and may receive special education services. Most provisions of P.L. 108-446 became effective on July 1, 2005 (National Dissemination Center for Children with Disabilities, 2008).

Pamella Settlegoode vs. Portland Public Schools (9th Circuit) Court upheld jury verdict, reinstated 1 million dollar award to special education teacher who was retaliated against and fired for advocating for her students; decision clarified freedom of speech for teachers (Wrightslaw, 2008).

M. L. vs. Federal Way School District (WA) (9th Circuit) Court found that the failure to include a regular education teacher on the IEP team was a serious procedural error that led to a loss of educational opportunity and a denial of FAPE (Wrightslaw, 2008).

Zachary Deal vs. Hamilton County TN Board of Education (6th Circuit) Wide-ranging decision about standard of review, additional evidence, judicial notice, procedural and substantive IDEA violations, FAPE, educational benefit, predetermination of placement, failure to include regular ed teacher and reimbursement (Wrightslaw, 2008).

Mackey vs. Arlington Central School District, State Education Department (2nd Circuit) In "stay-put"/pendency case, Court finds that parents are entitled to reimbursement for private school tuition because earlier denial was a result of delays and untimely decision by the state review officer (Wrightslaw, 2008).

2005 *J. S. vs. Isle of Wright Virginia School Board (4th Circuit)* Money damages were not available because Congress intended disabled children to pursue claims to FAPE through remedial mechanisms in the IDEA statute; extensive discussion of statute of limitations and federal "borrowing' doctrine (Wrightslaw, 2008).

2005 *Schaeffer vs. Weast* The parents of Brian Schaffer, a disabled child, sued their public school district under the Individuals with Disabilities Act (IDEA). Schaffer's parents claimed the Individualized Education Program that the school system devised for their son, and which IDEA required for each disabled student, was inadequate. In a 6-2 ruling, the Supreme Court held that the party bringing the suit bears the burden of proof, whether that party is the parents or the school system. In the majority opinion, Justice Sandra Day O'Connor wrote that "absent some reason to believe that Congress intended otherwise, . . . we will conclude that the burden of persuasion lies where it usually falls, upon the party seeking relief" burdens (The OYEZ Project, U.S. Supreme Court Media, 2008).

Judith Scruggs, Administratix of Estate of Daniel Scruggs vs. Meriden Board of Education, E. Ruocco, M. B. Iacobelli and Donna Mule (US District Court, Connecticut) Suit for actual and punitive damages against school board, superintendent, vice principal and guidance counselor under IDEA, ADA, 504, 42 USC 1983, 1985 and 1986. Child bullied, harassed in school for years while school personnel looked on, did nothing. Child committed suicide (Wrighslaw, 2008).

2006 *Arlington Central School District vs. Murphy, Pearl, et vir* In August of 1999, Pearl and Theodore Murphy filed a complaint on behalf of their son Joseph Murphy, who has dyslexia and several other cognitive disabilities, claiming that the Arlington Central School District did not prepare a proper individualized Education Program (IEP) for their son. Although the Murphy's won their case, they returned to court seeking $29,350.00 in fees for the services of an educational expert and consultant they had hired for their case. In a 6-3 decision, the Court ruled that prevailing parents are not entitled to recover fees for services rendered by experts in IDEA actions (On the Docket U.S. Supreme Court News, 2008).

Henrico County School Board vs. R. T. (E.D. VA) Tuition reimbursement case for young child with autism; comparison of TEACCH and ABA; FAPE and least restrictive environment; deference to decision of hearing officer; witness credibility; impact of low expectations and "an insufficient focus on applying replicable research on proven methods of teaching and learning." (Wrightslaw, 2008).

2007 *Jarron Draper vs. Atlanta Independent School System (N.D. GA)* School district misdiagnosed a dyslexic boy as mentally retarded, placed him in self-contained program for years where he did not learn to read. School district failed to complete three-year reevaluation, as required by law. The Court ordered the school system to provide Jarron Draper with compensatory education at private special education school for four years or until he graduates with a regular high school diploma (Wrightslaw, 2008).

2008 *Reauthorization of the Higher Education Act (H.E.A.)* reauthorizes the 1965 H.E.A. increasing support for: (1) collaboration between school districts and teacher-preparation programs, (2) keeping tuition costs down, and (3) simplifying the main federal student-aid application from 7-27 pages. This act was approved by a bipartisan majority in both the House and Senate. The H.E.A. of 2008, last renewed in 1998, has been in preparation since 2003.

REFERENCES

Martin, E. W., Martin, R., & Terman, D.L. (1996). The legislative and litigation history of special education.

Special Education for Students with Disabilities, Vol. 6, No. 1, p.25.

National Dissemination Center for Children with Disabilities. *(1999-2008). A User's Guide to the 2004 IDEA*

Reauthorization. Consortium for Citizens with Disabilities. Retrieved November 5, 2008 from http://www.ncld.org/content/view/274/321/

Wrights Law. (2008). *Special Education Caselaw.* US Supreme Court I Courts of Appeals District Courts 1

Noteworthy Cases. Notes to Non-lawyers. Retrieved January 20, 2008 from http://www.wrightslaw.com/caselaw.htm

Chapter Three

Special Education Curriculum

Curriculum can be viewed as anything that occurs in the education and program during the school day. This can begin the moment a student leaves home to begin the school experience and last until the time he or she returns home. More specifically, curriculum can be viewed as a composition of vision and structure. *Vision* for a curriculum is frequently what we see as important for people to experience in order to learn. How we view the people for whom a curriculum is developed and the environment in which we anticipate they live becomes the basis of the plan for the vision. The plan we develop for this to happen takes place within a specific *structure.* That specific structure is the way the organization of the information is implemented.

Once the vision and philosophy of what we want special education students to gain within the educational experience are clear, the development of curriculum becomes direct and purposeful. From knowledge and understanding obtained, skills and applications can be developed.

Eisner (as cited in Florida Department of Education, 1994) explains that *curriculum* comes from the Latin word "currere," meaning "the course to be run." Additionally, *curriculum* has been conceived of as all the experiences a child has during the school day; this includes the quality of the experiences, not just the lessons. A curriculum cannot ignore individual differences. Whatever the philosophy behind curriculum, the consequences of the concept are greater than solely educational; they influence people in a variety of ways. The development of skills is parallel to that of attitudes and values. The classroom actually becomes a social environment that serves as a microcosm for the social experiences to be experienced by each person.

According to Fogarty (as cited in Florida Department of Education, 1994) *integrating* the curriculum helps teachers make connections between new experiences and prior knowledge. "Innovative teaching models call for integrated, cross disciplinary instruction. As teachers begin to mix and match subject-matter using creative combinations, the restructuring process is actually generated from the inside out" (p. 259). In a traditional model, there are separate and distinct disciplines. In an integrated curriculum, relating ideas and concepts within and across disciplines gives a different emphasis. By tying thoughts, social skills, topics, and technology across disciplines, commonalties emerge.

The concept of the integrated curriculum is especially significant when viewing the academic and specific needs of the special education child. A curriculum that is developed for someone needing remediation of either the material or an area of the brain, that focuses on training all thought processes, and that utilizes more tools and technology allows the special education student to operate the same part of the thought process as the rest of the group.

Although the content of a curriculum is important, the *process* of curriculum development is equally important. When the process of curriculum development for at-risk and handicapped children is based on the concept of individual differences due to intellectual, cognitive, and physical disabilities, the strategies and activities can be planned more thoughtfully. In all probability, they will have more successful outcomes. Interventionists and curriculum planners need to be very aware of this.

When dealing with young children to develop annual goals and objectives, which drive curriculum development, the presence of a family member is mandatory. Additionally, it is important that specific health professionals or allied health professionals be present in such planning. Strategies developed as part of the curriculum will be more meaningful if that professional is part of the team. Whether the health professional or a resource person is providing the therapy or recommended procedure, at least the team will be knowledgeable of the best practice. A consultation model may be the best way to implement these specific responsibilities (Bricker, 1989).

CURRICULUM DEVELOPMENT INVOLVES A MULTIDISCIPLINARY TEAM

In addition to the special education teacher and the regular education teacher, related service personnel are involved in both the IEP and curriculum development, helping to create a multidisciplinary team. They include:

Social Worker/Visiting Teacher. The school social worker/visiting teacher may

- serve as liaison between student, family, community agencies, and the schools;
- coordinate social services for the student and the family;
- consult with families to assist them in child-rearing practices;
- contact social and medical agencies regarding referrals from the school; and
- assist in the return of the students to regular class placement.

Speech-Language Pathologist. The speech-language pathologist may

- provide speech and language assessments;
- provide speech and language therapy;
- interpret test information;
- provide in-service training for special and basic education teachers;
- provide parent training; and

- assist in the development and implementation of an appropriate individual educational plan.

Psychologist. The school psychologist may
- conduct formal observations and testing;
- interpret test information;
- supervise evaluation procedures;
- consult directly with teachers, other school personnel, and parents; and
- provide in-service training on behavior management techniques.

Behavior Specialist. The behavior special may
- provide technical expertise to address complex student behavior issues;
- assist school staff in development, implementation, and education of student behavior management plans; and
- provide technical expertise to assist parents in addressing complex student behavioral issues.

Guidance Counselor. The school guidance counselor may
- participate in screening, referral, and placement procedures;
- observe and participate in behavioral management strategies;
- consult with teachers with regard to specific interaction techniques designed to assist the student; and
- provide guidance and support to students who have specialized needs.

Vocational Rehabilitation (VR) Counselor. The VR counselor may
- determine specific strengths, weaknesses, needs, and interests of the individual as related to job placement;
- assist in appropriate job placement according to the individual's profile;
- provide for vocational training (whether on or off the job);
- provide for follow-up and job-related counseling; and
- participate in a support team of educational, career counseling, vocational, and job-training personnel.

School Nurses. The school nurse may
- facilitate referrals for medical and/or social services for students;
- serve as a consultant on matters related to student development, especially in the physical and social areas;
- serve as liaison between community agencies, family, and the school;
- provide screening for hearing, vision, or other health areas as indicated in the school health services plan.

Health Professionals (may include community nurses, pediatricians, psychiatrists, and neurologists). Health professionals may
- provide for the student's physical well-being;
- make referrals, as appropriate, to other health professionals;
- assist in coordination of health services between educational specialists and other medical personnel;
- communicate to the educational personnel the specific medical needs of the student;

- provide information related to medication for the students;
- provide assistance in implementing the school medical program; and
- provide specific diagnostic information.

Occupational Therapist. The occupational therapist may

- provide expertise in areas of motor development; positioning, adapting the environment; gross motor skills; posture; ambulation; cardiorespiratory functioning; joint mobility; muscle strengths; fine motor, perceptual-motor, and sensorimotor skills; sensory integration; and environmental and equipment adaptations to increase participation in functional daily activities;
- assist the student to achieve the goals and objectives on the IEP;
- integrate therapeutic practices noted above into the student's education program; and assist the student in integrating into and participating in normalized school, home, and community environments.

Physical Therapist. The physical therapist may

- provide expertise in the areas of motor development, positioning, adapting the environment, gross motor skills, posture, ambulation, cardiorespiratory functioning, joint mobility, and muscle strength;
- assist the student in achieving the goals and objectives on the IEP;
- integrate therapeutic practices noted above into the student's educational program; and
- assist the student in integrating into and participating in normalized school, home, and community environments.

CURRICULUM-BASED ASSESSMENT (CBA) AND EVALUATION APPROACH

Measurement tools linking assessment with curriculum are frequently called curriculum-based assessment (CBA). It is important to note that focusing on the assessment or evaluation takes away from the focus of the curriculum upon which that specific form of assessment is based.

Curriculums are usually based on certain developmental norms and patterns. Provisions for handicapped children must be very specific because these are not norms and patterns specifically developed for them. Developmentally arranged patterns are very general guidelines for a very different population. Children using augmentative communications systems especially cannot adhere to these. All this considered, developmental theory and research provides a general guideline. Curriculum goals have been broadened to include competencies that cut across all developmental and curriculum domains to include problem solving, creative thinking, and reasoning. Each emphasizes that at-risk children, as well as regular education children, need to be able to apply what they need to situations in the real world. Curriculum goals and objectives can be assessed on a broad basis as well as a specific basis. By having assessment based on specified curriculum goals and objectives, a greater understanding of results compared to expected outcomes can be achieved. A general assessment can be ascertained with specific assessments based on disability and level, compatible with goals and objectives in the IEP. This will provide a basis for comparison as well as a guide for planning additional experiences, if necessary (McAfee and Leong, 1990).

The curriculum can also be responsive to children's strengths and needs as determined by the assessment so that modifications can be made. Thus CBA becomes a circular plan—thought is given to the development, assessments are made, and new strategies are created based on those assessments to help achieve curriculum goals or to reevaluate those goals.

If students are assessed based on the curriculum they experience, and curriculum is developed based on individual goals and objectives developed for each child, the circle may become complete. Performance assessment will be based on what was initially determined to meet the special needs of the individual. Feedback based on the performance of the special needs child will have meaning, and new curricula goals can be developed. Additionally, successes and failures in both teaching and learning can more easily be determined. Clear goals, monitoring of progress, and revising of materials offer an alternative way to assess curricula success, in contrast to a narrow curriculum focusing on information to be covered in order to fit the demands of testing and accountability.

Lambert and McCombs (1998) point out that standardized achievement tests do not offer options for assessing what children have learned in a complex era when diverse curricula are being developed. These tests demonstrate only one way children learn and do not properly demonstrate what children with special needs or children from different cultures know. Alternate forms of assessment need to be given equal weight in the assessment process. In *How Students Learn: Reforming Schools through Learner-Centered Education,* Lambert and McCombs identify effective curricula as those that

- attend to affect and mood as well as cognition and thinking in all learning activities and experiences, thereby engaging the learner;
- include assessments from students, peers, and teachers to check for student understanding of the subject matter, including implications and applications of knowledge;
- have an affective and cognitive richness that helps students generate positive thoughts and feelings of excitement, interest, and stimulation;
- help students engage in higher-order thinking and practice metacognitive strategies, including reflective self-awareness and goal setting;
- help students to be more aware of their own psychological functioning and how it relates to their own learning;
- include authentic tasks (relevant to the real world) and assessments that help students integrate information and performance across subject matter disciplines while allowing students to choose levels of difficulty for challenge or novelty;
- are developmentally appropriate to the unique intellectual, emotional, physical, and social characteristics of the individual;
- incorporate meaningful materials and activities relevant to different cultural groups;

- help students to increase awareness and understanding of how thought processes operate to produce separate, self-confirming realities so that they can better understand different individuals, as well as different social, cultural, and religious groups;
- encourage students to see positive qualities in all groups of learners, regardless of race, sex, culture, language, physical ability, or other individual differences; and
- include activities that promote empathy and understanding, respect for individual differences, and valuing of different perspectives, including materials from a multicultural perspective.

INCLUDING THE AFFECTIVE DOMAIN

Along with the concept of a meaningful integrated curriculum is the desire to develop the *affective domain*—that is, emotion—through the experiences of the special education student. Group experiences always affect the development of the child in terms of interpersonal relationships. Because people are put together physically does not mean that they are a successful group. When someone is uncomfortable, he or she is not going to participate and often feels threatened, which can lead to inappropriate interaction, a breakdown in communication, inappropriate attention-getting behaviors, and conflict.

There is a distinction between *social skills*—specific behaviors that a person uses to perform competently on social tasks—and *social competence*—an evaluative term based on a person's adequate performance on social tasks. Social skills are *behaviors,* and social competence represents *judgments* about those behaviors. Because social competence deficits are used to identify children as emotionally disturbed or having behavioral disorders, fostering social skills among learning-disabled children is an important part of school success. Teachers react to more than academic success when identifying at-risk children. Those who exhibit behaviors different from model behavioral profiles and who are also mildly handicapped frequently are referred for testing. Additionally, children with mild disabilities (LD, MMR, BD, ADHD) are frequently rejected by peers in general education classrooms. Self-concept and self-esteem and their place in the affective domain can be addressed by becoming part of the curriculum. Failing to include the affective domain serves only to alienate the special needs student more and increase the likelihood of school failure (Gresham and MacMillan, 1997).

Simply taking time, or including in the daily curriculum, an explanation of an appropriate climate for living within a group can be the difference between successful and unsuccessful educational experiences. To omit the affective domain of any area of study leaves out an important piece of total development. Sharing experiences, providing for rules for common courtesy, empathy toward others, collective decision-making, values clarification, conflict resolution, and other steps toward the collective productivity of experiences can enhance the learning situation.

When teachers create conditions that foster an atmosphere of trust, the student becomes more secure with the teacher as the guide through the curriculum. This creates a more positive emotional environment for the special needs student. Specific teaching techniques to encourage development of the affective domain include modeling—imitating observed behavior; role-playing and simulation—acting out and trying social behavior without consequences; counseling—working with an adult on a specific skill; and values clarification strategies—activities used to examine choices, make decisions, and acquire self-knowledge. These strategies can be especially useful with special education students who may have several layers of acceptance issues.

ENCOURAGING A MORE PEACEFUL ENVIRONMENT

Students with disabilities find themselves subjected to a variety of unpleasant situations during the day, both outside and inside the school building. Not only are students who are rationally or culturally different subjected to cultural violence, but concern in this area for the special needs student and its contribution to low self-esteem is significant.

A teacher trained in this sensitive area will more probably (1) model such behavior and (2) include cultural sensitive experiences in the curriculum in order to create a less violent classroom and more peaceful, safe place. In the curriculum, structured reflections on experiences and classroom situations provide the opportunity to think critically about human relationships. The act of cooperative teaching and cooperative learning as part of the curriculum will enhance cooperation as opposed to competition. The classroom will set the scene for a more global application of peace education.

Within the curriculum, academic experiences can be offered through specific instructional strategies in order to create a philosophy of peace and acceptance in an educational setting. This can have enormous impact on the special needs child when experiencing a mainstreamed or particularly an inclusive setting. For the young child the act of sharing and caring can be a strategy; for the young adult, tools such as abstract reasoning to achieve higher-level conflict resolution can be employed. It appears that it is to the advantage of those involved in curriculum development for both regular and special education students to include experiences encompassing the cognitive as well as the affective domain. In other words, when academic experiences and accompanying goals and objectives are developed, some form of the affective domain encompassing communication involving values and socioemotional developmental needs to be included. An example of balancing both domains, cognitive and affective, might be to present historical and geographic *factual experiences* regarding both sides of a war (the cognitive domain) and to include *pictures of families* of both sides of the war (the affective domain), then discuss implications of the lack of conflict resolution and peace.

Violence in the curriculum goes beyond the traditionally physical violent act and can extend to verbal, visual, or physical acts intended to demean or harm another individual. If not addressed, bullying of a physically challenged student or use of racial epithets, for example, can, occur on a daily basis. By using concepts such as conflict resolution, curricula can contain elements to prevent this type of physical and nonphysical violence. Kopka (1997) identifies specific violence prevention curricula involving the following fourteen educational strategies:

(1) *Afrocentric curricula* aim to prevent violence through an awareness of African and African-American roots. They are designed to instill a sense of cultural identity and pride.
(2) *Aggression reduction/anger management curricula* convey the message that anger is a normal human emotion. They explore healthy and unhealthy ways to express and channel anger.
(3) *Conflict resolution curricula* help develop empathy; impulse control; and skills in communication, problem solving, and anger management.
(4) *Crime prevention/law-related education curricula* teach students how to reduce their chances of becoming victims of crime and encourage them to develop school and community projects to reduce crime.
(5) *Gang prevention/reduction curricula* build awareness of the consequences of gang membership among youth who are not yet gang members.
(6) *Handgun violence prevention curricula* alert students to the risk posed by handguns and help them recognize and avoid potentially dangerous situations.
(7) *Life skills training curricula* teach a range of social skills that students need for healthy development, such as problem-solving skills, decisionmaking skills, and strategies for resisting peer pressure or media influences.
(8) *Peace education curricula* look at violence prevention interpersonally and within and among societies as a whole.
(9) *Peer mediation programs* involve about fifteen to twenty hours of training for students and teachers. Afterward students identify and mediate conflicts that occur in the school.
(10) *Prejudice reduction/cultural awareness curricula* attempt to overcome stereotypes and prejudices that foster violence.
(11) *Promoting cooperation* is an education approach that emphasizes cooperative learning in which students achieve academic success through dependence on and accountability to each other.
(12) *Role model curricula* help students learn lessons in nonviolent behavior by exploring the lives of exceptional historical or contemporary figures.
(13) *Self-esteem development curricula* aim to raise students' self-esteem with the underlying assumption that doing so can raise academic performance and reduce violence.
(14) *Teen-dating violence/family violence/sexual assault curricula* address the increased incidents of domestic violence in recent years.

Continued support for students with disabilities who are victims of harassment is evidenced by the July 26, 2000, joint letter from the Office of Civil Rights and the Office of Special Education. Sent to principals, superintendents, and university presidents, this letter concerned the harassment of students with disabilities based on their particular disability. The letter asked administrators to advise related professionals to (1) develop greater awareness of this issue, (2) remind interested persons of the legal/educational responsibilities of institutions to prevent and respond to disability harassment, and (3) suggest measures that school officials should take to address the issue.

It is significant to understand that the curriculum in special education has to include the areas of exceptionalities as opposed to age or grade. In an inclusive curriculum/classroom, peer tutoring, special education consultants, and centers aid the regular classroom teacher throughout the educational experience.

MULTIPLE INTELLIGENCE AND ITS IMPACT ON THE CURRICULUM

Influencing the development of curriculum is are the beliefs that (1) the only limits to our intelligence are limits we set; (2) we can become more intelligent by increasing the activity of perception and knowing by working on higher levels of thought; (3) there are many ways we know, understand, and learn about our world beyond what the IQ tests measure; and (4) when there is a challenge, all of our "intelligences" work together in an integrated way. These beliefs considered together form the multiple intelligence theory first posited by Howard Gardner.

Gardner (1991) presents seven "intelligences," or distinct ways individuals learn and live within reality: (1) *verbal/linguistic intelligence,* responsible for the production of language and complex possibilities such as poetry, humor, grammar, and abstract reasoning; (2) *logical-mathematical intelligence,* scientific thinking or deductive reasoning, the capacity to recognize patterns, work with abstract symbols, and discern relationships; (3) *visual/spatial intelligence,* including visual arts (painting, drawing, and sculpture), navigation (map-making and architecture), visualization of objects from different perspectives and angles (e.g., chess playing), all which use the sense of sight to include the ability to form images and pictures in the mind; (4) *bodily/kinesthetic intelligence,* the ability to use the body to express emotion (dance and body language), participate in sports, and create an new product (devise and invention); (5) *musical/rhythmic intelligence,* recognition and use of rhythmic and tonal pattern sensitivity to sounds from the environment (human voice and musical instruments); (6) *interpersonal intelligence,* the ability to work cooperatively in a group as well as the ability to communicate verbally and nonverbally with others (and thereby notice distinctions such as moods, temperament, motivation, and intentions); and (7) *intrapersonal intelligence,* knowledge of the internal aspects of the self such as feelings, emotional responses, thinking processes (metacognition), and self-reflection. This is one's ability to transcend the self, the capacity to experience wholeness and unity and to discern patterns of our connection with the large order of things.

Gardner maintains that we use many different skills to solve a problem, and that those skills assist in the acquisition of new knowledge (Morrison, 1993). His theory of multiple intelligences can guide educators in designing curriculum and instruction that appeals to more than a single dimension of intelligence (Oliva, 1997). The theory has many implications for curriculum models and how teachers view and teach children.

The curriculum is the one place these multiple ways to learn can come together and serve as a basis from which instructional strategies can be developed. Curriculum strategies that involve the separate intelligences will awake more intellectual potential because they use more senses and have different areas of the brain working together.

The following example gives the view of a student who demonstrate s spatial, bodily-kinesthetic, and intrapersonal intelligences and how he can be helped to develop his linguistic intelligence.

> Trevor (12 years old) is a seventh grader who is just as proud of his collection of doodles and pictures as he is of his good grades (in math). Many of his drawings are done during school in classes that are lecture-based or "just plain boring," as Trevor puts it. Others are a result of long hours of detailed work on sketches and designs. While his classmates make simple book covers, Trevor creates covers with intricate and complex geometrical designs or cartoon characters. Trevor is drawn to classrooms that are picture rich. Slides, mobiles, photos, overhead transparencies, and other visuals that reinforce the lesson make all the difference in his motivation and understanding. He is easily frustrated by an overdose of words, whether he's reading, writing, or listening to them. His frustration about long writing assignments quickly changes to excitement, however, when he is encouraged to include visuals. Trevor's teacher can identify Trevor's reports without his name because they always have one picture on the front, one on the back, and several throughout.
>
> Trevor spends most of his free time putting together and painting models. He loves math class this year because, as he says, the teacher "keeps us really busy when we learn. We move around to different centers and use manipulatives."
>
> Trevor is definitely not a social butterfly. He has a small group of close friends and is happy to spend time alone. His mental and physical well being is very important to him, as is his academic achievement. (Gipe, 1998, p. 23)Based on this description of Trevor's learning skills and preferences, the best curriculum for Trevor would make use of his spatial talents, as well as his bodily-kinesthetic and intrapersonal intelligences. This type of child is one who is in almost every classroom, in every school, in every district. Reaching the Trevors of our schools, and providing a curriculum model that encourages them to succeed, is one of the great challenges of educators today.

Different types of intelligence are highly valued in individual cultures, and educators should be aware of this. For example, linguistic and mathematical intelligences are considered supreme among most Americans whereas spatial intelligence is most valued among Eskimo peoples, because knowledge and awareness of even slight differences in ice surfaces are significant to survival skills.

According to Gipe (1998) multiple intelligence theory is not the same concept as *learning styles.* Proponents of learning styles suggest that the learner approaches different contents (language, numbers, music, etc.) in the same way (global, analytical, or impulsive, reflective). Multiple intelligence theory supports the possibility that a learner may have more than one learning style. It is appropriate that curriculum models include the expansion of instructional methods that link learning to as much intelligence as possible. For example, in teaching a concept in social studies, the teacher can encourage the students to read about it (linguistic), draw it (spatial), build a model of it (bodily-kinesthetic), find music that complements it (musical), relate it to a personal feeling (intrapersonal), involve critical thinking (logical-mathematical), and work in cooperative groups (interpersonal). In this way, curriculum models will incorporate the theory of multiple intelligence and possibly assist educators in meeting the needs of all children. One of the most significant thoughts of using multiple intelligences is that educators can increase the self-esteem of youngsters in the classroom. In a kindergarten classroom in Colorado, a teacher discusses the different kinds of "smarts" with her five-year-olds. While pointing to a poster with pictures and symbols depicting the multiple intelligences, she discusses with the children that they are all smart in different ways. With choices of body-smart, people-smart, music-smart, picture-smart, word-smart, and number-smart, the children learn right from the beginning of their kindergarten curriculum that they each have individualized approaches to intelligence (Collins, 1998).

Gardner based his initial list of multiple intelligences on research in neurological, developmental, and cognitive psychology, as well as on anthropology. He believes that the various intelligences can be shown in areas of the brain, and that child prodigies are an example of the evidence of their existence. He has theorized about an eighth intelligence, "the naturalist" (sensitivity to the ecological environment), and a "half" intelligence, "the moralist" (sensitivity to ethical concerns), which serve to remind us that the concept of multiple intelligence is open to further speculation (Meyer, 1997; Checkley, 1997).

Some researchers feel that Gardner is just giving hope to parents and educators. Many researchers want to see further investigation into Gardner's theory. One study (Merrefield, 1997) found great success in including the multiple intelligence concepts with disabled preschoolers. Teaching with multiple intelligences in mind has been found to keep the lessons interesting, the assessment varied, and the strategies diverse (Emig, 1997).

CURRICULUM FOR BOTH GENERAL EDUCATION AND SPECIAL EDUCATION

Frequently, general education teachers have curriculum that is already set up for them by curriculum specialists. Examples of such curricula are:

(1) Grade-Level Curricula—which is specific content and related skills particular to a specific grade level. This is important because what is taught in one grade is contingent upon what is taught in the grade before it.
(2) Core Curricula—the basic areas of reading, writing, and arithmetic upon which further learning depends. Support areas such as social studies, science, and spelling revolve around the basic accomplishments of a core curriculum.
(3) Subject-Area Curricula—these are also content–area curricula, which differ throughout the states. For example, the subject area of social studies differs for New Jersey and Oklahoma as the specific content changes.
(4) Competency-based Curricula—involves setting competencies or proficiencies before a student can progress to the next level of learning. Part of this is competency-based testing, where the student must demonstrate an acceptable level of skill in competencies required before moving on or actually passing the material.

The special educator needs to be familiar with these in order to ensure successful student transfer, placement, or possibly inclusion. A large majority of mildly handicapped students spend part of the day in the regular classroom setting. Special education teachers and regular education teachers work together on curricular information and development in order to make this happen. It is important for the special educator to see where in the regular curriculum the student has difficulty, gets lost, or cannot intellectually progress. The special education teacher needs to be familiar with curricula developed for children with special needs, for the individual child, and how to adjust such curriculum. Examples of this:

(1) A Parallel Curriculum reflects, or parallels, the basic information and skills of the regular curriculum and focuses on shorter assignments, fewer objectives, untimed tests, alternative testing models, and breaking concepts into smaller steps.

(2) Community-based Curricula sets competencies for areas not able to be achieved in the classroom itself, such as basic experiences, for example, looking right and left before crossing a street, negotiating intersections, and trips downtown.

(3) Life Management Curricula involve areas necessary for independent living, such as grooming, communicating, traveling, and using a telephone.

(4) Specialized Curricula are developed for the individual special needs person. For example, some students need experience in social skills behaviors, career education, and vocational programming.

(5) Functional Curricula is a field unto itself with tremendous impact on the special needs population. It transcends the specific information that these children need to master with the reality of practical living. The curriculum helps children function appropriately in their own environment.

The fact remains, however, that with some special students, the individual challenge of the disabilities dictate that some specific instructional methodology be included into whatever curricular approach is advocated. For example, historically, the mentally handicapped were presented with a slower version of the regular education curriculum and set of experiences. Other than that, the most common educational placement for the mentally handicapped was the self-contained classroom. More recently, a functional curriculum has been developed to help these students acquire everyday skills that will help in everyday living—functioning within the community as well as at the workplace. "A functional curriculum approach is a way of delivering instructional content that focuses on the concepts and skills needed by all students with disabilities in the area of personal-social, daily living and occupational adjustment. What is considered a functional curriculum for any one student would be the content (concepts and skills) included in that student's curriculum or course of study that targets his or her future needs" (Clark, as cited in Florida Department of Education, 1994, p. 348).

The conflict arises between how this type of curriculum is to be viewed and provided for in an inclusive setting. To look at this as an *approach* as opposed to a specific order of curriculum makes possible the view that regardless of the environment in which this is delivered, the responsibility is on the regular classroom teacher and the special education consultant to comply with the goals and objectives of the individualized educational plan as mandated by IDEA. If the regular educational plan is on a more vigorous academic emphasis, how can a functional curriculum be delivered in an inclusive setting? The hope is that the desire to provide responsible adults in a more thoughtful society will allow both emphases to work together. The bonus of having disabled students interact more effectively with their nondisabled peers becomes a normal outcome of implementation of the functional curriculum within the normal classroom setting. Additionally, the goals and objectives of a functional curriculum are important for many of the regular education students as well as other challenged students operating within the inclusive classroom. This may provide enough diversity within the curriculum as well as within the social interaction of the classroom. If schools are to be concerned with addressing student diversity, then diversity needs to be addressed in the curriculum.

When dealing with students with severe handicaps, such emphasis on functional curricula is especially important. To wit:

> Today, most educators of individuals with severe handicaps consider it important to be familiar with the normal sequences of child development, but they recognize that their students often do not acquire skills in the same way that nonhandicapped students do and that developmental guides should not be the only basis for determining teacher procedures. For example, a 16-year-old student who is just learning to feed and toilet himself should not be taught in exactly the same way or with the same materials as a nonhandicapped 2-year-old child who is just learning to feed and toilet himself. The past experiences, present environments, and future prospects of the two individuals are, of course, quite different, even though their ability to perform certain skills may be similar. (Heward and Orlansky, 1992, p. 433)

CURRICULUM AND ASSESSMENT

Response to Intervention (RTI)

Response to Intervention (RTI) is a process focusing on several successive steps based on assessing student learning and implementing immediate intervention. Monitoring at specific intervals in order to provide interventions central to RTI and which intervention are to be implemented are based on research validated material. This process occurs in the general education classroom and helps clarify a need for different types of services that may go from differentiating instruction to more formal placement in order to receive services through IDEA.

RTI is viewed as a prevention model not actually an identification model for students who have learning disabilities. As part of this prevention model which focuses on a specific students learning need and creating effective instructional plans to meet that learning need, additional information can be gathered to help evaluate whether this student meets the criteria for service through IDEA and an IEP. Whether or not the child meets criteria for IDEA, research based RIT processes are in place which provide relevant help and critical information about the instructional needs of a student in order to create effective instructional interventions. Therefore, while IDEA 2004 and NCLB are working together to provide additional support for students struggling with general education and special education, RIT may identify factors such as inadequate instruction, cultural or language differences or, in some cases learning disabilities earlier.

As of 2004, IDEA has incorporated RTI as a source for identification of Learning Disabilities. Due to the steps involved (described below), educational decisions regarding instruction and a variety of on-going interventions are influenced by RTI. By incorporating an earlier process of intervention, the time needed for the current IQ achievement discrepancy may be drastically decreased. The outcomes involved in student learning are the focus, not the deficits and the specific disability or learning challenge may not be a learning disability. As in the beginning, assessment and intervention is monitored by the general education teacher, as the later steps involve the special education teacher. Both work well together to develop the best plan for the student (National Center for Learning Disabilities, 2006).

A 3 tier RTI model is described below:

(1) Screening and Group Interventions
(2) Targeted Interventions
(3) Intensive Interventions and Comprehensive Evaluations

1. Screening and Group Interventions—Students identified through their struggle with learning, frequently determined to be "at risk" for not meeting grade level standards through universal screening (see glossary) and/or statewide or district tests are monitored for a brief period (not to exceed 8 weeks) and over this period can receive supplemental instruction and interventions in small groups during the regular school day in the regular classroom. Monitoring through curriculum based measurement (see glossary) will indicate which students make significant progress in order to go back to the regular classroom program and which students are not making adequate progress.

2. Targeted Interventions—Students not making adequate progress are provided more intensive services and interventions. These are in addition to instruction in the general curriculum. By the end of the grading period, students who continue to show little progress move to more intensive interventions.

3. Intensive Interventions and Comprehensive Evaluations—These intensive interventions target the student's particular skill deficits. If the student does not respond to these targeted interventions, they are considered eligible for services through IDEA.

Just as RTI allows and encourages parents to participate in face to face meetings, review written intervention plans and work cooperatively throughout this process, IDEA also allows parents to request a formal evaluation to determine eligibility for special education.

Universal Design for Learning (UDL)

This method advocates creating lessons and classroom material flexible enough to accommodate different learning styles. Both special education and regular education professionals support making this a part of any reauthorization of NCLB. Instead of retrofitting existing materials to accommodate students with learning differences, lessons can be designed with accessibility to the physical environment; an example is for LEP students, gifted students, or students who employ different learning styles. By developing alternate methods in which students demonstrate they have mastered a concept, is a basis of UDL which reinforces the idea that children in schools come from diverse backgrounds to include: culture, socioeconomic, language and abilities/disabilities. Based on this philosophy, the application encourages that the same support provided during instruction is provided during testing. On-going assessment utilizes curriculum based measurement in both the learning process as well as the instruction. This is also addressed thru the use of technology, both through regular techniques (computers reading a book) and low-techniques (creating posters depicting main ideas as opposed to reports).

According to Rose and Meyer (2002) there are three UDL principles that guide the design of flexible curricula by calling for the embedding of options that support differences in recognition, strategic, and affective networks:

- To support recognition learning, provide multiple, flexible methods of presentation.
- To support strategic learning, provide multiple, flexible methods of expression and apprenticeship.
- To support effective learning, provide multiple, flexible options for engagement.

Associations such as National Education Association (NEA), National School Board Association (NSBA) and CEC are all supporting the UDI concept, developed by David H. Rose at the Center for Applied Specific Technology (CAST) in Wakefield Mass (1984). While first focusing on creating assistive technology based on existing lesson plans, it was later found that it is more important to rethink what the lesson is about and then develop software and hardware solutions for meeting those needs of students with disabilities. CAST helps educators rethink their lessons and customize them for students with different needs.

CAST has customized teaching methods to support these 3 UDL principles by setting up teaching methods supporting diverse media and formats, ongoing feedback, opportunities for repetition through practice, and choices of tools and rewards (Strangeman, Hitchcock, Hall &Meo, et.al, 2006).

HOW RTI AND UDL DIFFER YET INTERSECT

RTI and UDL differ in that RTI is a process for making educational decisions based on an at-risk student's success or failure during specialized intervention, while UDL is a process for making curriculum design decisions to maximize success in the general curriculum. RTI and UDL share the objective of improving educational outcomes for students with disabilities in several ways:

(1) Both RTI and UDL recognize that poor achievement does not necessarily reflect disabilities but may also reflect poor instruction, for example: a change within the curriculum or in the method of instruction with regard to the delivery of material. RTI supports this by prescribing that the general education curriculum incorporate research based validated instruction and

intervention by making learning disabilities identified contingent on the program of instruction and by acknowledging that there are cases where changes should be made to general classroom instruction in place of student intervention. UDL supports this by using research validated instruction and intervention as it recognizes it might be the curriculum not the student, who bears the burden of adaption;

(2) RTI and UDL both reflect the understanding that a curriculum effective for 1 student may not be effective for another. In RTI, there is an individualized progress intervention plan, while in UDL the curriculum is kept flexible in goals, methods and assessments in order to accommodate individual student needs;

(3) In both, assessment informs instruction and must be on-going with RTI having multiple interventions; in UDL multiple, ongoing assessments are also administered. Curriculum Based Measures referring to the effectiveness of instruction and guiding decision making about instruction and intervention are the greatest similarities between RTI & UDL.

(4) By integrating more technology through UDL into the RTI recommended intervention, the technology serves as an alternative means of instruction to meet the RTI suggested intervention; thus the classroom teacher can offer more diverse processes for adaptive instruction.

COMMUNITY-BASED INSTRUCTION (CBI) AND CURRICULUM

Decisions regarding appropriate curriculum and delivery models of instruction for the developmentally disabled are not, as explained earlier, based on developmental milestones. Such students have more difficulty generalizing from one instructional environment to another; therefore, targeting specific skills is more appropriate. The philosophy of a curriculum based on instruction within the real community is to use the classroom environment only as a beginning for simulation and infuse it with community-based instruction (CBI) in order to achieve applications of skills to actual adult life.

The special needs of students with moderate and severe disabilities are best met through direct instruction where they live, work, and play. The direct association between IEP objectives and skills required in order to function independently is essential and as often as possible needs to parallel the work environment. Local offices of the U.S. Department of Labor, Wage and Hour Division, need to be contacted to verify compliance with current labor laws. Part of this curriculum development may be the process of supported employment, a placement and training model for students who cannot succeed without intensive supportive individual on-the-job training with a job coach or employment specialist. The ultimate goal is for the intensive coaching to decrease so that the curriculum provides for decreased but continued monitoring (Department of Education/Vocational Programs, 1993).

Different from the previous exceptionality but equally important if we are to deliver appropriate services to all children is the curriculum developed for the gifted. Just as we prepare special education consultants and need to prepare regular education teachers for dealing with the mentally and developmentally disabled, the same rights apply to those children who are assessed to be gifted and talented. Controversy arises here in that often parents and teachers believe these children have been given more by nature or nurture to begin with and that others need educational funding more. This, however, is not the prevailing law, which funds the gifted and talented through IDEA as well as through the recently passed Educational Excellence for All Children's Act (1999, described in Chapter 2).

Concepts regarding high-order thinking can be accomplished in myriad settings, be they special classes, honors classes, resource rooms, or enrichment and acceleration programs. Models for teaching to the gifted include Bloom's Taxonomy of Educational Objectives, Renzulli's Enrichment Triad Model, Bett's Autonomous Learning Model, Clark's Integrative Education Model, and Maker's Integrated Curriculum Model.

Based on the amendments to the original P.L. 94–142, IDEA 1990, and IDEA 1997, the area of transition of young adults and the inclusion of specific plans for the continuation of services of these 14–21-year-olds into the workplace requires specific curriculum planning in the form of goals and objectives.

The strongest transition models appear to be those that include a functional secondary school curriculum that provides work experience. The law now requires an individualized educational plane stating the transition from school to work process. The coordination of this plan between the school vocational planner, the community, and an employer is a team approach that works best using a functional curriculum as previously described. Heward and Orlansky (1992) stress the importance of a continual curriculum beginning in the elementary years focusing on the functional curriculum. They stress that

Development of career awareness should begin in the elementary years for children with severe disabilities. This does not mean, of course, that six-year-old children must be placed on job sites for training. For example, elementary students might sample different types of jobs through classroom responsibilities such as watering plants, cleaning chalkboards or taking messages to the office. Young children with disabilities might also visit community work sites where adults with disabilities are employed.... Middle school children should spend time at actual job sites, with an increased amount of in-school instruction devoted to the development of associated work skills, such as being on time, staying on task.... Secondary school should spend an increasing amount of time receiving instruction at actual job sites. (637)Ultimately, curriculums need to provide for the type of residential choices available to these children, be they state residential facilities, group homes, foster homes, or apartment living. The ultimate goal is to open the doors to a more productive life as part of the greater community.

SERVICE LEARNING

Service Learning is defined as a "teaching method where guided or classroom learning is deepened thru service to others in a process that provides structured time for reflection on the service experience and demonstration of the skills and knowledge required" (Kaye, 2004, p.7).

Service Learning utilizes the concept of community service and introduces both a focus on: 1) the student providing the service and what that student will learn from performing the service and 2) reflection on how the service experience is part of a larger concept involving responsibility to others in the global community. Goals and objectives are an integral part of the planning with regard to outcomes achieved by the student. An IEP provides the perfect opportunity for Service Learning to be embedded into several areas of development for students with disabilities. It increases both communication as a skill as well as increases opportunities for social-emotional development. It provides a direct opportunity for creating inclusive situations. If Service Learning is embedded into the IEP, both the students with disabilities and regular education students will work together as part of the larger community beyond the school setting and sometimes beyond the immediate community.

Language differs from other communication services because the education of students and young people is always at its core. Students will come to know that communication develops first, then interaction, relationships, and knowledge of people, places, organizations, government and systems follow. Becoming active in communication builds a foundation for curriculum responsibility in later years.

According to Kaye (2004) there are different types of Service Learning such as:

- *Direct Service*—person to person—example: tutoring younger children; working with elders—encourages caring for others who are different (age or experience); developing problem solving skills; following a sequence from beginning to end; and seeing the "big picture" of a social justice issue.
- *Indirect Services*—do not provide service to individuals but benefit the community or environment—example: restoring a wetland; park construction; donating items to Head Start; and collecting clothes for a shelter. Students learn cooperation and work as a team organizing and prioritizing.
- *Advocacy*—create awareness of or promote actions on an issue of interest—example: writing letters; sponsoring a town meeting; public speaking; learn about perseverance; Understanding rules; systems; processes and civic engagement. Service Learning based on preparation, action, reflection and demonstration.

Websites to support and get ideas for service and action:

- The National Service Inclusion Project
  www.serviceandinclusion.org/index.php
- Children with Disabilities, an initiative of the Coordinating Council on Juvenile Justice and Delinquency
  www.childrenwithdisabilities.ncjrs.org/kids.html
- Special Olympics *www.specialolympics.org*
- Best Buddies International *www.bestbuddies.org*
- Project Linus *www.projectlinus.org*

Merging service-learning with the concept of inclusion is supported by the study, "Engaging Students with Disabilities in Service Learning: Findings from a

Statewide Program Evaluation" (Miller & Hinterlong, 2008) when the purpose is to "enable people with disabilities to become fully integrated in their communities ... the belief in one's ability to engage in civic life" (p.1). From this study the findings and implications for practice indicate benefits for students with disabilities participating in service learning encourage empowerment, teamwork and normalization. This supports goals of helping students become independent and plan for a more integrated adult life.

It is significant to note that many original Service Learning programs having students with disabilities were often the focus of the Service Learning through tutoring, mentoring, providing experiences for children in hospitals, advocacy work, etc. Service Learning actually provided a balance between serving the community and the needs of those providing the service.

Both the provider and one being served were equally important, valued and became partners in a win-win situation. As goals of the experiences were participatory and reflective, curriculum goals for students with disabilities thru IDEA and later NCLB stressed social-emotional development as part of the curriculum, the inclusion of students with disabilities as providers of Service Learning was a logical development.

According to Zlotkowski 1990; Trainor, Muscott and Smith1996; National Service Act 1993; (as cited in Muscott, 2001) The National and Community Service Act of 1990 (PL 101-610) defined Service Learning as a method:

- under which students learn and develop through active participation in thoughtfully designed service experiences that meet actual community needs and that are coordinated in collaboration with the school and community;
- that is integrated into the students' academic curriculum and provides structured time for a student to think, talk or write about what the student did and saw during the actual service activity;
- that provides students with opportunities to use newly acquired skills and knowledge in real-life situations in their own communities, and
- that enhances what is taught in school by extending student learning beyond the classroom and into the community and helps to foster the development of a sense of caring for others. (42 U.S.C. 12572 (a) (101) (p.9).

An area of special education where Service Learning has been utilized for the social and emotional development is with students with emotional or emotional and behavioral disorders

IDEA 1997 (PL 105-17) specifically identified emotional disturbance to contain characteristics such as: the inability to build satisfactory relationships with peers and teachers, negativism, depression and low interest level. Frequently these children have little opportunity to have structured opportunities to make changes. By providing opportunities to engage in authentic experiences meeting needs of the real world, their community, and include these curriculum experiences in the IEP, there becomes an integration of specific goals and objectives within reflective practice. Thus the learning of the students with disabilities includes higher level reflection and analysis regarding practice.

Students with emotional disorders may be able to begin the Service Learning experience in a less structural situation while students with more severe emotional behavioral disorders may need to begin with a system of highly structured activities based directly on an analysis of the individual learning needs of the student and the group benefiting from the service. Less complex experiences of a short-term that are of great interest to the student will ensure greater success and successively approximating more complex experiences should follow.

Additional examples of integrating Service Learning experiences into the philosophy of inclusion within IDEA and specific IEP have been led by states such as: New Jersey, Pennsylvania and Massachusetts. New Jersey has incorporated the "Learn and Serve America Program" (an example of Service Learning) in 13 school districts with their general education curriculum utilizing it as a basic curriculum methodology so that experiential learning is integrated into the IEP. Massachusetts developed the "Hampshire Educational Collaborative" curriculum for students with disabilities and students without disabilities to work together on an inter-generational cooking project for senior citizens in order to go beyond skill development and move toward critical reflection regarding civic responsibility. Pennsylvania's Service Learning Alliance, for students working through transition plans, operates a summer camp for small children. This experience, and others that developed as a result, were written into their transition part of the IEP for students with disabilities (National Service Resources, 2008).

Another statewide program model, Community Higher Education School Partnerships (CHESP) utilized quantitative data to support the belief that one's ability to engage in civic life, leads to a more integrated adult life for students with disabilities. This program fostered the creation of partnerships between the community, higher education, and K-12 schools. Themes that emerged of empowerment, teamwork learning and normalization are important in helping students plan for a more integrated life (Miller & Hinterlong, 2008).

In projects and programs such as the Resolving Conflict Creativity Program (RCCP) developed by Linda Lantieri (1999) in collaboration with Educators for Social Responsibility which focused on inclusion of children at-risk for school failure based on early identification, surveys and follow-up focus groups evaluations reported increased learning with regard to conflict-resolution, anger management, listening skills, ability to share and self-esteem.

DISCIPLINE AS PART OF THE CURRICULUM

IDEA 1990 provided for school personnel to remove a child to an interim alternative educational placement for up to forty-five days if that child brought a gun to school or a school function. Since the IDEA 1997 amendments became effective, the following disciplinary measures have applied to disabled and special-needs students:

- Removal of the child for up to ten school days at a time: The regulations clarify that school personnel may remove a child with a disability for up to ten consecutive school days and allow for additional removals of up to ten school days for separate acts of misconduct, as long as the removals do not constitute a pattern.

- Providing services during periods of disciplinary removal: Schools do not need to provide services during the first ten school days in a school year that a child is removed. During any subsequent removal that is for ten school days or less, the school must provide services to the extent determined necessary to enable the child to appropriately progress in the general curriculum and appropriately advance toward achieving the goals of his or her IEP. In cases involving removals for ten school days or less, school personnel, in consultation with the child's special education teacher, make the service determination. During any long-term removal for behavior that is not a manifestation of a child's disability, schools must provide services to the extent determined necessary to enable the child to appropriately progress in the general curriculum and appropriately advance toward achieving the goals of his or her IEP. In cases involving removals for behavior that is not a manifestation of the child's disability, the child's IEP team makes the service determination.
- Conducting behavioral assessments and developing behavioral interventions: Meetings of a child's IEP team to develop a behavioral assessment plan, or (if the child has one) to review the child's behavioral intervention plan, are only required when the child has first been removed from his or her current placement for more than ten school days in a school year, and when commencing a removal that constitutes a change in placement. If other subsequent removals occur, the IEP team members must review the child's behavioral intervention plan and its implementation to determine if modifications are necessary; they need and only meet if one or more team members believes that modifications are necessary.
- Change of placement; manifestation determinations: The regulations provide that change of placement occurs if a child is removed for more than ten consecutive school days or is subjected to a series of removals that constitute a pattern because they cumulate to more than ten school days in a school year, and because of factors such as the length of each removal, the total amount of time the child is removed, and the proximity of the removals to one another. Manifestation determinations are only required if the school is implementing a removal that constitutes a change of placement.Additionally, the 1997 amendments expanded the authority of school personnel regarding the removal of a child who brings a gun to school to also apply to *all* dangerous weapons and to *knowing possession* of illegal drugs or the sale or solicitation of the sale of controlled substances, and they added a new ability of appropriate school personnel to request a hearing officer to remove a child for up to forty-five days if keeping the child in his or her current placement is substantially likely to result in injury to the child or to others.

The 1997 amendments also require appropriate school personnel to assess a child's troubling behavior and develop positive behavioral interventions to address that behavior and to describe how to determine whether the behavior is a manifestation of the child's disabilities.

EARLY CHILDHOOD SPECIAL EDUCATION CURRICULUM

Curriculums for early childhood special education (ECSE) programs became a part of the responsibility of the U.S. Department of Education when P.L. 99–457 and IDEA 1990 mandated that family-focused intervention services had to be spelled out and provided for in an individualized family service plan. This interdisciplinary approach with screening, assessment, and specific programs led to a focus on curricular development. Appropriate curricula for children from birth to age five in both homes and centers needs to be based on goals and objectives. Most early childhood special education programs have a developmentally based curriculum, which means that each child can be measured against a normal developmental standard. Focus can include remediation, basic process skills, developmental tasks, psychological concepts, and preacademic skills. Essential to the success of early intervention is an interdisciplinary team of parent(s), teachers, and various ECSE specialists.

The following materials are commonly found in the ECSE curriculum:

Language Arts/Reading

- Steck-Vaughn Reading Comprehension Skills Series: Complements and supplements reading, phonics, and language arts programs; uses short, high-interest stories for low-level readers.
- Steck-Vaughn Phonics: A holistic and multisensory instruction approach.
- Steck-Vaughn Sight Word Comprehensive: Sight word program incorporating interesting topics and motivating activities.
- Steck-Vaughn Spelling: Integrates reading, writing, and language arts in a holistic approach.
- DLM Dolch Reading and Vocabulary: High-interest, low-reading-level paperback readers emphasizing sight word vocabulary.
- DLM Cove Reading Program: Workbooks in a thorough, sequenced program reinforcing decoding skills.
- DLM Survival Words Program: Low-reading-level readers with abundant structure and repetition reinforcing reading in context.
- Project Read: A multisensory reading program to teach and reinforce decoding and phonetic skills.
- Merrill Linguistic Readers: Low-level reading series reinforcing decoding and comprehension skills using the linguistic approach.
- Strategies Intervention Model (SIM): Includes teacher's manual for strategies with regard to word identification, sentence writing, paraphrasing, LINCS, paragraph writing, first-letter mnemonics, and error monitoring.
- Balance Materials/Curriculum: Blends precision teaching, direct instruction, and whole language instruction; addresses all academic areas with emphasis on reading and language arts areas.

- LinguiSystems No Glamour Grammar: Teaches "no-frills" grammar through structure practice of verbal and written skills.
- Moving Up in Grammar: A low-reading-level grammar skills kit.
- SRA/Distar: Build upon skills previously learned and introduce new skills continuously using a systematic, direct instruction approach to teach reading, spelling, writing, math, science, social studies, and reasoning and thinking skills through a variety of curricula. Individual programs are Distar Language, SRA Reading Mastery Series, SRA Corrective Reading Program, SRA Expressive Writing, SRA Your World of Facts, SRA Cursive Writing, SRA Spelling Mastery, and SRA Reading, Writing and Thinking Skills.

Mathematics

- Steck-Vaughn Mastering Math: A developmental program for low reading levels with sufficient practice, review, and assessment included.
- Steck-Vaughn Succeeding in Mathematics: Consistent step-by-step approach using practical applications at low reading levels. Provides frequent practice and review.
- DLM Math Problem-Solving Kits: An extensive program to develop and reinforce story problem skills on a low reading level.
- DLM Mathematics Big Box Kits: Comprehensive hands-on math centers providing instruction, reinforcement, and practice with manipulatives. Specific kits include Math Big Box, Math Manipulative Big Box, Time Big Box, and Money Big Box.
- DLM Moneywise: Comprehensive, developmentally sequenced instruction and practice in money concepts; includes manipulatives.
- Creative Publications Mathematics Their Way: An activity-centered math program to build and reinforce math skills.
- Creative Publications Hands-On: Concrete, sequenced activities using a variety of manipulatives.
- Creative Publications Base Ten Block Program: Teaches and reinforces the base ten number system and place value skills using concrete problem-solving activities with manipulatives.
- Creative Publications WorkMat Math Story Problems Series: Teaches logical thinking by interpreting problems with manipulatives.
- Mathematics for Daily Use: Math skills for everyday function are presented through visual means to assist students with low reading levels and/or motivation.
- Project Math: Especially for students with learning and/or behavior problems; skills are presented at four different mental age levels.
- Distar Math: Systematic, direct instruction approach to teaching math by building upon skills previously learned while introducing new skills.
- Innovative Learning Concepts, Inc., Touch Math: A multisensory method of teaching basis counting and computation skills by counting sequentially.

Science/Social Studies

- Steck-Vaughn The Wonders of Science Series: Complete science program presenting content in brief, high-interest, low-level readings.
- Steck-Vaughn Health and You: Comprehensive health program with controlled vocabulary at low reading levels.

Career-Vocational Skills

- Community-Based Instruction: Teach students the necessary skills for functioning within a community, including lessons in daily living and social/personal and career-occupational skills. Among the individual programs are Donn Brolin's Life Center Career Education (LCCE), Attainment Company's Stepping Out, SRA Reading, Writing and Math for Independence, and community-referenced curriculum guides by local school districts or BEES Clearinghouse/Information Center.

RECOGNITION & RESPONSE (R&R)

The three key features of Recognition to Response, an outgrowth of RTI which focuses on Pre-K are: recognition, response and problem-solving. Already part of early childhood appropriate practices has been screening for purposes of diagnoses and identification for early childhood eligibility for special education services. Different from this traditional application, screening and monitoring in the Recognition & Response process, are used for instructional goal setting (not a specific curriculum).

The response component of the Recognition & Response process is based on intentional teaching for all children and targeted interventions for those children needing additional support. The goal of Recognition & Response is to provide teachers with more systemic, intentional methods to use with their students, further, to rely on assessment information and link it to instructional planning and decision-making. The third component of Recognition & Response, problem-solving, is a collaborative process about how to proceed from the beginning, before it is applied to individual children (Buysse, 2008).

Collaboratively, teachers and other staff introduce this system to parents and involve the parents and other professionals in the problem-solving process.

CURRICULUM ACCOMMODATES DUAL EXCEPTIONALITIES

As discussed in Chapter 1, children with dual exceptionalities present unique curricular challenges. An environment taking into consideration both the gifts of the child and the disability while offering stronger emotional support tends to result in greater success. Developing a curriculum that offers remediation for the disability while at the same time focusing on the child's intellectual strengths may take time but will offer an enriched environment as well as higher self-esteem. According to Whitmore and Maker (1985) more gains are seen when intervention focuses on the gift rather than on the disability. Providing an environment through specific strategies in the curriculum for the gifted/learning disabled child can produce unusual productivity. For example, is a tedious book report any greater a documentation of acquired information than a student's production of a video focusing on what the message of the book was? Children with learning disabilities can produce more creative and probably more meaningful documentation when allowed to use their creative abilities. If a student has difficulties with handwriting, will learning to use a computer to record his or her thoughts and plans not serve the same purpose? Finding alternate ways to receive and document information does not make a curriculum less challenging but does encourage success. Technology provides organization, management, and access and is an integral part of curriculum development for many children with special needs but especially for gifted children with inconsistent abilities.

INCLUSION IN THE CURRICULUM

The scope of curriculum has changed over the years, yet some similarities have remained. One of the changes is in the inclusion of special needs students in general education classrooms, and how that affects the curriculum. Including students with disabilities in the regular education program is the "right thing to do and is the presumption of the special education law" (Schaffner and Buswell, 1998). When most of us attended school, the special education students were separated and away from us, in their own classes. Schaffner and Buswell (1998) believe that this may cause some perplexing fearfulness in the educators of today, who did not interact with special education students as youngsters. Whether we buy into that belief or not, the fact is, the "least restrictive environment" provision of the Reauthorization Act (IDEA 1997) states, "To the maximum extent appropriate, children with disabilities are educated with children who are not disabled, and special classes, separate schooling, or other removal of children with disabilities from the regular educational environment occurs only when the nature of severity of the disability of a child is such that education in regular classes with the use of supplementary aids cannot be achieved satisfactorily" [Section 612(a)(5)]. The general educational classroom must be the first placement considered. Therefore, in attempting to benefit special needs students and give them the best possible education, many students are now being educated in the least restrictive environment of the regular class, with a continuum of support available.

There is some debate of what *inclusion* actually means (see Dyal, Flynt, and Bennet-Walker, 1996). According to the Grapevine-Colleyville ISD Inclusion Task Force Report of 1997, inclusion is "a collaborative process among students, parents, and educators which enables students with and without disabilities to learn together in the same class to the greatest extent possible utilizing appropriate support services" (p. 1). As a report prepared for the Florida Department of Education (Stetson and Associates, 1998) notes, there are students who will succeed in school no matter what educators do, there are students who will fall through the cracks, and there are students who will not succeed in school unless something different is done. Inclusion is a possible answer to the problem that the highest dropout groups of students are those who fall between the cracks and those who did not succeed in school because something different was not done. In an inclusion setting, everyone is part of the solution. It includes collaboration and trust and a passion for learning and growing. There is a focus on the academic success of *every* student, not just some of them. Supporters believe that *inclusion* is just another word for "good teaching." As special education is a service, not a place, the general education setting may be appropriate for many students. How does this affect the curriculum of the general education class?

Curricula need to be adapted for all students, not just for students with identified disabilities. Adaptations of the standard curriculum can benefit "students all along the continuum, from students with disabilities to students 'at risk,' to students who need enriched curricular options ... adaptation increases the likelihood of success for more learners" (Ebeling, Deschenes, and Sprague, 1994, p. 68). Curriculum can be altered without compromising it in terms of content or accountability. Classrooms have always had students who learn at different rates, who have more background knowledge, who have varying abilities. Good teachers have always automatically and intuitively adapted the curriculum and instruction to meet the needs of each student. An inclusive curriculum that involves collaboration with colleagues makes this task even easier, enabling the educators to facilitate changes and adaptations (Snyder, 1999; Tapasak and Walther-Thomas, 1999; Tichenor, Heins, and Piechura-Couture, 1998).

Deschenes, Ebeling, and Sprague (1994) note a variety of instructional approaches to curricula that accommodate a wide range of learners:

- cooperative learning structures
- multidimensional student grouping
- thematic, integrated approaches
- multilevel instruction
- class projects
- outcomes-based instruction
- applied learning stations
- student presentation and projects
- role playing, skits, and plays
- peer supports
- community volunteers
- multimedia presentations
- concrete experiential learning activities
- community-referenced and community-based projects
- short-term skill-based grouping
- assignment menus and contracted grades
- community-based instruction
- portfolio or "authentic" assessments

Utilization of the above strategies in a curriculum allows all students the opportunity to participate and succeed. *Reciprocal teaching* is another strategy that has been successful in various classrooms (Lederer, 2000). In reciprocal teaching, the teacher and student take turns assuming the role of leader of the conversation. The purpose is to facilitate the group experience between teacher and student as well as to increase understanding of the meaning of the instructive activity.

Beliefs about students and learning form the foundation from which a curriculum is developed. According to Onosko and Jorgensen (in Jorgensen, Fisher, and Roach, 1997) these beliefs include: (1) All students can think and learn; (2) All students have value and unique gifts to offer their school; (3) Diversity within a school community should be embraced and celebrated; (4) All students differ in the ways they most effectively learn and express their understandings; (5) All students learn best when they are actively and collaboratively building knowledge with their classmates and their teacher; (6) All students learn best when studying interesting and challenging topics that they find personally meaningful; and (7) Effective teaching for students with disabilities is substantively the same as effective teaching for all students.

All students—with or without disabilities—"need to learn three types of skills: 1) dispositions and habits of mind, such as inquisitiveness, diligence, collaboration, work habits, tolerance, and critical thinking; 2) content area knowledge, in science, social studies, language arts, computers, the arts, etc; and 3) basic academic skills such as reading, writing, and mathematics" (Sizer, 1992, and U.S. Department of Labor, 1991, in Jorgensen, Fisher, and Roach, 1997). These three types of skills should be included in the curriculum of general education classes as well as in various types of inclusive settings.

Collaboration and teaming, problem solving, and using strategies in the classroom to accommodate a diverse group of learners are common approaches in quality inclusive curriculum (McGregor, Halvorsen, Fisher, Pumpian, Bhaerman, and Salisbury, 1998; Tichenor, Heins, and Piechura-Couture, 1998). These approaches help educators guide and support the efforts of teaching and learning, including success for all students.

REFERENCES

All Kinds of Minds. (2008). IDEA, Response to intervention and schools attuned. Retrieved July 10, 2008 from http://www.allkindsoffinds.org/

Bricker, D., 1989. *Early Intervention for At-Risk and Handicapped Infants, Toddlers, and Preschool Children.* 2nd ed. Palo Alto, CA: Scott, Foresman & Co.

Buysse, V. (2008). *How is recognition & response (TTI for Pre-K) different from what we're already doing?* Retrieved September 12, 2008 from http://cecblog.typepad.com/rti/2008/07/ho-is-recognit.html

Checkley, K., 1997. "The First Seven . . . and the Eighth: A Conversation with Howard Gardner." *Educational Leadership* 55: 8–13.

Collins, J., 1998. "Seven Kinds of Smart." *Time* 152, no.16: 94–96.

Department of Education/Vocational Programs, 1993. *Career Development Resource Guide for Students with Disabilities.* Author.

Deschenes, C., D. Ebeling, and J. Sprague, 1994. *Adapting Curriculum and Instruction in Inclusive Classrooms: A Teacher's Desk Reference.* Minneapolis: The Center for School and Community Integration Institute for the Study of Developmental Disabilities.

Dyal, A., S. Flynt, and D. Bennett-Walker, 1996. "Schools and Inclusion: Principals' Perceptions." *The Clearinghouse* 70: 32–35.

Ebeling, D., C. Deschenes, C., and J. Sprague, 1994. *Adapting Curriculum and Instruction in Inclusive Classrooms: Staff Development Kit.* Minneapolis: The Center for School and Community Integration Institute for the Study of Developmental Disabilities.

Emig, V., 1997. "A Multiple Intelligences Inventory." *Educational Leadership* 55: 47–50.

Florida Department of Education, 1994. *Specialized Curriculum for Exceptional Students: Florida Alternatives, Module 3.* Tallahassee, FL: Florida Department of Education.

Gardner, H., 1991. "Intelligence in Seven Phases." Paper presented at the Centennial of Education at Harvard. Precis published in the *Harvard Graduate School Alumni Bulletin* 36, no. 1: 18–19.

Gipe, J. P., 1998. *Multiple Paths to Literacy: Corrective Reading Techniques for Classroom Teachers.* 4th ed. New York: Merrill Publishing.

Grapevine-Colleyville ISD Inclusion Task Force Report, 1997. Grapeville, TX: Grapevine-Colleyville School District.

Gresham, F. M., and D. L. MacMillan, 1997. "Social Competence and Affective Characteristics of Students with Mild Disabilities." *Review of Educational Research* 67, no. 4: 377–415.

Heward, W. L., and M. D. Orlansky, 1992. *Exceptional Children* 4th ed. New York: Macmillan.

Jorgensen, C., D. Fisher, and V. Roach, 1997. "Curriculum and Its Impact on Inclusion and the Achievement of Students with Disabilities." *Policy Research Practice: Issue Brief—Consortium on Inclusive Schooling Practices.* Pittsburgh: Allegheny University of the Health Sciences.

Kaye, C. B. (2004). *The complete guide to service learning.* Minneapolis, MN: Free Spirit Publishing.

Kopka, D. L., 1997. *School Violence: A Reference Handbook.* Santa Barbara, CA: ABC-CLIO.

Lambert, N. M., and B. L. McCombs (eds.), 1998. *How Students Learn: Reforming Schools through Learner-Centered Education.* Washington, DC: American Psychological Association.

Lantieri, L. (1999). Hooked on altruism: Developing social responsibility in at-risk youth. *Reclaiming Children and Youth, 8, 83-87.*

Lederer, J., 2000. "Reciprocal Teaching of Social Studies in Inclusive Elementary Classrooms. *Journal of Learning Disabilities* 33, no. 1: 91–106.

McAfee, O., and D. Leong, 1990. *Assessing and Guiding Young Children's Development and Learning* 2nd ed. Boston: Allyn and Bacon.

McGregor, G., A. Halvorsen, D. Fisher, I. Pumpian, B. Bhaerman, and C. Salisbury, 1998. "Professional Development for All Personnel in Inclusive Schools." *Policy Research Practice: Issue Brief—Consortium on Inclusive Schooling Practices.* Pittsburgh: Allegheny University of the Health Sciences.

Meyer, M., 1997. "The Greening of Learning: Using the Eighth Intelligence." *Educational Leadership* 55: 32–34.

Miller, C. R., & Hinterlong, J. (2008). Engaging students with disabilities in service-learning: Findings from a statewide program evaluation. *Research That Matters.* Retrieved February 5, 2008 from http://sswr.confex.com/sswr/2008/techprograms/P7837.HTM

Morrison, G., 1993. *Contemporary Curriculum K–8.* Boston: Allyn and Bacon.

Muscott, H. (2001). Introduction to service learning for students with emotional and behavioral disorders. Answers to frequently asked questions. *Beyond Behavior, 10(3), p.8-15.*

National Center for Learning Disabilities. (2006). *A parent's guide to response-to-intervention.* Retrieved April 10, 2008 from *www.LD.org*

National Service Resources. (2008). *Integrating service-learning in individual educational plans for primary school students with disabilities.* Retrieved April 4, 2008 from http://nationalserviceresources.org

Oliva, P., 1997. *Developing the Curriculum.* 4th ed. New York: Longman.

Rose & Meyer (2002). *Universal Design for Learning.*

Schaffner, C. B., and B. Buswell, 1998. *Opening Doors: Strategies for Including All Students in Regular Education.* Colorado Springs, CO: PEAK Parent Center, Inc.

Snyder, R., 1999. "Inclusion: A Qualitative Study of In-service General Education Teachers' Attitudes and Concerns. *Education* 120, no. 1: 173–180.

Stetson and Associates, 1998. *A Step by Step Approach for Inclusive Schools: Together Is Better!* Tallahassee, FL: Florida Department of Education and the Florida Inclusion Network.

Strangeman, N., Hitchcock, C., Hall, T., Meo, G., et. Al. (2006). *Response-to Instruction and Universal Design for Learning: How Might They Intersect in the General Education Classroom?* Center for Applied Special Technology. The Access Center: Washington, DC. Retrieved April 1, 2008 from http://www.ldonline.org/article/13002

Tapasak, R., and C. Walther-Thomas, 1999. "Evaluation of a First-Year Inclusion Program: Student Perceptions and Classroom Performance." *Remedial and Special Education* 20, no. 4: 216–225.

Tichenor, M., B. Heins, and K. Piechura-Couture, 1998. "Putting Principles into Practice: Parent Perceptions of a Co-taught Inclusive Classroom." *Education* 118, no. 3: 471–477.

Whitmore, J., and J. Maker, 1985. *Intellectual Giftedness among Disabled Persons.* Rockville, MD: Aspen Press.

Chapter Four
Special Education Programs and the Law

Whereas policy- and lawmakers view results of regular education programs based on formalized testing and evaluation of large groups of children, special education programs focus on *individual* student assessment. Development of special education programs is based on the laws passed to create educational opportunities, and how those laws have developed and changed. In special education, educators spend a great deal of time on the goals and objectives identified in the IEP.

The successful delivery of services provided by several laws, including the Vocational Rehabilitation Act of 1973 and IDEA 1990, depends on how the local and state agencies choose to fulfill the laws' intentions. Neither the Vocational Rehabilitation Act nor IDEA have resulted in absolute equal opportunity and inclusion of all individuals with disabilities.

Although the federal government sets laws, if state and local governments do not agree with those laws, they will not implement them, resulting in lost opportunities. An example is the Head Start federal program, which includes a provision for the early education of young children who live in poverty. Beginning in 1972, Head Start was required to set aside 10 percent of its monies/opportunities to be available for children with disabilities. This was seen as such an important and positive step that in 1975, the Education for All Handicapped Children's Act (P.L. 94–142, now known as IDEA) was passed, requiring all states applying for and receiving funding under that act to ensure a free, appropriate public education (FAPE) for all children with disabilities between six and eighteen years of age. This mandate of services is referred to as a "zero reject" policy. What is important to note is that for children ages birth through five and eighteen through twenty-one, FAPE was at *state discretion.* The federal government offered financial aid to implement its vision, and state and local governments had the right to choose not to participate. Under IDEA, state governments apply for the federal funds for state and local initiatives and must implement the mandates—even, if necessary, changing the state law.

When IDEA was amended in 1986 (see Chapter 2), two important early childhood special education policies were established: States had to ensure services to children age 3–5 years (applying the "zero reject" policy down to age three), and a new program (Part C) for newborns through two-year-olds (the Infants and Toddlers Intervention Program) was developed. Therefore, in 1986, ECSE took a new place within the field of special education and related services.

These new policies highlighted the balance of power set forth in the U.S. Constitution: The federal government made a statement by making the necessary funds available for these programs, and each state was left to decide whether to apply for the funds, knowing that accepting the funds required compliance with significant federal procedures and rights.

The federal government also has been instrumental in supporting and funding research and development. The Handicapped Children's Early Education Program (HCEEP) was established in 1968 and for thirty years has funded research and development (R&D) efforts that have resulted in tests, curriculum, and models of delivery service used today. Additionally, the Personnel Development Program under IDEA has provided funds for training personnel since the 1950s. States and localities seldom see their role as supporting R&D efforts; they leave this to the federal government. Instead, they focus on providing services to the citizens of their state and enacting laws to ensure access to services rather than quality of services. Through the use of federally supported research demonstrating the importance of early intervention, the states implemented early intervention policies—so that by 1994 the number of infants and toddlers receiving services had increased almost threefold, and preschool–age children receiving services had increased by over 100,000. The balance of power between federal and state has tipped in favor of children and families (Smith, 2000).

SPECIAL EDUCATION AS IT IS IMPACTED BY GOAL 1 OF GOALS 2000

As a response to Goal 1 of The Goals 2000: Educate America Act (see Chapter 2), a position statement by the Division for Early Childhood, a part of the Council for Exceptional Children (CEC), was drafted. Goal 1 states: "By the year 2000, all children in the United States will start school ready to learn." The CEC decided to define and explain the implications of this federal act for children with disabilities, children placed at-risk for school failure, children of poverty, children who are non-English speaking, and children with gifts and talents.

The Division of Early Childhood's statement posits that to reach Goal 1, it is imperative to have healthy and competent parents, wanted and healthy babies, decent housing, and adequate nutrition. Its interpretation additionally offered that quality early education and childcare is a birthright for all children, and therefore, services to support this concept must be comprehensive, coordinated, and focused on individual family and child needs. Additionally, the division wrote, "it is inappropriate to screen children into or out of early education programs that give them a legitimate opportunity to learn." Finally, early educators must be schooled in and encouraged to use developmentally appropriate curricula, materials, and procedures to maximize a child's growth and development.

Prior to IDEA 1975, education of students with disabilities was at the discretion of local school districts, often a local school administrator. Historically, there has been some care and concern for the deaf, blind and physically challenged. A specific change took place after the National Defense Education Act of 1958 (NDEA) which was the beginning of federal support and involvement in elementary and secondary education. The Elementary and Secondary Education Act (ESEA) of 1965 followed this philosophy as it subsidized direct services to specific populations in public schools, although it did not specify grants for students with disabilities (Martin, Martin & Terman, 1996).

Through continued advocacy and lobbying for a government unit to coordinate efforts for these children, in 1966, Congress mandated a Bureau for the Education of the Handicapped (BEH) under Title VI of BEH this became more popularly known as the "Education of the Handicapped Act." From this act through the creation of the BEH, there was an increase in effort and public awareness on students with disabilities to include early childhood education, children who were deaf, blind or multiply handicapped, and learning disabled. In 1970, the Education of the Handicapped Act (EHA) brought many of these independently operated programs into a more comprehensive act (Martin, Martin & Terman, 1996).

Through the 1970's many students with disabilities were still unserved. Specific court cases such as PARC (1971-1972) and Mills vs. Board of Education (see Chronology Section) provided more attention and focus as well as served as an impetus for Federal Laws, beginning in 1975 through the present. Litigation, specifically around Section 504 and ADA served as vehicles for parents, with regard to discriminatory practices in the public sector while IDEA signed into Law by President Ford, served as a vehicle for specific access to a free and appropriate education (Martin, Martin & Terman, 1996).

PL 94-142 the Education for All Handicapped Act, was re-titled to the Individuals for Disabilities Education Act (IDEA) in 1990 due to amendments added in 1983 and 1990. Additionally, in 1980, the BEH was officially replaced by the Office of Special Education Programs (OSEP) which was later combined with other national offices to create the Office of Special Education and Rehabilitation Services (OSERS).

COMPARISON OF IDEA 2004 WITH IDEA 1997

Specific wording has changed between IDEA 1997 and IDEA 2004 that incorporates 7 years of new information, new legislation and new developments in the field of education impacting special education. Obviously, as technological advances bring more possibilities to aid children with disabilities, as well as higher levels of scientifically-based instructional practices and methods to assess those practices (mandated by NCLB 2001), are integrated into the field of special education, IDEA 1997 needed to be reauthorized in order to integrate and benefit from those advances.

Some of these are:

(1) Supporting high-quality pre-service preparation and professional development for all personnel who work with children with disabilities (to include everyone from paraprofessionals to highly qualified teachers) which help

ensure that all such personnel have skills and knowledge necessary to improve academic achievement as well as their functional performance, including the use of scientifically based instructional practices whenever possible;

(2) Supporting the development and use of technology, including assistive technology devices and services, to maximize accessibility for children with disabilities,

(3) Benefits and responsibilities of an increasingly diverse society to include both children as well as special education personnel who provide appropriate role models with sufficient knowledge and experience to address special education needs of students as more minority students in the general population will mean more minority students in special education as graduation rates for children with disabilities increases;

(4) Transition services from graduation to post-school employment, or further education, must be reviewed and assessed in order to measure the success of children with disabilities. IDEA 2004 has 2 new subsections to support this.

Section 1412, Subsection (24), Overidentification and Disproportionality, which focuses on a state's responsibility to set policies and procedures designed to prevent the inappropriate overidentification of or disproportionate representation by race and ethnicity of children as children with disabilities and Subsection (25) whereby the State or LEA personnel are prohibited from requiring a child to obtain a prescription for a substance covered by the Controlled Substances Act as a condition of attending school, receiving an evaluation, or receiving services (Wright's s Law, 2004, p.22).

(5) When initiating a request for an initial evaluation to determine if a child is a child with a disability, whether the request is made by the parent, SEA, or LEA, that determination must be completed within 60 days, not within 60 business or school days, a distinction not previously mandated in IDEA 1997, unless (a) a previous LEA has made the recommendation and subsequent LEA is making sufficient progress to ensure a prompt completion of evaluation and parent and subsequent LEA agree to specific time set or (b) the parent of a child repeatedly fails or refuses to produce the child for evaluation.

Reevaluations can take place annually unless a parent and LEA do not agree with the placement and parent requests a due process hearing; a reevaluation must take place at least once every 3 years unless parent and LEA agree reevaluation is unnecessary. Additionally, the LEA can not use a single measure or assessment as the sole criteria for determining whether a child is a child with a disability or determining an appropriate educational program for the child and that LEA must use technologically sound instruments to assess the contribution of cognitive and behavioral factors, in addition to physical or developmental factors. These assessments are selected and administered so as not to be racially or culturally biased and discriminatory; provided and administered in the language most likely to produce accurate information;

used for purposes which the assessments are valid and reliable; administered by trained and knowledgeable personnel; assess all areas of the suspect disability; and the assessments transfer from one school district to another school district in the same academic year coordinated between prior and subsequent school districts to ensure prompt completion of full evaluations. In evaluating all students tested for specific language disabilities, schools are no longer required to use a sever discrepancy between achievement and intellectual ability to find that a child has severe learning disabilities and requires special education devices.

(6) IEP Changes—Specific changes to one of the most important outcomes of IDEA 1975, the Individual Education Program (IEP), are: (a) a continuation of benchmarks and short term objectives *only* for students being assessed using alternative assessments. For standardized assessment requirements (as in NCLB), benchmarks and short term objectives are replaced with measurable, annual goals and a plan of how the students progress toward these goals will be measured; (b) not all members of the IEP team are required to attend IEP meetings in person, and may provide their input in alternative forms, for example: videoconferencing, e-mail and teleconferencing; (c) 15 pilot programs have been established to evaluate the use of multi-year IEPs. These pilot programs outline plans, are optional and must ensure parents are provided informed consent before a multi-year IEP can be developed for their child.

The multi-year IEP (not to exceed 3 years) would have long-range goals and have natural transition points in the student's education as well as annual review, and peer-reviewed research. Natural transition points mean those periods close in time to the transition of a child from preschool to elementary grades, from elementary to middle or junior high school grades, from middle or junior high school to secondary school grades, and from secondary school grades to post-secondary activities, but in no case a period longer than 3 years. A description of this process for review contains revision of each multi-year IEP regarding the annual goals outlined, amending the IEP when necessary and appropriate and LEA review within 30 calendar days if goals are not being met. It is the responsibility of the LEA to reconvene the IEP team to find other strategies to meet any transition objectives set forth in the IEP that are not being met.

(7) A change to IDEA 2004 provided for provisions with regard to the National Instructional Materials Accessibility Standard (NIMAS). As specified in IDEA 2004, NIMAS is the approved standard established regarding Braille, audio or digital texts used exclusively by blind or other persons with disabilities. This refers to print instructional materials (books, textbooks and related printed core materials) that are purposefully published for elementary and secondary school students required by the SEA or LEA for use with children served under IDEA as blind or persons with print disabilities. Additionally, the National Instructional Materials Access Center (NIMAC) through the American Printing House for the blind, provides instructional materials to blind persons or persons with print disabilities. An

> SEA or LEA can choose to or not to coordinate with NIMAC but must demonstrate assurance that instructional materials will be provided to blind persons or persons with print disorders in a timely manner. Whether through NIMAC or not, access to print instructional materials, including textbooks, in accessible media, free of charge, to blind or other persons with print disabilities in elementary or secondary schools, must be available (Office of Special Education and Rehabilitative Services (OSERS, 2005).

The most recent studies to benefit students with disabilities are often pilot studies using a small number of students in order to refine the study and follow with administration to larger groups if the information from the pilot proves significant to special education. Such is the case with several pilot studies being considered by the National Instructional Materials Accessibility Standard (NIMAS) on behalf of the U.S. Department of Education created under IDEA 2004, housed at the Center for Applied Special Technology in Wakefield, Massachusettes. NIMAS will be reviewing findings from researchers in Kentucky studying "the effects of digital mathematics textbooks that speak words and equations aloud while highlighting those elements on a computer screen. The students studied all had print disabilities, an umbrella term for a variety of physical, visual or learning issues that interfere with the ability to read text on the printed page. Students in the study had learning disabilities, including dyslexia, attention deficit disorders, cognitive issues or other conditions, but not visual impairment (Trotter, 2008).

Findings from this pilot study were positive for students using the digital version versus students who did not. Improvements were made in both algebra and prealgebra skills, and the study will be increased from 14 to 26 students. Students in the study shared that hearing the formula so that they could now repeat it and the highlighting features gave them more independence. The digital software involved is called Mathematical Markup Language (Math ML) which presents formulas and other math expressions. Modifications after the pilot included the speech quality of the system and earbuds rather than headphones for the students. Commercial companies supporting previous and present studies in digital math accessibility technology are: Prentice Hall, a division of Pearson LLC, Texthelp Systems Inc., a Woburn, Massachusettes subsidiary of the British company Texthelp System Ltd, and Design Science Inc., based in Long Beach, California (Trotter, 2008).

SECTION 504 OF THE VOCATIONAL REHABILITATION ACT AND IDEA COMPARED

Identifying the similarities and differences between Section 504 of the Vocational Rehabilitation Act of 1973 and IDEA will help the reader understand the difficulties lawmakers as well as advocates encounter in having just one group of laws on which they can rely. Originally enacted to "level the playing field," Section 504 applies to all persons with disabilities regardless of age.

Whereas IDEA is more remedial, often requiring the provision of services and programs in addition to those available to persons without disabilities, Section 504 is meant to preclude hurdles to participation, whether physical (steps to preventing a person in a wheelchair from accessing a building) or programmatic (excluding a child with aids from a classroom). Additionally, while IDEA requires more of schools for children with disabilities, it also provides routes to funding. Section 504 does not provide for financial support of its recommendations.

The definition of a disability under Section 504 is much broader than the definition under IDEA. Section 504 is less discriminatory in that it protects all persons with a disability who have a physical or mental impairment limiting one or more of life activities, and have a record of this impairment.

The Americans with Disabilities Act (ADA) of 1990 has its roots in Section 504. Whereas Section 504 applies only to organizations receiving funding from the federal government, ADA applies to a broader spectrum. Also, Section 504 is broader than IDEA with regard to a "free and appropriate public education." IDEA defines FAPE to include special education and related services, whereas Section 504 includes the provision of special or regular education and related services. IDEA focuses on the unique educational needs of the student; Section 504 compares the education of students with or without disabilities.

Child Find originated under Section 504, which puts the responsibility for identifying and locating children with disabilities on the school. The schools in turn must designate some agency to identify and locate every qualified child in the school's jurisdiction who is not receiving a public education and its related services. Public elementary and secondary schools must develop standards and procedures for evaluating and placing students who are believed to have a disability needing special education and or related services. Because the definitions under Section 504 are broader than IDEA, even if there is no reason that a student is in need of special education under an IEP, a district's procedures and staff training may require an evaluation. These evaluations must have (1) reliable and valid evaluation measures, (2) administration by trained personnel, and (3) evaluations assessing specific educational needs. Unlike IDEA, Section 504 does not mandate a multidisciplinary team, and parents do not have to be included.

Section 504 covers preschool and adult programs as well as elementary and secondary education, requiring equal and accessible transportation, architecture, educational programs, and nonacademic services. Graduation and textbook standards may not be discriminatory, nor may evaluation systems. Different treatment is justified only if it is necessary to provide services to persons with disabilities that are as effective as those provided to others.

Section 504 guarantees an appropriate special education as well as accessibility to regular education programs. It requires that all handicapped children be provided a free, appropriate public education in the least restrictive environment. A handicapped person under Section 504 is (1) any person who has physical or mental impairment that substantially limits one or more major life activities, (2) has a record of such impairment, or (3) is regarded as having such an impairment. This definition differs from that found in IDEA, which defines specific disabling conditions. Because of this difference, some individuals who are not qualified for special education under IDEA may be qualified for special services under Section 504.

Like IDEA, Section 504 requires identification, evaluation, provision of appropriate services, notification of parents, an individualized accommodation plan, and procedural safeguards. These activities must be performed in accordance with Section 504 regulations, which have some requirements that differ from those of IDEA.

Because Section 504 comes under the Office of Civil Rights within the U.S. Department of Education (DOE), students with disabilities have been granted additional support with regard to transportation and facilities. Transportation schedules must not cause students with disabilities to spend appreciably more time on buses than students without disabilities, and arrival and departure times must not reduce the length of the school day. With regard to facilities, room sizes must be adequate to accommodate the educational, physical, and medical needs of the students. Classes for students with disabilities should not be held in storage rooms, partitioned offices, or other inappropriate locations. Teachers of students with disabilities must be provided adequate support and supplies to give their students an education equal to that of nondisabled students (ERIC Clearinghouse on Handicapped and Gifted Children, 1992).

According to deBettencourt (2008) the differences between IDEA and Section 504 are as follows:

(1) IDEA is enforced by the US Department of Education, Office of Special Education; Section 504 is enforced by the US Department of Education, Office of Civil Rights;
(2) IDEA requires parental consent; 504 does not;
(3) IDEA provides a "stay put" provision (a student's IEP and placement continue to be implemented) until all proceedings are resolved; 504 has no "stay-put" provisions.
(4) IDEA parents must receive 10 days notice prior to any change in placement; 504 does not require that parents are notified prior to a student's change of placement, but they must be notified;
(5) IDEA children have highly specific criteria to be identified for placement to include specific time frames and formal paperwork; 504 has less specific procedural criteria;
(6) IDEA addresses the specific education of students with disabilities from preschool to graduation only (ages 3-21); 504 covers the lifespan and safeguards the rights of persons with disabilities in many areas of their lives to include: employment, public access to buildings, transportation and education.
(7) IDEA's guidelines cover all children who fall within 1 or more specific categories of qualifying conditions such as autism, specific learning disabilities, speech or language impairments, hearing impairments or other health impairments; Section 504 covers individuals who meet the definition of a handicapped person limiting a major life activity such as: walking, seeing, hearing, speaking, breathing, learning and caring for oneself.
(8) IDEA requires a reevaluation every 3 years; Section 504 requires periodic evaluation.
(9) IDEA requires an IEP; 504 does not require an IEP but does require a plan.

(10) IDEA "appropriate" education means a program designed to provide educational benefit for persons with disabilities; 504 appropriate means an education comparable to the education provided to non-disabled students.
(11) IDEA placement may be any combination of special education and general education classroom; 504 placement is usually within the general education classroom.

NCLB & IDEA

NCLB & IDEA work in tandem as they both focus on improving academic achievement through high expectations, high quality programs, school accountability, teacher quality, parental involvement and evidence-based instructions. NCLB specifically addresses these and IDEA focuses on how students with disabilities meet academic goals.

- NCLB recognizes that all students receive needed support to achieve high standards to include students with disabilities and hold schools accountable for that. By specifying the inclusion of students with disabilities in NCLB, states, districts and schools have to allocate resources to improve achievement of students with disabilities and monitor the quality of services provided by IDEA as outlined in the IEP, the map of what achievement is expected and those services mandated to meet those standards.
- Prior to IDEA 1997 and NCLB 2001, the federal law improving America's Schools Act of 1994, required schools to include the assessment results of students with disabilities in their accountability of Title 1 Schools. NCLB 2001 as well as the reauthorized IDEA 2004 reaffirmed the commitment to this (IASA of 1994). By including students with disabilities in the assessment process, expectations for those students are higher and schools have the data they need to help *all* children become successful. While NCLB specifies the academic goals, IDEA specifies specific resources and services necessary to help students with disabilities achieve those goals.
- Although Adequate Yearly Progress (AYP) may be missed by a school due to inclusion of any one subgroup, states, districts and schools can disaggregate their data (separate the results of specific subgroups), ensuring that all schools and districts are accountable for the performance of that subgroup of students, not just the school as a whole. This can become an important part of an improvement plan.
- By having (NCLB) all students held to the same academic standards and participate in annual state assessments, schools know how to better serve their students. One of the foci is to make tests more accessible and valid in order for all students to achieve higher scores. Necessary accommodations, outlined in IDEA, specified in the IEP, such as repeating directions or extending time do not invalidate tests scores but measures what the students with disabilities actually know and not the disability.
- While NCLB includes students with disabilities in participation and achieving proficiency, on state assessments, there are certain students with more

severe cognitive disabilities (about 10% of all students with disabilities) and, therefore, acknowledges this need for alternative achievement standards which are less difficult and more tailored to their needs; this proficient score can be counted in the same way as other general education student's proficient score on a state assessment. Example of what IDEA includes students in the most significant cognitive categories are: autism, multiple disabilities, and traumatic brain injury (TBI) in this 10% of students with disabilities.

If a student, due to their cognitive disability, has significant difficulty achieving grade-level proficiency, even with excellent instructions, this student may be able to be tested through a "modified achievement standard" which is a standard created that is aligned with this academic content for that grade in which the student is enrolled but may have reduced depth. If the student is assessed through this modified achievement standard, and found to be proficient in the academic content, then the score is proficient for the school's AYP report for accountability purposes only. Certain cases of these "modified achievement standards" specifically must provide students with disabilities access to grade level curricula in order to attain a regular high school diploma.

- Both NCLB and IDEA reinforce the goal of accountability for all children, and must include students with disabilities. State performance goals under IDEA must be aligned with state's definition of AYP. New provisions in IDEA 2004 allow Local Education Agencies (LEAs) to use federal special education funds to provide early intervention services for students who are at risk of later identification and placement in special education. This reinforces the NCLB focus on implementation of scientifically based instructional practices like curriculum based measurement to identify and address academic problems early.

HIGHLY QUALIFIED SPECIAL EDUCATION TEACHERS

NCLB requires teachers of all core academic subjects, including special education teachers to be highly qualified. IDEA 2004 reinforces this requirement. Core Academic subject are: English, Reading and Language Arts, Math, Science, Foreign Language, Civics and Government, Economics, Art, Music and Geography.

(1) Special education teachers must be endorsed in special education and if they are teaching core academic subject to students with disabilities, they must be endorsed/demonstrate content knowledge in the subject they teach.
(2) Special education teachers who teach core academic subjects to students being assessed against alternate achievement standards and complete evaluations of their progress must demonstrate content knowledge of student achievement in the subjects they teach.

(3) Special education teachers who instruct students in core academic subjects, in consultation, or co-teaching with NCLB qualified teachers who assign grades, do not need to be NCLB qualified in those core subjects.
(4) States may design a High Objective Uniform State Standard of Evaluation (HOUSSE) which impacts elementary special education teachers in that a state may elect to consider courses completed, years of experience teaching elementary special education or professional development as long as it does not establish a lesser standard for the content knowledge requirements of special education teachers compared to standards for general education teachers (Nebraska Department of Education, 2008).

FUNDING AND OPPOSITION

Funding provided to programs developed in IDEA 1990 and the amendments of 1997 has proven to be enormous when compared to the cost of educating the regular education student. In March 2000, the Supreme Court declared that school districts should additionally pay the costs of nursing care during the school day for disabled persons, which could cost as much as $15,000 annually, per pupil. The increase in the number of special education students is approximately 3 percent each year. To keep up with this, 23,000 more special education teachers will be needed. These factors alone present enormous implications for universities and state and local governments.

Opponents to special education believe these programs and expenditures are taking money away from school construction, books, and teacher salaries. Opponents also believe that vague wording in IDEA produced frivolous lawsuits.

Proponents for special education counter with the thought that the lack of funding and programs based on such funding so far has caused many special education problems and challenges to increase; for example, learning disabled students account for one-half of the special education students, and early identification is equally critical. Additionally, school districts must continuously collect meaningful data to document student progress toward IEP goals, thus documenting program validity. Data needs to be collected throughout instruction so that student progress is continually monitored, which can support the decisions as to whether or not a program or instruction is continued (Yell and Drasgow, 2000).

Both political parties support increased spending for special education. The Republican Party recently went on record in support of an increase in the funding level to the legal maximum, and the Democratic Party has responded with support for the largest increase in funding for education ever.

Progress is continually being made from the laws that were passed to legislative and congressional effort being put forth now with regard to the special education movement. According to a progress report on National Disability Policy, IDEA is becoming an achievement of bipartisan compromise. Parts of the 1997 IDEA amendments provided for disciplinary action and payment of attorneys' fees to parents (described in Chapter 2). A nine-month study of the effect of federal special education protections on the ability of schools to maintain discipline is currently being planned by the U.S. General Accounting Office. Advocates for special education work to keep these areas of provision alive.

NCLB 2001—IMPLICATIONS FOR SPECIAL EDUCATION POLICY AND PRACTICE

Under NCLB, each state plans and demonstrates that it has developed an accountability system to be employed by all state LEAs, public elementary and secondary schools, that ensures they make adequate yearly progress (AYP) as defined by that state which:

(1) impacts all children (to include students with disabilities);
(2) is statistically valid and reliable,;
(3) results in continuous improvement, to include measurable annual objectives supporting such improvement.

Reasonable accommodations in assessments for students with disabilities, which parallel IDEA 1997—Section 602 (3). Results within each state, LEA and school can be disaggregated for students with disabilities as compared with non-disabled students. Funds available for improving basic programs operated by LEAs must supplement and not supplant state and local funds provided to the school for special education. Children with disabilities are eligible for services under NCLB as general education children. The special education group eligible for such provider services must have goals consistent within the ones outlined in the IEP, consistent with IDEA. NCLB acknowledges that highly qualified teachers have professional development that provides instruction when teaching children with special needs as well as training and hiring special education teachers, including the hiring of special education teachers to team-teach in classrooms containing both children with disabilities and non-disabled children.

Additionally, training will be provided in how to teach and address the needs of students with different learning styles, particularly students with disabilities. Principals who demonstrate a record of improving academic achievement of all students, but particularly students with disabilities, will receive incentives to include financial incentives.

The hiring of highly qualified teachers, including teachers who become qualified through state and local alternative certification programs, and special education teachers with the goal of reducing classroom size, particularly in the early grades (Council for Exceptional Children, 2002).

According to the Council for Exceptional Children (2002) the "No Child Left Behind Act of 2001" indicates the following implications for Special Education Policy and Practice regarding the improvement of educational programs impacted by IDEA 2004 and interacting with SEAs and LEAs.

Title 1 Pt. A, Plans Required SEA Section IIV—coordinate a plan in consultation with LEAs and with IDEA that includes: academic standards, academic assessments, accountability, academic yearly progress (AYP), measuring objectives, school improvement, public school choice, supplemental educational services, and qualifications for teachers and paraprofessionals.

Activities for professional development based on NCLB, must be aligned and related to curriculum and academic standards with funds providing professional development activities as they relate to the needs of students with disabilities with different learning styles, particularly students with disabilities and identifying early and appropriate interventions. Additionally, programs must be created to enable paraprofessionals to become certified and licensed teachers in relation to IDEA.

Title II—Pt. A—Teacher and Principal Training and Recruiting Fund

- Developing and implementing initiatives to assist in recruiting highly qualified teachers and principals;
- Training and hiring regular and special education teachers, which can include special education teachers to team teach in inclusion classrooms;
- Improving knowledge of teachers and principals and in appropriate cases, paraprofessionals, to provide training to teach and address needs of students with different learing styles, particularly students with disabilities and students with specific learning needs;
- Providing incentives, including financial, to principals with a record of improving the academic achievement of all students, but particularly students with disabilities; and hiring highly qualified teachers in order to reduce classroom size particularly in the early grades including special education teachers.

POLICY BASED ON THE LAWS

Modified Academic Achievement Standards—(MAAS)

An expectation of performance that is challenging for eligible students, but less difficult than grade-level academic achievement standard; must be aligned with a state's academic content standard for the grade in which the student is enrolled. Only academic achievement standard is modified, not the content standard; may be less difficult when compared with general test and grade-level achievement standards. Example—The content is the same but the questions are less difficult.

A student is eligible for MAAS participation if he/she is a student with a disability under IDEA in any of the disability categories listed under IDEA.

The IEP team (including student's parent) determines how student will participate in State and District—wide assessments. If a State uses MAAS for assessment, criteria must include: 1) objective evidence demonstrating that the student's disability has precluded the student from achieving grade-level proficiency, 2) student progress to date in reading to appropriate instruction, including special education and related services designed to address student's individual needs, so that even if significant growth occurs, IEP team believes student will not achieve grade-level proficiency within the year covered by the IEP; 3) IEP must include grade level academic content standards.

A state may modify or develop a new assessment but cannot use an outside of level assessment (designed for student at a lower grade level) because content would be different. The State is responsible for making certain staff learn to write IEP goals tied to State academic content standards. This helps facilitate students with disabilities making progress towards grade—level proficiency, improved exposure to subject matter in order to focus instruction on more challenging goals, and offered greater collaboration between special and general education teachers when working with a student whose IEP goals were aligned with State academic content standards (U.S. Department of Education, 2007).

CHARTER SCHOOLS AND CHILDREN WITH SPECIAL NEEDS

Charter schools are based on a specific philosophy and *charter,* or contract, about what objectives the school wants to meet. The charter is held accountable for academic and operational results. Some parents of special-needs children believe charter schools provide less bureaucracy and can more easily meet their children's needs.

Charter schools sometimes can provide a lower student-teacher ratio, and they may be more open to adopting a variety of instructional techniques—in part because they are at liberty to exhibit more autonomy, which may lead to a more individualized program. The programs available at the charter school may provide what the parents believe are significant to their child's academic and social development. A charter school may also provide simply the opportunity for a fresh start. McKinney (1996) explains that few of the twenty-five states that have passed charter school legislation have resolved whether the charter schools are separate school districts or part of the regular school district. If they are, in fact, legally autonomous school districts, they act as the local education agencies (LEAs), which are required under IDEA to provide a free, appropriate public education. If a charter school accepts special education children as part of the general population being served according to the charter or contract—and therefore receives funding for these children—it is required to follow the regulations set forth by Section 504 of the Rehabilitation Act of 1973 and the Americans with Disabilities Act (ADA). All public school districts, including charter schools wholly funded by the state, are bound by Section 504, which prohibits discrimination on the basis of disability by any agency that receives federal financial assistance.

What happens if a charter school's administration believes it cannot meet the needs of special education students? *Charter Schools: A Reference Handbook* (Weil, 2000) several reasons why some charter schools eliminate students with specific needs. Primary among them is cost. As Secretary of Education Richard W. Riley commented, it is often more expensive to educate a child who is disabled or emotionally troubled (p. 128). Many charter schools therefore determine to improve their bottom line by leaving the education of students with special needs to the regular public schools.

It is important to note that parents who choose charter schools give up some of their individual rights under IDEA, as the charter school selected may not have as many specific resources on site to meet the special needs of the child. However, parents may choose the charter school experience in order to receive what they believe are better educational services. This has implications for future planning, programs, and funding allocations (Lange and Lehr, 2000).

TECHNOLOGY PROGRAMS BASED ON THE LAW

The Department of Education has since 1991 funded projects at the state level to promote systems change and advocacy activities enhancing access of children and adults with disabilities to assistive technology devices and services. These projects were originally authorized under the section Technology Related Assistance in IDEA. In October 1998, Congress passed the Assistive Technology Act (see Chapter 2). Disability advocates continue to lobby for more access and training, including use of the Internet at public libraries. The latter has revolutionary potential for individuals with special needs because of the extraordinary potential to empower them in education, employment, and civic activities (National Council on Disability, 1999).

ASSISTIVE TECHNOLOGY—SEC 300.105

(a) Each public agency must ensure that assistive technology devices or assistive technology services, or both as those terms are defined in Section 300.5 and 300.6, respectively, are made available to a child with a disability as a part of the child's—
   1) special education (under Section 300.36);
   2) related services (under Section 300.34); or
   3) supplementary aids and services (under Section 300.38 and 300.114 (a) (2) (ii)).

(b) On a case by case basis, the use of school- purchased assistive technology devices in a child's home or other setting is required if the child's IEP Team determines that the child needs access to those devices in order to receive FAPE.

The Association of Assistive Technology Act Programs (ATAP) representing 50 of the state Assistive Technology Programs funded under the Assistive Technology Act of 2004 (PL 108-364), supports Assistive Technology loan programs, demonstration centers, financial loan programs, technical assistance and training and related services. For purposes of IDEA 2004 related to delivery of AT needed for a free, appropriate public education (FAPT) as well as universal design, the ATAP offers expertise that can be included collaboratively. The main difference regarding AT between IDEA 1997 and IDEA 2004 is the exclusion of a surgically implanted cochlear implants, implanted electrodes related to computer controlled prosthetics and similar devices. In all other IEP meetings, including ATAP, a group familiar with utilizing technology to maximize curricular access might serve as a critical resource. Additionally, collaboration between the ATAP and State Education Agencies (SEA) and Local Education Agencies (LEA) might also ensure delivery of technology in a more timely manner. Having greater collaborative involvement might also ensure the increased use of technology in curricular programming for universal design principles (National Organization Representing State Assistive Technology Act Programs ,2005).

PROGRAMS FOR AT-RISK INFANTS AND TODDLERS

The Department of Education's twenty-first annual report on the implementation of IDEA acknowledges a sharp rise in the number of children two years old or younger who are receiving special education services. Between 1988 and 1997, that number soared from 34,270 to 197,376. A majority of these children—55 percent—received services in their home. Children from birth to age two are also receiving services in early-intervention classrooms and outpatient service facilities.

The rise in the number of infants and toddlers receiving special education services can be attributed to better identification practices over that ten-year period. This is especially due to the fact that the 1997 revision of IDEA added a category for the developmentally delayed, giving more flexibility to define needs based on academics and more for young children (Galley, 2000).

It is important to note that when IDEA was adopted in 1975, lawmakers decided that the federal government should pick up 40 percent of the additional costs associated with the law's requirements. Congress has never come close to that goal, though spending for IDEA rose by 66 percent in the five years since the Republicans took control of congress. But federal aid still amounts to an estimated 13 percent of the total state and local costs for special education, according to the Department of Education. For the fiscal year 2000,Congress allocated $5.75 billion for state grants under IDEA; most of that money, about $5 billion, went to educate students ages 6–21; the rest went to early childhood and preschool programs.

Again, there are bipartisan efforts to continue the support. A new grassroots group from Concord, New Hampshire, the National Campaign to Fully Fund IDEA, is attempting to collect a million signatures of support to bring to Washington in the year 2001. The CEC has recommended spending nearly $7 billion on IDEA, Part B, alone with an additional $1 billion for early childhood and preschool programs. The National School Boards Association is requesting that Congress approve an additional $2.2 billion a year for the next ten years. Additionally significant is that two representatives, Matthew G. Martinez (D–Calif.) and Bill Gooding (R–Penn.), have introduced legislation to authorize an appropriation of an additional $2 billion each year until 2010, at which time the federal government's contribution would meet its 40 percent mark—the original goal of 1975 (Sack, 2000).

POLICY VS. PROGRAM IMPLEMENTATION

Sections of IDEA 2004 continue to clarify important components related to Early Intervention (Part C of IDEA). A purpose of early intervention is to lessen the effects of a disability; the emphasis are on services occurring in the child's natural environment as soon as the disability or delay is identified. The natural environment can include the home and community setting in which children without disabilities can participate. An exception to this policy would be when early intervention can not be achieved satisfactorily for the infant or toddler in a natural environment.

The same goals and guidelines for the federal grant program that support these programs for infants and toddlers, ages birth-2 years and their families, with a lead agency receiving the federal grant and administering it were supported in 2004, with the reauthorization of IDEA.

Although there are many requirements states have to meet, the states do have some discretion in setting the criteria for child eligibility, to include whether or not to serve at risk children. Therefore, definitions of eligibility may differ from state to state to include which state agency is the lead agency. If the state agency and designated professionals determine a child eligible, an Individualized Family Service Plan (IFSP) is created.

Early Intervention Transition

Transition from Part C, services provided to Infants and Toddlers to Part B, special education services begins between 30-32 months and no less than 3 months prior to a child's 3rd birthday. Not all children are eligible to transition; the multidisciplinary team decides this at a transition meeting with a plan of how the parent and team transition the child out of Part C and develop an IEP. In this IEP, services the child needs after transition are specified under the guidance of a service coordinator to ensure rights and procedural safeguards.

In the reauthorization of IDEA 2004, provisions were made for school districts to use up to 15% for "coordinated, comprehensive early-intervention services." This decrease in the special education budget must be put back through another source. The focus on this may be pupils in grades K-3rd who need extra academic or behavior support. In actuality, programs such as Response to Intervention (RTI), not solely directed to students with disabilities but to general education students as well, can benefit from these funds. Specific tracking of this 15% for non-special education students takes place for 2 years. This application of the law to applied policies attempts to offer assistance to general education students while teachers and intervention specialists can better focus on specific support for the students with disabilities (Samuels, 2008).

Similarly, in the reauthorization of IDEA 2004, focus is placed on the special education student's need for assistive technology. Once this need is documented in the IEP, it must be provided. An outcome of this becomes the need for collaboration between the information technology (IT) specialist and the assistive technology specialist to work together to create technological assistance to create the most successful learning environment. This can be accomplished through conversations around planning so that the IT specialist implements what the AT specialist is trying to accomplish for the students with disabilities. The IT specialist can better understand what the specific technology is attempting to focus on while the special education teacher and administrator explain why and how the IEP has included the specifics (Samuels, 2008).

According to Davis (2008), as presented in Quality Counts, Special Education Technology Tips are as follows:

(1) Make sure special education teachers know what software is already available in the district. Sometimes, existing software just needs to be loaded on a new computer.
(2) Communication is key. Help forge good working relationships between special educators, assistive-technology specialists, and the information-technology department. Have regular meetings to share progress and update goals. Work together when planning and carrying out assistive-technology projects.
(3) Make sure IT staff members understand what technology does for special education students. Ask assistive technology staff to do a show-and-tell with software or other technological devices. Have IT staff members visit classrooms to see how technology aids students with disabilities.
(4) Keep special education teachers informed about repairs to technology. Tell them when their problem is likely to be fixed so they can make alternative lesson plans for the interim.
(5) Help special education staff members understand what will and will not work on a network and the reasons why. Be creative in coming up with solutions for making new technologies work for special education students.

Policy vs. Program ImplementationAs Garrett, Thorp, Behrman and Denham (1998) point out, when the vision of policymakers is turned into specific services and actions, policy implementation takes place. It is here where the decision maker's ideas become real for the intended beneficiaries of the policy. With regard to Part H of IDEA 1990 (reauthorized in 1997 as Part C of IDEA), the policy becomes actuality when (1) an early intervention system is put in place, and (2) when infants, toddlers, and their families receive appropriate services. Practicality comes in when modifications are made by the implements. Each agency applies its own version of the legislation and is affected by the knowledge of the implementers and availability of resources. When Congress passed Part H of IDEA, "appropriate intervention services" were to include multidisciplinary, interagency coordination; the funding was never intended to be solely the responsibility of the federal government. Congress required each state to develop an interagency coordinating council (ICC) to assist state agencies in developing and implementing the early intervention system, with parents of young children with special needs composing one fifth of each state's ICC membership.

Garrett, Thorp, Behrman, and Denham (1998) also discuss a study employing in-depth interviews with local interagency coordinating councils, observations, review of materials, and additional interviews at two expanded data collection sites, results demonstrated that policy intentions and implementation frequently differ. In this case the early childhood intervention legislation had both positive and negative effects. Local impact in areas of family-centered activities and service coordination, improved Child Find, and referral for services, funding, networking, and developmental outcomes were very positive. However, negotiating system bureaucracies, increased paperwork, reduction in at-risk services, increased financial responsibility for parents, and budget impacts from non-reimbursable services were noted drawbacks.

Early childhood intervention is one of the few special education legislations of IDEA, which requires much coordination on the part of funding that does not predominately come from the federal government. The program is so significant in the hearts and minds of special education policymakers and practitioners that the local application and effort from advocates of the law's success will not fade.

The major laws providing services to children with special needs were enacted in the 1970's principally Section 504 and Public Law 94-142 (IDEA 1975). Prior to that, in the 1960's and early 1970's special education advocates brought the need for services to the forefront through specific court cases and litigation. Thus, the enormous number of court cases, Reauthorization of Acts, is relatively recent.

HIGHER EDUCATION ACT AND IMPLICATIONS FOR SPECIAL EDUCATION

On July 31, 2008, the House and Senate passed the Higher Education Act (H.E.A.) the reauthorization bill was signed by President Bush, August 14, 2008. Under Title II, Partnership Grants, the "eligible partnership evaluation" requirements for partnership, in keeping with NCLB and its emphasis on highly qualified teachers, has a focus on high needs areas such as special education. There are five new programs in Title II and two specifically address students with disabilities: *Teach to Reach Grants* which provide funds to institutions to help pre-service teacher education candidates to teach children with disabilities with emphasis on inclusive and Graduate situations and *Fellowships to Prepare Faculty at Colleges and Universities* with funds supporting doctoral candidates who will become faculty in areas to include special education. (Klein & Sawchuk, 2008).

REFERENCES

Council for Exceptional Children. (2002). *No Child Left Behind Act of 2001 Implications for Special Education Policy and Practice.* Arlington, VA: Author.

Davis, M. R. (2008). Technology Cooperation Vital in Special Education. *Education Week*.Retrieved September 24, 2008 from http://www.edweek.org/dd/articles/2008/01/23/3spec.ed.h01.html?qs=special+education

deBettencourt, L. U. The Differences Between IDEA and Section 504. Retrieved June 6, 2008 from http://school.familyeducation.com/specialeducation/ada/38439.html

ERIC Clearinghouse on Handicapped and Gifted Children, 1992. Section 504: The Rehabilitation Act of 1973 and the Americans with Disabilities Act of 1990. Reston, VA: The Council for Exceptional Children, Office of Educational Research and Improvement, U.S. Department of Education.

Galley, M., 2000. "Report Charts Growth in Special Education." *Education Week* 19, no. 32: 35.

Garrett, J. N., E. K. Thorp, M. M. Behrmann, and S. A. Denham, 1998. "The Impact of Early Intervention Legislation: Local Perceptions." *Topics in Early Childhood Special Education* 18: 183–190.

Klein, A., and Sawchuk, S., 2008. "Congress OKs Renewal of Higher Education Act" *Education Week 27, no. 45. Retrieved September 8, 2008 from http://www.edweek.org/ew/articles/2008/07/30/45hea_web.h27.html*

Lange, C. M., and C. A. Lehr, 2000. "Charter Schools and Students with Disabilities: Parent Perceptions of Reasons for Transfer and Satisfaction with Services." *Remedial and Special Education* 21, no. 3: 141–151.

Martin, E. W., Martin, R., & Terman, D. L. (1996). The Legislative and Litigation History of Special Education. *The Future of Children. Special Education for Students With Disabilities (6)1, p. 25-39.*

McKinney, J. R., 1996. "A New Barrier for Children with Disabilities." *Educational Leadership* 54 (October): 22–25.

National Organization Representing State Assistive Technology Act Programs. (2005). *Assistive Technology Act Program.* Retrieved June 10, 2008 from http://www.ataporg.org

Nebraska Department of Education. (2008). *NCLB/Special Education Frequently Asked Questions and Implementation Guidance.* Retrieved February 10, 2008 from www.nde.state.ne.us/federal programs/pdf/faqNCLBqualftchrreqmts1-8-08.pdf

National Council on Disability, 1999. *National Disability Policy: A Progress Report.* Washington, DC: National Council on Disability.

Office of Special Education and Rehabilitative Services. (2005). *National Instructional Materials Accessibility Standard (NIMAS).* U.S. Department of Education. Retrieved May 10, 2008 from www.ed.gov/about/offices/list/osers/index.html

Sack, J., 2000. "Congress Poised to Increase Funding for Special Education." *Education Weekly* 19, no. 31: 39.

Samuels, C. A. (2008). Special Education is Funding Early Help. *Education Week.* Retrieved September 24, 2008 from http://www.edweek.org/ew/articles/2008/-9/10/03ceis_ep.h28.html?qs=special+education

Smith, B., 2000. "The Federal Role in Early Childhood Special Education Policy in the Next Century: The Responsibility of the Individual." *Topics in Early Childhood Special Education* 20, no.1 (Spring): 10.

Sung, E., 2000. "At What Cost Special Education?" *The Policy News & Information Service,* VoxCap Network, *http://www.policy.com/news/dbrief/farc480.asp.*

Trotter, A. (2008). Math Study Evaluates Digital Aids. *Education Week* Retrieved October 10, 2008 from edweek.org/go/digitaled

U. S. Department of Education. (2007). *Final Regulations on Modified Academic Achievement Standards.* Retrieved January 21, 2008 from http://www.ed.gov/policy/speced/guid/modachieve-summary.html

Weil, D., 2000. *Charter Schools: A Reference Handbook.* Santa Barbara, CA: ABC-CLIO Publishers.

Wurtz, E., 1999. *Promising Practices: Progress Toward the Goals 1999.* Washington, DC: National Education Goals Panel.

Yell, M. L., and E. Drasgow, 2000. "Litigating a Free Appropriate Public Education: The Lovaas Hearings and Cases." *Journal of Special Education* 33, no. 4: 205–214.

Chapter Five

Politics and the Special Education Challenge

THE DEVELOPMENT OF TEACHER UNIONS AND THEIR IMPACT ON SPECIAL EDUCATION

Concerned about the neglect of parents in the training of their children, the Puritans of the Massachusetts Bay Colony, a religious society, proposed and supported the Massachusetts Law of 1642, which called for an investigation of the ability of children to read and understand the principles of religion and the laws of society. In 1647 the Old Deluder Satan Laws passed, requiring communities in Massachusetts Colony to establish and support schools. At that time in the American Colonies, there were no licensing or professional standards to be met.

In the early 1800s, most Americans lived in farm communities with one-room schools and a single teacher. By the mid-1800s a reform movement called "the common school movement" attempted to bring schools under state control, teaching a common body of knowledge to children from different social and economic backgrounds. The first teacher organizations and teacher unions were organized around this time.

In 1857 ten state teacher associations met with the objective of upgrading teaching to a profession. They called their combined organization the National Teachers' Association. Years later, when it merged with the National Association of School Superintendents, the two organizations became the National Education Association (NEA). Because the NEA was dominated by superintendents and college professors, teachers themselves had little influence on issues and advocacy.

It was left to two women, Margaret Haley and Catherine Goggin, working tirelessly for the benefit of classroom teachers, to form the Chicago Teacher's Federation (CTF) in 1897, the forerunner of the American Federation of Teachers (AFT). In 1902 the CTF formed an alliance with the Chicago Federation of Labor that resulted in heightened antagonism against the Chicago Board of Education. The board had voted not to increase teachers' salaries and required teachers to sign yellow-dog contracts, which prevented them from joining a union (if they did, they would be discharged).

By 1917 the NEA had become an association pledging professionalism encompassing education training and scientific inquiry. In April 1916, the CTF regrouped in order to organize the American Federation of Teachers, an organization that had minimal impact up to World War II.

Major differences between AFT and the NEA were evident from the beginning. AFT was a teacher's union organized and lead by teachers, whereas the NEA membership was largely school administrators, including school district representatives. Although by the 1960s NEA membership was mostly composed of teachers, administrators still led the organization, resulting in adversarial bargaining when conflicts arose. It wasn't until fairly recently that teachers and administrators came to respect each other's rights and roles and cooperate for the good of their students.

In recent years, school districts and unions have worked together to establish conditions conducive for the success of special education programs. Both groups recognize that federal laws for programs and practices related to special education require the teacher's unions to advocate and districts to provide appropriations so that special education teachers are able to effectively do their jobs. Proof of this are the special certifications developed by most state departments of education in areas such as learning disabilities; mental, physical, and visual handicaps; hearing impairments, and giftedness.

State departments of education, school districts, and teachers unions have demonstrated that special education teachers and the population they teach have definite and important needs. To include teachers in decision making is one of the missions of teacher's unions. This ability is essential if, for example, inclusion of special education students in regular education classrooms is to come about successfully. Other good examples of this are special education programs serving students with various disabilities that "years ago, the public schools did not attempt to serve" (Streshly and DeMitchell, 1994, p. 32).

In education there is a flow from politics to economics to collective bargaining. Education advocacy groups have supported the political debates regarding the setting of values for education. These values support special education and are evident in the laws that have been passed to protect children with special needs. Collective bargaining ensures that the advocate's initial work gets into the special programs the politics support. The distribution of funds is something teachers unions have kept a close eye on.

The unions have specifically made issues important for the equal education of special needs students part of their political agenda. For example, both the NEA and AFT have stated that charter schools (discussed in Chapter 4) must be open to all students, including those with special needs. This was part of a conscious effort to not allow charter schools to create a multitiered choice system discriminating against some students (Weil, 2000).

Teachers unions have developed collaborative relationships with local universities to help teachers gain more academic background in their fields as well as meet requirements of the Department of Education. A new partnership, the United Teachers of Dade (UTD) in Miami-Dade County, Florida (an affiliate of the American Federation of Teachers), has forged a pioneering relationship with a national university, the Union Institute, based in Cincinnati, Ohio, in order to develop an innovative model designed to make learning more accessible and available to teachers and other related school personnel. Its aim is to provide the most highly educated people possible to work with our most treasured resource—our children. The National Education Goals Panel in its publication *Promising Practices: Progress Toward the Goals 1998* proposed important educational goals for the year 2000, among them "the nation's teaching force will have access to programs for the continued improvement of their professional skills and the opportunity to acquire the knowledge and skills needed to instruct and prepare all Americans for the next century." One objective of this goal was that "Partnerships will be established, whenever possible, among local education agencies, institutions of higher education, parents, and local labor, business and professional associations to provide and support programs for the professional development of educators" (National Education Goals Panel, 1998). The partnership between the Union Institute and UTD is an ideal example of an educational institution and a labor association joining forces to support professional education for teachers.

Recently the NEA and AFT locals have come together to develop TURN, the Teachers Union Reform Network, headed by Roger Erskine of the Seattle, Washington, NEA and Adam Urbanski of the Rochester, New York, AFT. These joint union/association leaders have committed to helping to bring to the forefront educational reform issues such as quality teaching, pay for performance, evaluation, and parental involvement.

One of the outcomes of TURN's mission statement is to "promote in public education and in the union democratic dynamics, fairness and due process for all" (Urbanski, 1998). This is parallel to the goals of IDEA, which identified that due process for special-needs children is essential. The goals of TURN appear to be consistent with the goals of the federal government and special education advocates.

Teachers unions organize around school reform as well as salary benefits, and a report by the AFT calls for stricter requirements for new teachers with regard to standardized tests, higher grades, and more student teaching experiences. The efforts by teacher associations and unions to influence policy are continual.

Specifically, in resolutions set forth by the AFT at the 1994 national convention in Anaheim, California, support was unconditionally given for major issues related to special education. With regard to inclusion, a concept with no legal mandate or consistent definition, the AFT recognized (1) a working definition of inclusion to be "the placement of all students with disabilities in general education classrooms without regard to the nature or severity of the students' disabilities, their ability to behave and function appropriately in the classroom, or the educational benefits they can derive"; (2) that two years before the twentieth anniversary of the passage of the Education of All Handicapped Children's Act (P.L. 94–142), Congress's continuing cynicism with funding the mandates of the law at under 10 percent instead of the 40 percent promised compromised schools' ability to provide appropriate services to children with disabilities; and (3) that there is a high percentage of minority children in some classes for students with disabilities, and inclusion is viewed by some advocates as the only means of getting minority children out of some of these placements.

Convention attendees discussed eleven other issues regarding children with special needs and passed seven resolutions, including:

(1) The AFT will continue to seek high national achievement standards for all education, applicable to all students, disabled and nondisabled alike.
(2) The AFT opposes inclusion based on placing all students with disabilities in general education classroom regardless of disability, their ability to behave or function appropriately.
(3) The AFT opposes administrative practices placing too many students with disabilities in the general education classroom, often without services, and changing IEPs in order to do this.
(4) The AFT seeks alliances with organizations supporting alternative placements and the educational placement of students with disabilities in the LRE (American Federation of Teachers, 1994).

It is important to note that the AFT represents *all* teachers, many more regular education than special education. In trying to make the educational experience in the regular education classroom the highest academically, and by recognizing the needs of the regular education teacher and restating the desire to support both students with and without disabilities, the AFT is supporting all of its membership.

Another demonstration of AFT support for special education is its Educational Research and Dissemination (ERD) Program, which disseminates research to help promote effective teaching and learning with a variety of courses related to special education. Additionally, AFT is involved with the Association of Service Providers Implementing IDEA Reforms in Education (ASPIRE) partnership. ASPIRE develops materials to support special education teachers as well as regular education teachers.

POLITICS ON SPECIAL EDUCATION PROGRAMS FOR YOUNG CHILDREN

The first U.S. preschools were affiliated with colleges and universities, who developed them in an effort to find better ways to care for children. Garwood (1983) points out that federal legislation under the Works Progress Administration Program of the 1930s and the Lanham Act during World War II was instrumental in providing funds for the spread of preschools beyond the university community. Thus began the traditional nursery school.

During the so-called War on Poverty in the 1960s, the young economically disadvantaged child became a focus of discussion. Many believed that if the disadvantaged child had the same advantages middle-class children had, especially in the early years, the educational achievement of the disadvantaged child would increase. Thus evolved the *enriched curriculum* exemplified by the Bank Street Program and the Erickson Institute Program. Both the cognitive and affective domains were promoted, with development of language as well as a positive self-image of paramount importance. In an enrichment model, structure is low, flexibility is high, and there are no lists of measurable objectives; developing one's own choice of activities and projects is stressed.

Another model of curriculum evolving from 1960s political philosophy was the direct instruction curriculum of Bereiter and Engelmann, in which the desire to increase the linguistic and cognitive levels of disadvantaged children was so imperative that a highly structured direct teaching system was developed. Aligned with the theories of B. F. Skinner, the curriculum's results appeared dramatic and quick. Garwood (1983) describes the Bereiter and Engelmann theory that " disadvantaged children have a severe language deficit in thinking about and describing experiences .... The teacher was the key to this instructional model focusing initially on language" (415). From this model developed the Distar curriculum, which follows all the initial premises but added reading and arithmetic. All curriculum goals and objectives are in measurable terms, instructed in groups with children responding orally in unison.

The politics of this time was to raise the level of education of the disadvantaged because the social consciousness of the country was high. The flame of this desire, as evidenced by the laws being enacted for special education beginning in the 1960s, has continued to the present through hundreds of federally funded, state funded, and community supported programs.

POLITICAL CHANGES AFFECTING THE EDUCATION OF DISABLED CHILDREN

Changes in society that affect aspects of daily life produce actions and reactions by political and educational leaders. This has certainly been the case concerning the recent trend in students bringing weapons to school. The original Individuals with Disabilities Act stated that disabled students who carry guns to school could be removed for more than ten days without parental consent or court approval. In 1997 Congress approved changes that gave schools the power to suspend for up to forty-five days disabled students who bring guns or other weapons to school. Additionally, the 1997 revision streamlined the procedure for removing dangerous students from the classroom by allowing placement decisions to be made by a hearing officer rather than a judge. A loophole allowing (1) students to claim disability status after committing a crime, and (2) the school district to call police without penalty when disabled students commit crimes has since been closed.

Also affecting special education students is the Class Size Reduction Program, enacted in 2000, which seeks to help schools improve student learning by providing reduction funds to hire additional qualified teachers so that classes contain no more than a nationwide average of eighteen pupils. A guidance memo for the program specifies that if a special education class has more than eighteen students, the local education agency (LEA) may use the reduction funds to achieve a reduced class size. Since mainstreaming and inclusion are important to special education, LEAs may also use these funds to pay professional development costs for regular education classroom teachers to help educate them to the needs of special education children. LEAs may also use these funds to hire special education teachers to team-teach with regular education teachers when needed.

Another political act allocating funds to create programs for special education students is the Reading Excellence Acts (REA) Program. On July 26, 2000, the Secretary of Education announced the award of $198.4 million in grants to help improve the reading skills of prekindergarten through third-grade children. The funds will help nine states and Washington, D.C., use scientifically based research to improve the reading skills of up to one million elementary school students, particularly at-risk students during the critical grades of kindergarten through grade three. One of the key purposes of REA is to provide early intervention to children who are at-risk of inappropriately being identified as having special needs.

Political support for special education has continued in the form of federal mandates to accommodate students with disabilities, as evidenced by the greater number of critical issues being addressed and funding being allocated through the Americans with Disabilities Act, the Individuals with Disabilities Act, Section 504 of Title V of the Rehabilitation Act, and advisory guidelines from the U.S. Architectural and Transportation Barriers Compliance Board.

Further evidence of political support for special education and the rights of the disabled is found in the Consortium on Inclusive Schooling Practices, a collaborative effort to build the capacity of state and local education agencies serving children and youth with and without disabilities in school and community settings. It is a five-year project funded by the U.S. Department of Education/Office of Special Education Programs to states participating in the Allegheny University program. (Participating states are California, Missouri, and New Mexico, in conjunction with the National Association of State Board of Education.)

Here's how the consortium works: Policies and practices within the participant states are first audited, and the results are communicated to policymakers. This allows monitoring of the policy objectives and reveals which are being accomplished and which need to be changed. If individual schools need to develop more inclusive educational experiences, consortium staff will provide training and technical assistance. Additionally, the consortium facilitates conferences, workshops, and forums on critical issues throughout the participating states. By linking key personal at the state and local level of the target state, the groups can be directly involved in policy and implementation issues.

Within the institution of the school itself, special education is dependent on politics at the national, state, and local levels: It is the politics of the nation that enacts laws that ultimately determine who is included or excluded in the schools; the state budget determines what basic or enrichment programs can be allotted; and the local educational settings are responsible for developing and presenting the curriculum content. The selection of knowledge included in a curriculum is often a political act. Political ideology directs social and political action, which manifests itself in school philosophy and, ultimately, in what is taught. English (1992) states that "curriculum construction goes on in schools within the unspoken and dominant education ideology, the dominant political ideology that serves as 'hidden' screens for the actual process of writing the acceptable work plans in schools" (p. 30). The political agenda directly affects practical educational aspects of the special education child.

An additional example of how political funding is impacting special education is an increased understanding of support for secondary school students with disabilities. National Research and Development Center on Serious Behavior Disorders at the Secondary Level has been created which is composed of a consortium of 7 universities. This group has received a 9.6 million dollar grant from the federal government to research more successful methods for children with behaviorial disorders at the secondary level.

"According to a 2006 report from the U.S. Department of Education, the high school graduation rate for students identified as emotionally disturbed was only 35 percent in 2002, the latest year for which figures were available, while 56 percent of those students dropped out. No other group of students with disabilities monitored by the department had a lower graduation rate or higher dropout rate, the report showed, and the numbers hadn't changed substantially in 10 years" (Samuels, 2008, p. 12).

While special education historically focuses on the elementary level and identification at the preschool level, this research emphasis focuses on secondary school students with diagnosed behavioral and emotional disorders, traditionally a more difficult population with which to work. This program will include parent training, as intervention cannot be limited to the time spent solely in school, along with teacher training. Behavioral focus on organizational training as well as decision making. The first two years will include a pilot program between Lehigh University, PA, James Madison University VA, and University of Missouri, (Columbia). After the first 2 years, the more successful techniques will be expanded to the larger group of 500 students from 4 additional universities: University of Maryland (College Park), University of Kansas (Lawrence), University of Louisville (KY), and Miami University (Oxford, OH) who will administer and assess the interventions employed (Samuels, 2008).

SPECIAL EDUCATION AND ADVOCACY

Chapters 2 and 4 identified the development of specific laws and their applications to the field of special education. This chapter takes the laws to their next level: advocacy.

The School As an Advocate

Because education in the public schools is mandatory for all children, schools are the great equalizer. They are the one place in the United States where we can be certain that the rights of all children are protected and appropriate placements are implemented.

Throughout our country's history, schools have functioned as an advocate for immigrant populations and lower socioeconomic groups—a ladder up which countless individuals have climbed to reach opportunity and security. Generally speaking, our public schools allow all children to achieve personal and academic success through merit and hard work rather than by elitism.

By advocating the rights, privileges, and needs of children with disabilities and exceptionalities; by including the challenged in the mainstream; and by providing services that help special children fit in, our schools may make accessible to them all the wonders available to normal children. Following are specific examples of how schools may advocate for a child to receive appropriate services:

- The regular education teacher makes a referral to the school psychologist (or that school's designated person) based on the regular education teacher's observations that the child cannot learn in the regular education classroom.

- The regular education teacher contacts the special education teacher for that special education teacher to come into the regular education classroom and observe the child for concerns that the regular education teacher has expressed.
- The regular education teacher contacts the parents with concerns to obtain their input, or if it might be more expedient, based on the regulations of that school district, have the parents request the referral for special education services.
- The staffing specialist, a person designated by the school district to coordinate all efforts, presents the special needs of the child in order to obtain either appropriate placement or appropriate services.
- A person is designated at the school district level to look beyond special services authorized by the school district toward national programs or services available for the most appropriate education.
- A person is designated by the school district to connect the parents of the special needs child with any of the appropriate organizations, associations, agencies, or services listed in Chapter 7.

Development of Advocacy Groups

The civil rights movement of the 1950s and 1960s drew attention to social injustices experienced by minorities, the poor, and women. The first advocacy groups for the disabled grew out of the protests and legal actions of that time. Advocates for persons with disabilities worked tirelessly to obtain access to rights for these individuals, as well as the funding, programs, and facilities that go with them. Litigation and legislation were the major tools used to access educational programs as well. The same parents who had complained to school boards and community representatives for years now discovered that the lawsuit was a more effective tool. These parents formed groups of advocates that could influence the voting for or against congressional and other political leaders. Most of the successful outcomes of individual court cases and appropriate administration of the federal and state laws concerning special education can be attributed to advocates, be they parents or other professionals in the field.

Legislators usually do not just decide that special needs children and adults require laws to ensure their rights. Parents, committees from advocacy groups, or representatives from professional groups with related interests are almost always the initiators, supporters, and organizers of proposed legislation. In their book *Mental Retardation,* Patton, Beirne-Smith, and Payne (1990) describe four types of advocacy:

- **Systems advocacy:** Advocacy by an independent collective of citizens in order to: (1) represent the rights and interests of groups of people with similar needs, and (2) pursue human service system quality and progressive change.
- **Legal advocacy:** Advocacy by attorneys at law in order to represent individuals or groups of individuals in the litigation or legal negotiations process.
- **Self-advocacy:** Advocacy by individuals whose rights are at-risk of being violated or diminished in order to represent one's own rights and interests as well as to speak on one's own behalf.

- **Citizen advocacy:** Advocacy by a mature, competent, volunteer citizen in order to represent, as if they were his or her own, the rights and interests of another citizen.

In any of the above types of advocacy, the concept remains the same; citizens are coming together to create, first, *awareness* of social policy regarding rights of the individual, and, second, *legislation* to make the policy a reality in order to eliminate barriers of access. Organizations such as those listed in Chapter 7 help make certain that persons with disabilities exercise their rights as individuals as well as a group.

Among the advocates for persons with disabilities and special needs have been many unheralded parents whose names are lost to history. In 1921, the National Society for Crippled Children, organized by parents, became the first national advocacy group for children with disabilities. As in most early organizations of this sort, medical professionals played a major role in providing organizational impetus. Physical and medical needs (as opposed to educational needs) were the original emphasis of such groups, though they eventually began to focus efforts on improving education for children with special needs (Gearheart, Mullein, and Gearheart, 1993) Two parent groups, the National Association for Retarded Children (NARC), which later became the National Association for Retarded Citizens, and the United Cerebral Palsy Association (UCP) strongly influenced early federal legislation and encouraged even those who were not parents of children with disabilities to support their cause.

Parent Advocacy

Parents working alone and as members of organized lobbying forces—such as the Association for Children with Learning Disabilities, which began to influence legislation in the 1960s—have long been the grassroots of all support for children with disabilities. When in the 1970s it became obvious that federally mandated services and federal financial support were needed, parents and other primary caregivers banded together to revolutionize special education through the passage of P. L. 94–142, the Education for All Handicapped Act. Today, parents continue to be the foremost advocate for their children's educational needs. After all, who can speak more effectively about the abilities and obstacles to their children's emotional and academic success than an involved and loving parent?

Peterson (1987) offers the following as rationale for parental involvement in securing rights and opportunities for their special-needs children:

(1) Parents (or their substitutes) are the key teachers, socializing agents, and caregivers for children during their early years.
(2) Parents can be effective intervention agents and teachers of their own children.
(3) Parents are in a particularly strategic position to enhance or negate the potential benefits of educational programs.
(4) Involvement offers a mechanism for helping parents build a positive perspective about their child.

(5) Intervention works best when parents and professionals are working toward common goals for their children and when all are applying compatible strategies.
(6) Involvement of parents in planning and implementing special services for a young child is a parental right.
(7) Involvement brings parents into contact with a great variety of resources that can help them in their parenting roles.

In addition to the above rationale for parental involvement where parents work as advocates for their children with special needs, parents can also serve as not only an advocate but as a mentor. Parenting a child with learning disabilities can be hard work, requiring one to become knowledgeable about the skills necessary for healthy development and developing strategies to address daily living. It can be exciting, fun, frustrating, invigorating and extremely gratifying (National Center for Learning Disabilities, 2008).

The National Center for Learning Disabilities (NCLD) (2008) indicates that "learning the essential skills necessary to becoming your child's advocate and ensuring your child receives an appropriate education, does not require lots of money or even years of schooling, it requires learning five (5) basic skills and consistently implementing them with the school community" (para. 3, p.1).

The Five Essential Skills as cited by NCLD (2008) are as follows:

Skill 1: Become informed about your child's learning disability. Understand your child's strengths and weaknesses, as well as the strategies that enable your child to compensate for weaknesses or deal with challenging activities.

Skill 2: Learn about your child's educational rights. Three federal statutes guarantee your child's access to a Free and Appropriate Public Education (FAPE) as well as accommodations as a person with a disability. The three federal laws are:

- Individuals with Disabilities Education Act (IDEA 2004)
- Section 504 of the 1973 Rehabilitation Act
- Title II of the American Disabilities Act

Skill 3: Learn to become a clear communicator. Be sure to document all conversations in writing, especially verbal conversations and meetings with any member of the school community. It is essential for you as a parent to have accurate records and written documentation. These summarize all conversations and document your understanding about the next steps or follow-up actions to be taken concerning your child.

Skill 4: Learn to work collaboratively with your child's school. Remember to focus on the positives. It is vital to recognize efforts of individuals and provide support, encouragement, and recognition of the difficulties involved in working with your child. [When a staff member has acted inappropriately or insensitively towards your child or yourself, put your concern in writing. Address it to the individual involved, with a copy going to the district office. Share your point of view, as well as your suggestions for remedying the situation.]

Skill 5: Learn to be in charge of your emotions. As Kenny Rogers says, "know when to hold 'em and know when to fold 'em." As parents, we need to learn to step back and bring in others to help us when we are having difficulty with our child's school. Oftentimes, our natural reaction is to push harder and scream louder, thinking that the school will then do what we want. Unfortunately, more often than not, what occurs then is a "battle of wills," with both parties expending emotional energy to be right. They may lose focus on the real issue—a child's success in life and school. It is vital, as a parent advocate, that you learn how to step back, reflect, rally your troops, and encourage others to think outside the box, be creative, and find common ground. Compromise does not mean one is "giving in" or losing, it means meeting one another halfway.

A recent example of parent advocacy is the film *Including Samuel*, created by Dan Habib, Samuel's father, a photojournalist. With inclusion of Samuel, a child with cerebral palsy, who ambulates with a wheelchair and has speech difficulties, as the focus, the impact of the film, which also features the struggle of 4 other families attempting to include their members into society, goes beyond one family's struggle.

The focus is on the impact of inclusion on changes within society as well as the rights of the disabled community action advocates, national policies, and civil rights. Through the medium of film, Samuel's parents have the viewer join in the wheelchair assisted T-Ball games, family dinners as well as his development from infancy to boyhood. The 4 other families offer different insights into inclusion, some more successful than others (Hollingsworth, 2008). For more information on *Including Samuel*, visit *www.includingsamuel.com*. In addition, *Including Samuel* can also be purchased from the EP Bookstore at *www.EPBoostore.com*

Popular Culture and Advocacy

In recent years, fictional characters in books, in movies, and on the stage have brought international attention to persons with special needs. Either the individual's advocate or the person him- or herself is featured. Such portrayals often result in (1) the disabled person or disabled group getting looked upon with more respect, and (2) an increase in the funding for programs that serve members of the disabled group. Although negatives and inaccuracies are certain in the presentation of some portrayals, on the whole, they have served to increase awareness and understanding of special-needs audiences.

The films *Mask, Rain Man, Children of a Lesser God,* and *The Miracle Worker* all brought special-needs individuals to the center of public attention, and all four received Academy Awards. *David and Lisa,* the story of two special education students attending a residential school for emotionally disturbed adolescents, is a cult classic among black-and-white films. The popularity of these films suggests a wide acceptance of their message and portrayals.

In *Mask,* the main character, Rocky Dennis (played by Eric Stoltz), is afflicted with craniodiaphysealdysplasia, a physical disorder that affects development of a part, system, or region of the body, in this case the head, face and clavicle; Rocky's specific affliction is commonly called lionitis. The film:

> presents Rocky Dennis as a high functioning adolescent. A great deal of his strong self-esteem is attributed to his advocate mother [played by Cher] and supportive friends, who,

> as members of a motorcycle gang, are social outcasts. It is the depth of the love of the significant adult, the mother that draws the viewer to support her advocacy for her son. The strength of her determination becomes clear when she confronts the principal of a local school to which Rocky has been assigned. The principal wants to place Rocky is a special, separate school for handicapped students, simply because of the way he looks. Rocky's mother insists that he stay, and proceeds to explain Rocky's rights and to display appropriate documentation, including his last report card, demonstrating that he has been in the top fifth of his class. This experience demonstrates the ongoing struggle over school placements for Rocky. The principal demonstrates the desire of the school to hide, rather than mainstream, the exceptional student. (Farber, Provenzo, and Holm, 1994, p. 193).

A similar situation to the one found in *Mask* can be assessed in *Rain Man.* The main character, Raymond (played by Dustin Hoffman), has an advocate younger brother, Charles (played by Tom Cruise), just as Rocky in *Mask* had his mother. Raymond is autistic and so exhibits severe disturbances "characterized by bizarre behavior, developmental delays, and extreme isolation" (Meyen, 1990, p. 514). Here, too, the advocate supplies the force that changes the situation for the special needs person. The film simplifies and distorts autism, asking informed viewers to suspend their understanding of the autistic person's need for a quiet, undisturbed routine when Raymond spends time with Charlie in a Las Vegas casino. Another scene, however, deals quite realistically with the act of touching, a very difficult experience for the autistic. As Farber, Provenzo, and Holm (1994) note in their analysis of *Rain Man*:

> If there is to be success, the full picture of reality must be taken into account. If not, the fantasy, and whatever positive effects it may have in generating heightened awareness and support for the autistic, must be weighed against the impact of any misconceptions and disappointments that result from the film's tendency to simplify and distort what is known. (196)

In *Children of a Lesser God,* the main character, Sarah (played by then-newcomer Marlee Matlen), and the advocate, her teacher (played by William Hurt), draw the public's attention to the issue of educational achievement for the deaf and the hearing impaired.

In this film, the teacher takes his students in a school for the deaf to new heights of experience by teaching them to dance to music vibrations felt through large speakers. After some conflict between Sarah and her teacher, Sarah eventually becomes her own advocate. Even the controversial issue of total communication, an approach involving all forms of communication—speech, signing, and finger spelling—is presented in the movie.

The Miracle Worker is the well-known film version of the story of young Helen Keller, blind and deaf, who achieves some normalcy in life through the efforts of teacher/advocate Annie Sullivan. Helen (played by Patty Duke) is at first angry and resentful of her new teacher but eventually comes to accept Annie (played by Anne Bancroft) , who first reaches Helen in the pivotal water pump scene. Viewers learn that Helen is far from being mentally disturbed and is, in fact, a brilliant and inquisitive child who just needed the right advocate to help her achieve her potential.

David and Lisa is the story of two special education students at a residential school for emotionally disturbed adolescents. David (played by Keir Dullea) is severely emotionally disturbed and believes that touch can kill; he is arrogant and difficult and seems incapable of developing interpersonal relationships. Lisa (played by Janet Margolin) communicates through rhyme, exhibits wide mood swings, and has a personality disorder that manifests in the persona of "Muriel." The significant advocate in the film is their psychiatrist (played by Howard DeSilva).

Through the development of the relationship between David and Lisa and the intervention of the advocate, David teaches Lisa to speak without rhyme, and she encourages him to allow touching. The film proposes that emotional disturbance can be overcome through advocacy and support, appropriate placement, and good psychiatric care.

Of course, this is not always the case in the real world—disorders don't just melt away, and the "right" advocate is not always miraculously found, but the film wins credit for its realistic portrayal of special-needs individuals.

Advocacy and Politics

As South Dakota governor Bill Janklow stated in his 1999 State of the Union Address, "It's so politically easy and convenient to talk about kids and children and use them for rhetoric" (Sconyers and Levy, 1999, p. 22).

The National Association of Child Advocates examined the responses of Governor Janklow and thirty-five other governors elected in November 1998 in order to determine whether they were incorporating campaign promises to children in their policy decisions. The association specifically considered how the governors followed through on children's health insurance, Head Start, childcare subsidies, and programs for at-risk youth and others. It found that "Analyzed by region, candidates in the West most frequently supported children's issues (67%) while candidates in the East supported them the least (54%). By party, Democrats showed stronger support than Republicans (79% verses 58 %) did. The positive information was that there was a follow-through rate of almost 80% of the increased funding for at-risk youth" (Sconyers and Levy, 1999, p. 22). The success rate of advocates and their organizations in influencing policy at the state level is thus considerable.

REFERENCES

American Federation of Teachers, 1994. Resolution on Inclusion of Students with Disabilities. National convention. Anaheim, CA. Available at http://www.aft.org/about/resolutions/1994/inclusion.html.

English, F. W., 1992. *Deciding What to Teach and Test.* Thousand Oaks, CA: Corwin Press.

Farber, P., E. Provenzo, and G. Holm (eds.), 1994. *Schooling in the Light of Popular Culture.* Albany, NY: State University of New York Press.

Garwood, S. G., 1983. *Educating Young Handicapped Children.* Rockville, MD: Aspen Publications.

Gearheart, B., R. Mullein, and C. Gearheart, 1993. *Exceptional Individuals and Introduction.* Belmont, CA: Brooks/Cole Publishing.

Hollingsworth, J. C. (2008). Including Samuel. *EP Magazine.* Retrieved October 1, 2008 from *www.eparent.com*

Meyen, E. L., 1990. *Exceptional Children in Today's Schools.* Denver: Love Publishing.

National Center for Learning Disabilities. 2008. *Parenting Strategies.* Retrieved August 11, 2008 from *http://www.ncld.org/content/view/1160/456164/*

National Education Goals Panel, 1998. *Promising Practices: Progress Toward the Goals.* Washington, DC: National Education Goals Panel.

Patton, J. R., M. Beirne-Smith, and J. S. Payne, 1990. *Mental Retardation.* Columbus, OH: Merrill Publishing.

Peterson, N. L., 1987. *Early Intervention for Handicapped and At-risk Children.* Denver: Love Publishing.

Samuels, C. A., 2008 *Center Researching Approaches That Work With Troubled Teens.* Education Week, Eye on Research.

Sconyers, N., and T. Levy, 1999). *Promises to Children.* State Government News, The Council of State Governments, Lexington, KY: The Council of State Governments.

Streshly, W. A., and T. A. DeMitchell, 1994. *Teacher Unions and TQE: Building Quality Labor Relations.* Thousand Oaks, CA: Corwin Press.

Urbanski, A., 1998. "Turning Unions Around." *Contemporary Education* 69, no. 4: 186–190.

Weil, D., 2000. *Charter Schools: A Reference Handbook.* Santa Barbara, CA: ABC-CLIO Publishers.

Chapter Six

Primary Documents and Quotations

INTRODUCTION

Special Education is a constantly evolving field, based on federal laws, funding, and research that is continually being developed and revised. The challenges and controversies surrounding this field are inevitable based on the numerous concepts, information and allocation of resources to those who are diagnosed, serviced and impacted. As Special Education becomes more fully integrated into regular education, new information and conversation by those in the field, as well as by those affected by Special Education, will present itself. Therefore, the ideas and concepts, i.e. brain plasticity, presented in this chapter are the best and brightest of current thinking but not, by any means, the last word on the subject.

The material included here supports the right and need for Special Education to exist in educational systems. The individuals quoted range from experienced professionals to lay society, all of who have raised their voices regarding the continuation and improvement of Special Education. Certainly, they don't all agree on the how, what, when, or where of Special Education, but they do all agree on the basic right of all children to an education.

This chapter incorporates many of the newer laws and interventions that have come about since the first edition of this title in 2001. Still, great challenges in the field of Special Education exist, such as:

1. **Classification**—important in determining eligibility and services, but not uniform throughout the states. Children diagnosed and classified with a disorder in one state may or may not be classified as such in another;
2. **Diagnosis**—some disabilities diagnosed by physicians or brought to the attention of a physician by the parent provide clear diagnosis, while other disorders are diagnosed by the classroom teacher after poor achievement or behavior is exhibited;

3. **Definitions**—the term "mild disabilities" is sometimes confused with "learning disabilities" or "normal abilities," a confusion that could impede academic progress. The concept of "instructional disability" impacts this confusion; and
4. **Representation**—disproportionate representation of minorities, attributed to poverty, cultural bias, inherent differences or other causes.

The future of Special Education based on new and ongoing research virtually has no limits. It may involve reforming categorical classifications to focus on skills upon which an educational plan might be based. Negative connotations due to labeling might be addressed by transferring from categorical classifications such as disabilities of any kind, to functional classification of specific skill deficits (reading decoding skills) and the services needed (tutoring in phonics). Confusion between "instructional disability" (changing the instruction) and a "learning disability" might more easily be identified and remedied. It bears repeating that Special Education is a constantly evolving field.

Certain quotes and excerpts on the following pages are preceded by editorial comments, which appear in italics. Bold first letters easily identify each new element. Articles that appear in their entirety include an author byline.

"The process of formal education has changed dramatically over the century. The design of the classroom, the roles of the teacher and student, and the methods of instruction have all been targets of experimentation and modification. Yet the essential objectives—to impart skills, values, and information from one generation to the next—remains basically the same."

Barbara M. Newman and Philip R. Newman, Development Through Life (1999)

"Of all the civil rights for which the world has struggled and fought for 5,000 years, the right to learn is undoubtedly the most fundamental. The freedom to learn has bought by bitter sacrifice. And whatever we may think of the curtailment of other civil rights, we should fight to the last ditch to keep open the right to learn, the right to have examined in our schools not only what we believe, but what we do not believe; not only what our leaders say, but what the leaders of other groups and nations, and the leaders of other centuries have said. We must insist upon this to give our children the fairness of a start which will equip them with such an array of facts and such an attitude toward truth that they can have a real chance to judge what the world is and what its greater might have thought it might be."

W.E.B. DuBois, The Freedom to Learn *Views Regarding Special Education (1939)*

An old man and a child went fishing on a river. No sooner had they gotten their lines into the water than they noticed a child floating down the river in distress. Quickly, they pulled the child into their tiny fishing boat. Soon another child came floating by, then another, both of whom they rescued. The old man starting rowing toward shore when the child pointed upstream and yelled, "Wait, we have room for one more." To this, the man replied, "No, we must go ashore and find out who's throwing all these children into the water."

This was the allegory Sam Goldstein, Ph.D. used to begin his presentation, "Developing Resilient Children: Changing the Lives of Challenged Children," at a recent Learning and the Brain Conference for educators and parents. His message? Creating resilient children requires a paradigm shift in our thinking. To really help them, he says, we need to focus on prevention, rather than on treatment alone, which has traditionally used a wait-and-see approach.

"Our kids are falling into the 'river' at a rate faster than we can pull them out," says Goldstein, editor-in-chief of the *Journal of Attention Disorders* and co-author of two books on resilience in children. This is an urgent matter, he says, especially because our children are experiencing greater rates of depression with each generation.

A concept with increasing relevancy since September 11th, resilience implies an ability to spring back "to function competently under stress" to recover from setbacks, trauma, or adversity.

According to Goldstein, three powerful predictors of resilience are:

- A temperament that elicits positive responses from others;

- Family relationships that promote trust, autonomy, initiative, and connections, and
- Community support systems that reinforce self-esteem and self-efficacy.

Excerpted from Developing Resilience in Children With Challenges *by Dr. Sam Goldstein.* *For more information, visit LD.org.*

"I am speaking out about this because I was an educator for twenty years before I became a Senator. I speak out because as a Senator, I have been in a school almost every two weeks for the past ten years and I have seen, as you have, the inequality so many children confront. I also have seen how much difference a good system, a good school and a good teacher can make for a child.

"That all citizens will be given an equal start through a sound education is one of the most basic, promised rights of our democracy. Our chronic refusal as a nation to guarantee that right for all children, including poor children, is a national disgrace. We cannot be so blind that we do not see that meeting the most basic needs of so many of our children condemns them to lives and futures of frustration, chronic underachievement, poverty and violence.

"But, in the end, this is a spiritual issue for me. We must invest in the skills and intellect and character of our children, not because we know that if we do, they will be more likely to graduate from high school and less likely to be involved in crime although that is true. We must invest in children not because they will be more likely to go on to college and to lead more productive lives, although that is also true. We should invest in the skills and intellect and character of our children because they are all under four feet tall, they are all beautiful and we should be nice to them."

Senator Paul Wellstone, Center for Law and Education. (2008)

"I introduce ... a bill ... to insure equal opportunities for the handicapped by prohibiting needless discrimination in programs receiving federal financial assistance ... the time has come when we can no longer tolerate the invisibility of the handicapped in America ... These people have the right to live, to work to the best of their ability-to know the dignity to which every human being is entitled. But too often we keep children whom we regard as 'different' or a 'disturbing influence' out of our schools and community altogether ... Where is the cost-effectiveness in consigning them to ... 'terminal care in an institution?"

Senator Hubert H. Humphrey, on introducing to Congress a bill mandating education for children with disabilities (1972)

"Unfortunately, this bill promises more than the federal government can deliver, and its good intentions could be thwarted by the many unwise provisions it contains

. . . Even the strongest supporters of this measure know as well as I that they are falsely raising the expectations of the groups affected by claiming authorization levels which are excessive and unrealistic . . . [This bill also contains a] vast array of detailed complex and costly administrative requirements which would unnecessarily assert federal control over traditional state and local government functions."

President Gerald Ford, upon signing federal legislation to mandate education for children with disabilities (1975)

As with any new law, act or regulations implemented, in this case NCLB 2001, modifications found to be important in order to serve the vision of educating each of our nation's children are proposed as part of Title I of the ESEA. The following are changes proposed to help with regard to areas of assessment, accountability, and supplemental educational services that particularly impact students with disabilities and public school choice.

1) in order to clarify a misunderstanding that accountability is based on a single measure or form of assessment, measures of student academic achievement may include:
    a) multiple question formats—example: multiple choice, extended response, and
    b) multiple assessments within a subject area—example: reading and writing
2) to create a National Technical Advisory Council (NTAC) of approximately 10-15 members, to provide advice and guidance on technical issues related to state standards, assessments and accountability issues affecting all states.
3) to ensure all subgroups of students are included in the AYP by requiring each state to explain in an accountability workbook how all components defining AYP are statistically reliable and how all students and subgroups are included. The newly formed NTAC will help develop guidelines by which state accountability workbooks are reviewed and these accountability workbooks will be submitted within 6 months after the new regulations are passed.
4) to require states and districts to report how students are performing on state assessment tests when compared with how those students are performing on the National Assessment of Educational Progress (NAEP); this is to be reported on the same report card as the state test results in the hopes of empowering parents to be able to assess their states educational systems and results.
5) to provide a uniform definition of graduation rate "consistent with the definition agreed upon by the National Governors Association (NGA)." The recommendation would be, the number of students with a regular high school diploma, divided by the number of students who entered high school 4 years earlier. This would adjust for transfer students and for stu-

dents who, due to certain conditions, may need longer than the standard 4 years. A specific alternative definition would be developed for the latter group.

6) to increase a presently low graduation rate goal of 50% to a high goal of 90% or demonstrate continuous, substantial AYP from the previous year.
7) to disaggregate graduation rates by the academic year 2012-2013, using the NGA rate within data broken down by different subgroups.
8) to restructure requirements focusing on interventions. Particularly significant for students with disabilities as well as regular education students the restructuring plan of a school needs to be rigorous and comprehensive with regard to intervention beyond the corrective action plan implemented after it was identified as in need of improvement. Even if the principal is replaced, that alone does not constitute restructuring; the focus is on the entire school staff.
9) to continue newly announced (2008) Differentiated Accountability Pilot Programs. This requires differentiating between schools in need of high level intervention and those close to meeting AYP. Examples are teacher effectiveness, using data to determine methods of differentiation and categories of intervention.
10) to address specifically Supplemental Education Services (SES) in order to help parents make more informed decisions regarding their child's educational options:
    a) notify parents of SES through information that is clear, concise, and distinguishable from other information sent to let them know their child's school is in improvement status;
    b) include on websites lists of SES providers approved to serve the district as well as their locations as well as schools available for transfer;
    c) the provider's of SES can offer information about their services proving they are research based and parallel state academic content and standards supporting increases in student achievement;
    d) inform parents of providers that are approved due to the state's examination of the provider's instructional programs and increased student academic proficiency.

Excerpted from NCLB 2008—Proposed Changes as they Impact Title I of NCLB

Additional controversies regarding the implementation of NCLB 2001 that might impact changes to take place in any reauthorization after 2009 surround the accountability system. Two oppositional proposals come from hard-line educational reformers advocating a national test with national standards and progressives advocating local assessments that could vary from school district to school district. One of the challenges of local assessments is that there is no way to make comparisons with students being held to different standards though those students might be applying to the same colleges or for the same jobs.

"Poor and minority students and students with disabilities, who historically have been held to lower standards might return to a time when they repeatedly were told they were dong fine, only to graduate from high school and discover they did not have the skills needed to succeed in college and the workplace. Resources that are now allocated on the basis of accountability systems geared to a single and comparable set of state tests-those, for example, for after-school and summer programs, tutoring, teacher-training, and new curricula-might be misdirected away from areas that actually need them most, because each district or school would then be measured by different standards and different yardsticks."

As first appeared in Education Week *November 2008. Reprinted with permission from the author, Charles Barone.*

Examples of professionals supporting the hard-line national tests and standards approach are New York City School Chancellor, Joel Klein, and former Assistant U.S. Secretary of Education, Chester Finn, Jr. Supporting the progressive approach advocating local or district assessments is Linda Darling-Hammond, Stanford University, advisor to Barak Obama during the 2008 presidential campaign.

A compromise to both national tests and local test adversaries proposed by Charles Barone, former California Democratic deputy staff director for the House Education and Labor Committee, is to create a national databank providing an "open source" system of testing.

"A nonprofit entity could empanel a group of experts to create items in line with national standards, perhaps those used as a basis for the National Assessment of Educational Progress or for international comparisons by the Program for International Student Assessment. The panel would have to represent a broad range of stakeholders-teachers, principals, testing and policy experts, higher education faculty members, college presidents and business leaders. Over the course of one or two years, the panel would create a pool of test items that would be piloted and subjected to the usual analyses and psychometric rigor."

U.S. Department of Education. Elementary & Secondary Education. Accountability, Assessments and Transparency. (2008)

Bellevue Community College, which is located near Seattle, Washington, offers one of the first of its kind, a Program in Occupational and Life Skills degrees for high functioning developmentally disabled students who are able to work at a minimum of fourth grade level in academic studies. Although this program offers an opportunity for students with developmental disabilities to earn a degree which will help them to become self-sufficient, many parents have voiced concern about the college's promise to admit student's with Downs Syndrome as there has not been a student accepted with Down's since 2004. While the controversy continues regarding admissions, on

June 13, 2008, four graduates of Bellevue Community College received their degrees, ready to test the skills that they have learned.

"Heralded as a modern-day extension of the civil rights movement, the pioneering degree program for developmentally disabled students at Bellevue Community College has a loyal fan base and a history of great press. But some parents—and a former instructor at the college—now say there have been efforts to force out students who face some of the biggest challenges."

Inside Higher Education, Uneasiness in Uncharted Waters (2008)

Similarly, Gallaudet University in Washington, DC, the leading university for deaf and hearing impaired undergraduate students, has been using special applications of lecture capture system technology to help its students. Such applications can be adopted by any institution serving the hearing impaired. For example, lecture caption video can record the instructor using American Sign Language. The recording can be modified to add a transcript or closed-captions for hearing impaired students.

Among educators of the hearing impaired, two major controversies still prevail. The first deals with integrated vs. segregated types of school. By definition, education is education in special schools designed for the hearing impaired with specially trained teachers using techniques, methods and aids for teaching. The rooms are acoustically designed for the hearing impaired. Integrated education incorporates a hearing impaired child in a general education setting.

In whichever facility a hearing impaired child participates, the important factors are to have highly qualified professionals, adequate supportive devices and aids, and, if an integrated system is selected, a resource room unit is advisable.

The second controversy is over oral and manual communication. As hearing capacity is linked to the ability to speak more clearly, problems associated with hearing are related to speech. Originally, the combined difficulty caused people to consider the hearing impaired "deaf and dumb." We have known for decades this is not true and that the hearing impaired can acquire better speech. Due to this, some advocates for the hearing impaired believe that oral communication, from the earliest opportunities, must be stressed. Others believe this is not the approach to take, but rather learning sign-language, a manual format, should be taught.

"But most of the educational programmes are of neither type [oral or manual]. These vary in terms of amount of specialized input and amount of social/communicative integration with the hearing world. Ideally, educational integration includes a resource unit and a resource teacher. Resource unit is the unit that is supposed to take care of the hearing impaired students' needs in a non special school. Under the supervision of such resource educational programmes are planned with various degrees of integration/segregation. There can be hearing impaired students who sit with non impaired children in a classroom only for co-curricular activities, or for science/math or only for social studies.

"Hence the controversy oral versus manual mode of communication. There are scholars who think that since speech can be developed it should be developed. Speech can be developed successfully only with a lot of preconditions like the child has to be tested very early in life below the one year age or even six months, it has to be fitted with hearing aids immediately after that, its rigorous training must begin by professionals and parents etc. Therefore, some scholars believe that rather than trying to develop speech, sign language can be introduced to the hearing impaired child. According to them language is important more than speech and hearing impaired individual can function fully well without speech."

Ali Yavar Jung, National Institute for the Hearing Handicapped (2008)

Reaching an Autistic Teenager

By Melissa Fay Greene

On a typical Monday morning at an atypical high school, teenage boys yanked open the glass doors to the First Baptist Church of Decatur, Ga. Half-awake, iPod wires curling from their ears, their backpacks unbuckled and their jeans baggy, the guys headed for the elevator. Arriving at Morning Meeting in the third-floor conference room, Stephen, his face hidden under long black bangs, dropped into a chair, sprawled across the table and went back to sleep. The Community School, or T.C.S., is a small private school for teenage boys with autism or related disorders. Sleep disturbances are common in this student body of 10, so a boy's staggering need for sleep is respected. Nick Boswell, a tall fellow with thick sideburns, arrived and began his usual pacing along the windows that overlook the church parking lot and baseball diamond. Edwick, with spiky brown hair and a few black whiskers, tumbled backward with a splat into a beanbag chair on the floor.

"O.K., guys, let's talk about your spring schedules," said Dave Nelson, the 45-year-old founding director. He wore a green polo shirt, cargo shorts and sneakers and had a buzz haircut and an open, suntanned face. After his son Graham, 19, was given a diagnosis of autism spectrum disorder (A.S.D.) as a young child, Nelson left the business world and went into teaching and clinical and counseling work. On that Monday, he was instantly interrupted.

"I had a very bad night!" Edwick yelled from the floor. "Nightmares all night!"

"What was disturbing you, Edwick?" Nelson asked.

"What do you think?" Edwick cried in exasperation. "It's St. Patrick's Day!"

"What's upsetting about that?" Nelson asked.

Edwick dropped his shoulders to relay how tiring it was to have to explain every little thing. "Leprechauns," he yelled.

"Oh," Nelson said. "I thought maybe it was the tornado that hit downtown on Friday night."

"No, not the tornado!" Edwick yelled.

Nick stopped pacing to comment: "Edwick's not scared of tornados; he's scared of leprechauns." I burst out laughing and so did the faculty members, while Nelson seemed to relish the interruption rather than find it a hindrance to the morning routine. His hidden agenda was precisely to entertain outbursts like Edwick's, while making room for a sardonic intelligence like Nick's. No matter the stated purpose of Morning Meeting, the true purposes were always the same: conversation, debate, negotiation, compromise and the building of relationships. T.C.S.'s only serious admissions requirements are that a boy should have at least some functional language and that there's a good chance he can become part of the "community" of the school name.

The group turned to registering for spring classes. In addition to biology, algebra 2/trigonometry, English literature and U.S. history, there were the electives: Dragon Lore, Comic Books, How to Shop for Bargains and the History of Snack Food. Past electives included All About Pirates, Spy Technology, Ping-Pong, Dog Obedience, Breaking World Records, Unusual Foods and Taking Things Apart. ("I just wish they'd come up with a second-quarter class, Putting the Things Back Together," Nelson told me.)

"I knew it!" Edwick complained, mashing about on the beanbag chair. He was disappointed because no one picked the elective he'd proposed: the History of Meat.

What makes the Community School unusual is not its student body—plenty of schools around the country enroll teenagers with an autism spectrum disorder. But, like about only two dozen schools in the country, it employs a relatively new, creative and highly interactive teaching method known as D.I.R./Floortime, which is producing striking results among T.C.S.'s student body. (D.I.R. stands for developmental, individual differences, relationship-based approach.) The method is derived from the work of Stanley Greenspan, a child psychiatrist and professor of psychiatry, behavioral science and pediatrics at George Washington University, and his colleague Dr. Serena Wieder. D.I.R./Floortime can be effective with all kinds of children, whether they have developmental challenges or not. As applied by T.C.S., it is an approach that encourages students to develop their strengths and interests by working closely with one another and with their teachers. The goal for students is neurological progress through real-world engagement.

With the skyrocketing diagnoses of A.S.D.'s in recent years, parents and school systems are challenged as never before to find techniques to keep these teenagers engaged, productive and nondespairing. Boys with A.S.D. (they outnumber girls four to one) who were difficult to console, to teach, to restrain at age 4 or 8 can be nearly impossible for parents and teachers to manage and to steer at 14 and 18. While a 25-pound toddler's tantrum is wearying, a 150-pound teenager's tantrum is dangerous. Puberty and young adulthood take many of these young people unawares.

How best to serve this population remains a subject of debate, because autism is a "final common pathway" diagnosis, meaning children arrive here from different points of origin, are troubled by a wide variety of issues and respond to different strategies. "You meet one child with autism and, well, you've met one child with autism," says Linda Brandenburg, the director of school autism services at the Kennedy Krieger Institute in Maryland. Given the wide range of expression in autism and related disorders, there is no one-size-fits-all intervention. "We now know that there are several different models that seem to work—some more behavioral, some more developmental, some more eclectic," Dr. Fred R. Volkmar, director of the Yale Child Study Center, told me. "What we really need to be doing, what the law says, is design programs around the kids rather than force kids into a program."

The vast majority of programs for autistic youth in the U.S. use an approach called Applied Behavior Analysis, in which teachers and therapists use well-established techniques of reward and punishment to shape a student's actions toward goals like toilet training, learning vocabulary or completing a puzzle. A typical A.B.A. lesson rewards memorized responses, specific behaviors and compliance to external directives—"Pick up the fork, Jared." An instructor may move the child's arm, hand and fingers to model the desired behavior. The child is then rewarded—with praise, with hugs, with a treat—when he performs the act correctly. As the first method to work with profoundly self-absorbed children and to demonstrate that progress could be made, A.B.A.—which came to national prominence in the late 1980s—has been a lifesaver for countless families. Critics worry that the method focuses on modifying the symptoms rather than addressing the underlying disabilities, and many say they fear that A.B.A.-trained children often do not "generalize," that is, take a behavior learned in one setting and apply it in another. A child may learn to make eye contact in response to "How are you?" and to reply, "Fine, how are you?" But such rote memorization does not give the child the intuition to know when a stranger is to be greeted warmly and when to be avoided, and it does not enable him to meet his grandmother with greater warmth than the grocer.

"All teachers and therapists use elements of behaviorism," Nelson told me. "As an intervention for autism, the A.B.A. movement was one of the first to suggest how intensive the intervention has to be—maybe 40 hours a week—to see results. This notion of intensity has been valuable to everyone that followed."

The Community School—with a teaching staff of 12 and a $25,000 tuition—employs the intensity but not the methodology of A.B.A. Rather than spend time on a student's mastery of a skill preselected for him by an adult, the idea is to harness a student's energy and desire to learn. As a student interacts with peers and teachers, solves problems and expresses his ideas, his behavior should naturally begin to lose its rough edges. The essence of Floortime is that a person learns best when self-motivated, when an inner drive sparks the acquisition of skills and knowledge.

As with A.B.A., achieving D.I.R./Floortime's far-reaching goals for students requires intense interaction—a wooing of a child from his or her remove—for as many hours of the day as parents and teachers can physically sustain. Dr. Greenspan would like to see an autistic child productively interacting with an adult for most of his waking time, seven days a week. Those drained parents who have the means hire therapists and trained baby sitters to help them approximate that schedule, during either home-schooling days or out-of-school hours.

Because the goal of D.I.R./Floortime is the kindling of a student's curiosity, intelligence, playfulness and energy, the lessons can take on a spontaneous, electric quality. I have seen sessions with young children during which the child and his or her therapist or parent tumbled across the house, behind the sofa, into closets or onto the porch, picking up balls, puppets, costumes, books and snacks along the way. At T.C.S., classes can look like debates between equals; school days can include board games, sports, plays, science experiments, music, art, ropes courses or rafting trips in which all students and teachers playfully compete, contribute and perform. All the boys at the school probably have average or better intelligence. Onlookers might call a few "high functioning" (though that adjective has no clinical meaning), and T.C.S. is an accredited high school and middle school, offering college prep and high-school courses to students able to complete a conventionally rigorous course of study. (Other students pursue less-demanding tracks oriented toward getting a G.E.D., attaining job skills or developing independent-living skills.) So it's not all fun and social time. But rote learning is never the goal; the goal is that the students should be able to think, to feel, to communicate and to learn. Most of the kids are making the first friends of their lives here.

T.C.S. does not promise miracles. It does not promise to be a perfect fit for every teenager with an A.S.D. Dave Nelson does not invest great faith in the possibility of leaving the autism spectrum behind, no matter how much parents (like himself) would love to believe it. The breakthroughs at T.C.S. are subtle rather than headline-grabbing, noticeable at first only to the adults closest to the kids and to the students themselves. But for these families, any forward motion can inspire a moment of real hope and happiness, and quite remarkable progress happens every day.

Stephen, 17, a solidly built boy with a sweet face under a heavy thatch of bangs, entered T.C.S. in 2005 prone to blowups of alarming power. His parents adore their son and have been whipped about like sailboats by his furies. His first year at school, during group construction of an outdoor marble-run, a boy fumbled and a marble dropped. "I am going to assassinate him," Stephen exploded. "I. Will. Behead. Him." Stephen's academics are top-notch, but the stance of the Community School is not to ignore a student's psychological deficits while skipping ahead to schoolwork or life skills. It doesn't matter that Stephen is at home with algebraic theorems if he is going to react like a toddler when ambushed by a mad or sad feeling.

Ty Martin, 14, is a cute and curly-haired guy who lives in terror of loud or strange noises. The faux thunderstorm in the produce aisles at the grocery store makes it difficult to take him shopping. A classmate's coughing or a siren in the distance distracts him from schoolwork. His mother often was obliged to retreat to a windowless basement room at home, hugging and soothing her son when the outside world—especially lawn crews next door with leaf-blowers—overwhelmed him. "He doesn't like crows," Judy Martin told me last spring. "If crows are at a park, he'll go from happy to berserk in five seconds. If we go to a restaurant, we're all on edge, praying the bartender doesn't turn on the blender."

Sam Gross visited San Francisco with his mother two years ago at age 15. During a tour of Alcatraz, the handsome olive-skinned boy climbed a nearby fence and prepared to dive. Had his mother not spotted him and screamed, Sam would have been injured or killed by falling onto the rocks. But he was not trying to kill himself. He planned, as he explained in his monotone voice, to turn into a merman and swim back to the mainland.

Then he began to deteriorate. For two years, he spent every day in a ball under his blankets, rising only to pound either side of his head with such ferocity that two bald spots bloomed under his fists, then dangerously swelled. He had to be sedated to stop the self-battery. By the time Sam reached the Community School, he was nearly incommunicative. Whenever he began using his head like a punching bag, the teachers asked him to stop, and he did, but otherwise showed no sign that he heard them.

Students arrive at T.C.S. trailing long histories of school failure and humiliation, suspension, expulsion, truncated transcripts, social isolation, victimization, self-loathing, suicidal ideation or years of home-schooling patched together by mothers forced to leave their jobs. "On our first visit with Dave Nelson, Ty started screaming: 'I hate this place! I want to leave right now!' " Judy Martin says. "Most principals don't want to work with a kid like that. But what I saw on Dave Nelson's face was 'I can work with a kid like this.' "

Many prospective parents begin to weep during their intake interviews with Nelson. For them and their children, this place represents something of a last chance.

While there is no direct relationship between Dr. Stanley Greenspan and the nation's D.I.R./Floortime schools, other than one of mutual respect, the theoretical underpinning of these schools relies on his argument that human intelligence itself is constructed out of the warm back-and-forth signaling between child and parent, beginning at birth. Jean Piaget located a child's investigation of causality in the material world, for example, with experiments like pulling a string attached to a bell, but Greenspan and his colleague Serena Wieder see these insights occurring in the emotional realm, when a baby learns that his or her smile brings the parent's smile. Brain development is not a solo pursuit but a rich and complex flowering that occurs only in the hothouse of human relationships.

What does this have to do with autism? A child born at risk of an A.S.D. has cognitive and sensitivity issues that inhibit engagement. Pleasures enjoyed by a typical baby can upset him: a mother's face seems too close, so the infant cranes away; the father's tickles may produce fear reflexes rather than laughter. Meanwhile the sunlight is burning his eyes, the diaper scrapes his skin and the baby begins avoiding interaction with people at the cost of normal brain development.

I begin to picture the brain metaphorically as a tangled ball of Christmas lights. When you plug it in, there are strands that light up perfectly and there are dark zones where a single burned-out bulb has caused a line to go out. If the bulb for Exchanging-Smiles-With-Mother doesn't light up, then Empathy won't be kindled farther along the strand, or Playfulness, or Theory of Mind (the insight that other people have different thoughts from yours). The electrical current won't reach the social-skill set, the communication skills, creativity, humor or abstract thinking.

According to the D.I.R. perspective, emotion is the power source that lights up the neural switchboard. D.I.R./Floortime's goal is to connect autistic students with other people as a way of fueling their cognitive potential and giving them access to their own feelings, desires and insights. The latest findings in the field of neuroplasticity support D.I.R.'s faith in the capacity of the human brain to recoup and to compensate for injury and illness. "Early intervention is optimal," Dr. Greenspan told me, "but it's never too late. The areas of the brain that regulate emotions, that sequence ideas and actions and that influence abstract thinking keep growing into a person's 50s and 60s."

T.C.S. students are masters of withdrawal, and for the D.I.R. model to work, each student must be an active partner in his own education. But how do you ignite the enthusiasm of an autistic teenager who has long since walled himself off from the outside world; who uses little language or who screeches in random yelps or vulgarities; who flips out when pried away from his computer game; who speaks to you, if at all, in long monologues on arcane subjects with zero interest in your response? What do you use as a staging ground for a relationship with an increasingly furious and despairing adolescent?

The Floortime technique might be summed up as: "Follow the child's lead and challenge the child." It is most easily visible on the videotapes documenting Dr. Greenspan's 25 years of clinical work with younger children. In each video, the gangly psychiatrist crouches on the floor of his comfortably shabby home office in Bethesda, calling instructions to parents about how to catch the attention of and interact with their remote-seeming children. "I treat everything the child does as having a reason—to feel calmer, for example, or to feel excited," Dr. Greenspan told me. "Often the parents have notions of what the child should be doing, so they're trying to control the child rather than build on the child's natural interests."

In my favorite video, a 30-something husband and wife flank their 4-year-old daughter; the husband, in round horn-rim glasses, sits forward on the sofa; his wife curls up on the floor nearby. Their daughter, with chopped-off blond hair and a doughy face, looks to me like Helen Keller, pre-Anne Sullivan. Seeming almost blind, deaf, mute and mentally retarded, she bounces from sofa to table to wall. She is without affect, her movements ungainly and her eyes unfocused. She makes slurping sounds, as if she has reached the bottom of a drink with a straw. "We're going to try to get a continuous flow of back-and-forth going here," Dr. Greenspan says.

The mother smiles sadly, knowingly. "That would be nice," she says.

"We're going to build on what she does," the doctor says.

The girl is flapping a plastic toy in her hand. "Will she give it to Daddy?" Dr. Greenspan asks.

"Can I see that?" the father asks as the child roams the room. The child seems not to hear him. But then the girl, traveling by, indifferently drops the toy into his outstretched hand. Delighted, the father says: "There's a star on it! And there's a triangle!"

"Here you're losing her, Daddy," Dr. Greenspan says, and sure enough, the girl escapes and heads for a wall. "If you're trying to educate her with complicated language that she's not processing, then you're going to lose her. You want to change your orientation from educating her to interacting with her."

The child picks up a bright plastic flowered eyeglass case off a table and twiddles it. "See if she'll give it to you," the doctor prompts.

"Can you give it to Mommy?" the mother asks, and surprising everyone, the girl hands it over. "Thank you!" the mother says.

The mother hides the eyeglass case behind her on the floor. The girl treads in place for a moment, swinging her arms and slurping. She begins to laugh a strange, heaving laugh. "Huh-huh-huh!" The mother moves a little to show that she's sitting on the eyeglass case, and the child dives for it.

"Good, good!" Dr. Greenspan cheers.

"Can I have it back?" the mother asks. The mother hides it inside her own sweater, half-exposed.

"Let her get it! Let her get it! Let her get it!" Dr. Greenspan says in excitement. It is of paramount importance to him that the child initiates her own ideas and motor plans. Every time her parents start to physically turn or steer her, he stops them, crying: "Let her do it! Let her do it!"

The mother next slips the eyeglass case into the bib of her daughter's pink overalls, and the girl stops in her tracks. Dr. Greenspan is prepared to leap over furniture to block the parents from giving her a clue. Suddenly, slowly, the girl's gaze drops. . . . She finds the eyeglass case! In her own pants! "Ooh! Ooh! Ooh! Ooh!" she says.

"Make it more complicated!" the psychiatrist pleads.

"Can we go give it to Daddy?" the mother asks.

The mother walks over to the father, who hides the eyeglass case in his shirt. The girl freezes in confusion. The psychiatrist loves a moment like this and tries to prolong it. He sees momentary frustration as a vitally creative occasion. He urges parents to be "playfully obstructive." He's not after results; he wants to see a child thinking. "She can do this," he advises them.

The girl slowly looks down, plucking at her overalls. For a moment it seems they have lost her. But—no—she's looking inside the bib, where she last found the eyeglass case. It's not there. Again she freezes. She must be thinking, "Mommy went to Daddy. . . . " Slowly she turns toward her father.

The expression on the father's face, when his daughter plucks the eyeglass case from his shirt, is of heartbreaking gratitude. A moment later, he pitches the eyeglass case over her head to his wife. The girl turns and beholds her beaming mother holding the eyeglass case. "Ooh! Ooh! Ooh!" she says. Mom pitches the case back to Dad, and when the child turns to run to her father, she skips in her delight, her face radiant, making a hoarse sound of laughter.

Children with autism—especially Asperger's—are famous for all-consuming interests in Matchbox cars, bus maps, train schedules, oscillating fans, Civil War battles, baseball statistics, black holes, dinosaurs, chess or Star Wars. While most programs try to discourage these obsessions, D.I.R./Floortime argues that they can offer openings into relationships. Does this work? Parents of T.C.S. students say that it does. Most speak in glowing terms about the school's lifesaving impact on their families. Outside experts are more cautious, reluctant to give any one approach a gold medal when there are so many variables, including the profiles of the students admitted to T.C.S. in the first place. "Stanley Greenspan is an engaged and enthusiastic clinician," Dr. Volkmar says. "People are attracted to Floortime because it is respectful of the child and the child's wishes. He wants to follow the child's lead. I would imagine that more able children do produce leads that are worth following—I've seen kids with Asperger's do well in Montessori programs too—but what if the child isn't doing much that you'd want to follow? I wonder if following the lead of a child who's doing nothing but body rocking results in a roomful of people all body rocking with him."

Dave Nelson says: "T.C.S. is a school, so I'd argue that our success should be measured by how well we educate our students. The boys have far better attendance rates than at their previous schools. They have far better emotional regulation—many could not attend school before due to their outbursts; while here, emotional regulation is core curriculum. Many were depressed to the point of suicidal ideation at their previous schools; that's not happening here. Some were victims of bullying, some were aggressors at their previous schools; not here. All our parents report that their children are functioning better, are happier and are better communicators, thinkers and learners."

Judy Martin says: "My son Ty's progress has been monumental. He doesn't cry in dark basements anymore. He isn't entirely focused on himself; he is learning real empathy. He never liked school, and now he loves it. Every day this past summer he asked me when he could be with Dave Nelson. This is a child who never cared about teachers or friends. Now he tells me he loves them. I chatted with Stephen the other day by the vending machine as his money got stuck. He was problem-solving rather than blowing up. We rode the elevator together, chatting about the problem, while he decided to go find a teacher to help him."

One morning at school, the fire alarm went off. My first thought—like everyone's—was, Oh, my God —Ty! We descended the stairs to the parking lot. Ty was within a circle of T.C.S. teachers. "It was Elana!" he yelled to everyone about one of the teachers, who had been trying to prepare a snack for her class. "Elana burnt the popcorn in the microwave!" Poor Elana Himmelfarb, covering her face, not knowing whether to laugh or cry, said again and again, "I am just so, so, so, so sorry, Ty."

He was trying to forgive her, but he kept asking, "Elana, why did you make the fire alarm go off?" His face was red, his curls were plastered back with perspiration and he was rocking a bit, long after the alarm had been silenced. Back upstairs, when the smoke cleared, Ty huddled in a beanbag chair with Rebecca Richter, one of the teachers, beside him.

"I hate that noise," Ty said. "That's a bad noise. That has a witch's voice."

"You really didn't like that noise," she agreed.

"This can NEVER HAPPEN AGAIN," he sobbed, demanding that Rebecca promise him. "This will never happen again, will it? This can never happen!

"I need you to call my mom," he said, weeping. "I'm having a very bad day. Will you call my mom? I need her to come get me." I imagine a region of Ty's brain blinking hard, a fistful of tiny red lights setting one another off: Panic! Panic!

"If we can keep Ty engaged with us, it means that he is harnessing and organizing his energies in order to interact," Nelson told me later. "By keeping him connected, we won't let him be kidnapped by random fragmented thoughts. If you aren't engaged with other people, then you are completely at the mercy of your own regulatory system. Think about a situation where you were overcome with distress and how being able to tell someone helped you avoid becoming uncontrollably distraught."

Gently Richter moved Ty from unreality ("the witch's voice") onto solid ground ("I'm having a bad day"). Given the tools to hang on, Ty survived until the end of the school day. And the breakthroughs continued. "When Ty came home that day, we talked through the events, as the school has trained me to lovingly do," Judy Martin told me recently, "and Ty said, 'Mom, I feel bad for Elana, because she didn't mean to do it.'

" 'Do you think she felt embarrassed?' I asked him, and he said yes. This moment was huge: Ty has always struggled with seeing the viewpoint of others, and here he was able to take a moment that frightened him and look at it from Elana's viewpoint. We go to restaurants all the time now, and Ty couldn't care less about the blenders. Lawn crews arrive next door, and they don't faze him."

When Sam Gross, now 17, arrived at T.C.S., he tripped along down the hall on the balls of his feet, rolling his head, thrumming on his chest with his fingers, humming to himself, lost in other worlds. The only points of entry he offered were during serious flights of fancy. "What this school needs," he murmured in his low, resonant voice one day to a teacher, Lucie Canfield, "is a magic cabinet."

"What would it do, Sam?" Lucie asked, delighted.

After a long pause he said, "Turn Sam into Samantha." Sam wanted to travel back in time, he explained, to when he was a little girl; then he changed his mind and wanted to use it for teleporting.

Sam's parents and his psychiatrist were initially less than enthusiastic about the magic cabinet: "Let's not get started with this stuff here," they said. But Lucie had already asked Sam, "What would a magic cabinet look like?"

Sam had replied: "Cow-colored."

Lucie pushed poster board and colored pencils at Sam and said, "Show me."

Dave Nelson agreed. This was the clearest opening they'd had from Sam Gross. Everything Nelson knew about Floortime told him to follow the boy's lead. "Let's see where this goes," he told Sam's parents.

Sam finished several quite beautiful drawings of a tall, rectangular closet. It would have a blue curtain and a bell stand on top, with a chain he would pull when he was finished transforming or teleporting. Nelson brought in a refrigerator box, and Lucie and Sam painted it in a nice Holstein pattern of black on white. "We made a point of always saying to Sam not that we were building a magic cabinet, but that we would pretend with him," Lucie tells me. "I explained that magicians used tricks to make people think they disappeared." T.C.S. would facilitate this exploration, with Sam, of the frontier of fantasy, with the expectation that he would encounter some reality along the way.

The special day arrived, and Sam stepped into the cabinet and drew the curtain. Dave waved a magic wand and read words Sam had written: "Abracadabra-a-whirl. Let Sam turn into a girl."

There was silence inside the box. Then Sam called, "Do it again!" Dave chanted the words again. Silence. Then: "Let Lucie do it!" The teacher took the wand and gave it a try.

Sam peeked out, still male. "This is not the right cabinet for turning into a girl," he said in consternation. "This is the cabinet that turns you into Paul McCartney." He exited. At home that night, Sam looked up magicians in the Yellow Pages and booked one to come to school the next day. Dave Nelson canceled. It was time for reality to intervene.

Back at school, Sam spent the week focusing on how to teleport out of the cabinet to surprise folks in the cafeteria on the ground floor. Then one day he made an unusual request of Lucie Canfield: he needed help cutting a back door in the box that would allow him to slip away like a stage magician. It was a striking and brave acknowledgment of the material world.

Sam never staged his trick, as it was real magic that excited him. And he muttered, over the next few weeks, seditious thoughts along the lines of, What kind of school is this that doesn't provide a real magician? The Magic Cabinet still stands in the art room, bell-towered and cow-colored. Many of the students enjoy stepping behind the blue curtain now and then for a moment of quiet remove from the world or to prepare to burst back upon the room in an assumed role. "It's expanded from a product of Sam's fantastic imagination to something of real purpose," Judy Martin told me. "Kids peek out their heads as characters from books they've been reading, changing their voices and facial expressions." The Magic Cabinet has come to stand for what the Community School offers these students: the possibility of transformation.

New Jersey has historically advocated for children with A.S.D. as well as houses the well-known Princeton Child Development Institute. Many families with children with autism have migrated to New Jersey due to the many opportunities and available services for these children.

"In the classroom at Caldwell, students study the principles of behavioral learning to break tasks into their component parts, to reinforce success with tangible rewards like pretzels and intangible ones like praise, to meticulously chart progress, to make course corrections and foster what works and to generalize skills mastered in a controlled classroom for the messier circumstances of everyday life. They study language and social deficits—the hallmark of Autism Spectrum Disorder—as well as challenging behaviors common to autistic children, like hand flapping, tantrums or self-injury. They also do the equivalent of student teaching in New Jersey's private schools and in dedicated public-school programs for autistic children."

Controversies are reported between the U.S. Department of Education (USDOE) and several states required by the 2004 re-authorization of IDEA to collect and report extensive data on students. In IDEA 2004, the states are required to collect data in order to comply with 34 indicators needed to track eligibility for special education services. Of the 34, 20 refer to students ages 3-21, who are covered under Part B of IDEA while 14 refer to infants and toddlers with disabilities.

Examples of these indicators are: requiring states to track how many students IEPs graduate from high schools with a regular diploma; requiring states to report on percentages of youths with IEPs who drop out requiring states to send yearly surveys to parents reporting on schools facilitating parent involvement as a means of improving special education services.

The USDOE and representatives of the National Association of State Directors of Special Education (NASDSE) have opposing views. The USDOE mandates that the states comply and the NASDSE believe the requirements for compliance will divert funds needed to service the children. NASDSE members disagreeing include: Mary Watson, Director of Exceptional Children, Division for the North Carolina Department of Education who believes hiring a statistician for data collection was necessary as opposed to literacy coach; Paul Raskopf, Director of the Office for Finance and Data Services for the Virginia Department of Education believes the extensive collection of data is too time consuming and may not be worth the effort. Somewhat in between these opposing views is Chris Thacher, Systems Consultant for Information Technology for the Kentucky DOE, who believes though extensive collection of data is extraordinarily difficult, it is also a tremendous asset.

Reprinted with permission from Education Week. *Vol. 28, No. 13, 11/19/2008.*

The Ethics of Inclusion: Three Common Delusions

by John O'Brien, Marsha Forest, Jack Pearpoint, Shafik Asante & Judith Snow

We want to begin a dialogue on the expectations about personal behavior that go along with a commitment to Inclusion. Unattainable expectations confuse good people and fragment efforts for change into factions organized around hurt feelings. We who care about Inclusion can reduce this drain on the energy necessary to work for justice by being clear about three delusions, which are common, but mostly unconscious among advocates for Inclusion. When we replace these false and destructive beliefs with simpler expectations of decency and working constructively in common, we will all be better able to live out the real meaning of Inclusion by honoring and growing from our shared struggle with our diverse gifts, differences, and weaknesses.

[In writing this article, we have struggled for clarity. We talked about whether to use "delusion" or "illusion". Delusion means "a mistaken idea or belief". Illusion a "false appearance or deceptive impression of reality". They are synonyms—but we have chosen "delusion" because it is stronger.]

Delusion 1

Inclusion means that everybody must love everybody else or "We must all be one big, happy family!" (OBHF) This delusion is at work when people who care about Inclusion feel shocked and offended to discover that other Inclusion advocates don't really like one another. Sometimes this delusion pushes people into pretending, or wanting others to pretend, that real differences of opinion and personality don't exist or don't really matter. The roots of this delusion may be in a desire to make up for painful experiences by finally becoming part of "one big happy family," (OBHF) where there is continual harmony and peace. The "one big happy family" (OBHF) delusion is the exact opposite of Inclusion. The real challenge of Inclusion is to find common cause for important work that cannot be done effectively if we isolate ourselves from one another along the many differences of race, culture, nationality, gender, class, ability, and personality that truly do divide us. Educating our children is one such common task. The reward of Inclusion comes in the harvest of creative action and new understanding that follows the hard work of finding common ground and tilling it by confronting and finding creative ways through real differences.

The "one big happy family" (OBHF) delusion destroys the possibilities for Inclusion in a complex community by seducing people into burying differences by denying their significance or even their existence. People in schools or agencies or associations which promote this delusion lose vividness and energy because they have to swallow the feelings of dislike and conflict they experience and deny the differences they see and hear. Denial makes a sandy foundation for inclusive schools and communities. Community grows when people honor a commitment to laugh, shout, cry, argue, sing, and scream with, and at, one another without destroying one another or the earth in the process. We can't ever honestly celebrate diversity if we pretend to bring in the harvest before we have tilled the ground together.

Delusion 2

Inclusion means everyone must always be happy and satisfied or "Inclusion cures all ills." A group of good people came together to study inclusive community in an intensive course. One person, Anne, angrily announced her dissatisfaction from the group's first meeting on. She acted hostile to everyone else and to the group's common project.

At first, the group organized itself around Anne's dissatisfaction. A number of members anguished over her participation. It was hard for the group to sustain attention on anything for very long before the topic of how to satisfy Anne took over. The group acted as if it could not include Anne unless she was happy. And, they assumed, if they could not be an inclusive group (that is, make Anne happy) they would be failing to live up to their values. Two other members dropped out the group, frustrated by their inability to overcome the power of this delusion and move on to issues of concern to them.

The group broke through when they recognized that true community includes people who are angry and anguished as well as those who are happy and satisfied. After overcoming the delusion of cure, the group gave Anne room to be angry and dissatisfied without being the focus of the whole group. Let out of the center of the group's concern, Anne found solidarity with several other members, whom she chose as a support circle for herself. In this circle of support her real pain emerged as she told her story of being an abused child and a beaten wife. She did not go home cured or happy, but she did find real support and direction for dealing with the issues in her life.

The delusion that Inclusion equals happiness leads to its opposite: a pseudo-community in which people who are disagreeable or suffering have no place unless the group has the magic to cure them. Groups trapped in this delusion hold up a false kind of status difference that values people who act happy more than people who suffer. This delusion creates disappointment that Inclusion is not the panacea.

Real community members get over the wish for a cure-all and look for ways to focus on promoting one another's gifts and capacities in the service of justice. They support, and often must endure, one another's weaknesses by learning ways to forgive, to reconcile, and to rediscover shared purpose. Out of this hard work comes a measure of healing.

Delusion 3

Inclusion is the same as friendship or "We are really all the same."

Friendship grows mysteriously between people as a mutual gift. It shouldn't be assumed and it can't be legislated. But people can choose to work for inclusive schools and communities, and schools and agencies and associations can carefully build up norms and customs that communicate the expectation that people will work hard to recognize, honor, and find common cause for action in their differences.

This hard work includes embracing dissent and disagreement and sometimes even outright dislike of one person for another. The question at the root of Inclusion is not "Can't we be friends?" but, in Rodney King's hard won words, "Can we all just learn to get along—to live with one another?" We can't get along if we simply avoid others who are different and include only those with who we feel comfortable and similar. Once we openly recognize difference, we can begin to look for something worth working together to do. Once we begin working together, conflicts and difficulties will teach us more about our differences. If we can face and explore them our actions and our mutual understanding will be enriched and strengthened. To carry out this work, our standard must be stronger than the friendly feelings that come from being with someone we think likes and is like us. To understand and grow through including difference we must risk the comfortable feeling of being just like each other. The question that can guide us in the search for better understanding through shared action is not "Do we like each other?" but "Can we live with each other?" We can discover things worth our joint effort even if we seem strange to one another, even if we dislike one another, and it is through this working together that we can learn to get along.

The delusion of sameness leads away from the values of Inclusion. It blurs differences and covers over discomfort and the sense of strangeness or even threat that goes with confronting actual human differences. Strangely, it only when the assumption of friendship fades away that the space opens up for friendship to flower.

An ethic of decency and common labor Inclusion doesn't call on us to live in a fairy tale. It doesn't require that we begin with a new kind of human being who is always friendly, unselfish, and unafraid and never dislikes or feels strange with anyone. We can start with who we are. And it doesn't call for some kind of super group that can make everyone happy, satisfied, and healed. We can and must start with the schools, and agencies, and associations we have now.

The way to Inclusion calls for more modest, and probably more difficult, virtues. We must simply be willing to learn to get along while recognizing our differences, our faults and foibles, and our gifts.

This begins with a commitment to decency: a commitment not to behave in ways that demean others and an openness to notice and change when our behavior is demeaning, even when this is unintentional. This ethical boundary—upheld as a standard in human rights tribunals around the globe—defines the social space within which the work of Inclusion can go on. This work calls on each of us to discover and contribute our gifts through a common labor of building worthy means to create justice for ourselves and for the earth through the ways we educate each other, through the ways we care for one another's health and welfare, and through the ways we produce the things we need to live good lives together.

In this common labor we will find people we love and people we dislike; we will find friends and people we can barely stand. We will sometimes be astonished at our strengths and sometimes be overcome by our weaknesses. Through this work of Inclusion we will, haltingly, become new people capable of building new and more human communities.

http://www.inclusion.com, Inclusion Press International.

Expecting Longer Lives With Greater Risk, Reward

Down Syndrome Generation First to Outlive Parents

By Fredrick Kunkle, Washington Post *Staff Writer*

Like many people her age, Jennifer Holden wants to be on her own. But for the 20-year-old Springfield woman, crossing streets can be frightening. Keeping track of money is difficult. And fending for herself is challenging at times for a person who loves to read but has difficulty with novels above a fifth-grade level.

"A stranger could set a trap on me," she says between bites of a cheeseburger at a Wendy's. "Kidnap me."

Holden belongs to the first generation of people with Down syndrome who will probably outlive their parents. The life expectancy of people with Down syndrome has increased from about 25 years in 1983 to more than 50, thanks largely to medical advances. Although achieving independence has long been the goal for any person with a disability, increased life expectancy has made the goal more urgent now that the baby boomer generation is graying.

"It's a big question we all ask," said Gail Williamson, 55, executive director of the Down Syndrome Association of Los Angeles. Williamson's 29-year-old son, Blair, has Down syndrome and a résumé that many actors in Hollywood would envy, including performances on television dramas including "CSI," "Nip/Tuck" and "ER." But he also participates in a supported-living day program and will probably need similar guidance when he is totally on his own, she said.

Estate planning is tricky, as families have to create special trusts to ensure that their children will be provided for without jeopardizing their eligibility for Medicaid and other programs. Openings in group homes and supervisory programs are hard to find. Deciding whether to make a sibling a guardian can be difficult.

"It's a huge problem, and it's not just a problem involving Down syndrome but for all people who have an intellectual disability," said Peter V. Berns, executive director of the Arc of the United States, whose headquarters is in Silver Spring. "There's a serious crisis brewing. There are actually huge waiting lists for services across the United States."

In 2006, 61 percent of people with an intellectual disability were living with their families, and more than 700,000 of them were living with parents or family members who were older than 60, Berns said.

"The reality is that the services are not available to take care of these people in the event that their family member either becomes sick or passes away," Berns said. "In a sense, their very freedom is at stake."

Anita Mahood of Leesburg said she and her husband encountered many difficulties, including waiting lists for group homes and other programs, before finding their 34-year-old son, Bill, a subsidized apartment to share with another man who also has an intellectual disability. Mahood's son is enrolled in Community Systems, a supervisory program whose staff drops by her son's apartment to check on him, and a group called Every Citizen Has Opportunities, which provides job training and placement for people with disabilities.

"This is the first generation of children who will outlive their parents," Mahood said. "That's why we worked so hard to find a solution for Bill."

Mahood, 69, said she and her husband have set up a special-needs trust that will provide support for their son after they die. Although her daughter and son-in-law offered to take Bill in, Mahood said she decided that she did not want them to accept primary responsibility.

"I don't feel it's the right way to go," Mahood said. "Both need to have their own lives. I feel very strongly about that."

The LIFE Program that Holden attends at George Mason University's Helen A. Kellar Center for Human disAbilities is in its sixth year, and it is not cheap. Tuition, which is $16,500 a year for a non-degree program, is about the cost of a GMU degree for out-of-state students.

But it also offers a shot at independence.

"With each stage, as with a non-disabled child, you're giving them a little freedom and watching to see if they can handle it," said Jeanne Holden, Jennifer's mother. She knows that her daughter might not realize her dream of becoming a professional teacher and that she probably will be unable to live by herself without support. But her daughter also surprises.

"More often than not, they rise to the occasion," Jeanne Holden said. "Sometimes you've got to take a deep breath. You take that same deep breath earlier with your other kids. But you have to let them go. If they're going to go as far as they can, you've got to let them try."

Jennifer Holden loves movies and musicals, especially "The Three Musketeers" with Charlie Sheen and "High School Musical." She often goes to the movies with friends. She also has been serving as an assistant religion instructor for young children at her synagogue in Alexandria and this summer worked as an assistant counselor in a Fairfax County recreation program. Last year, she spent a week living in a GMU dorm, preparing microwaved meals and navigating the campus. She loved it.

"Independent living is to live by yourself in dorms without my parents and without my siblings—by ourselves and without my siblings bothering me sometimes," she says. She adds that she really enjoyed fixing her own meals. "I cooked for myself—I loved that. Hardest thing to do—cross a street. That's a big problem. Sometimes I don't like it when there's an accident. I don't like cars" crushed up, she says.

A trip to the Metro and a fast-food restaurant with her class last week illustrates the rewards and possible perils that she faces along the way.

Holden's classes in independent living and community access combined classroom work and a field trip with four instructors, 21 students and three former students who work as interns. The students, who have intellectual disabilities including Down syndrome, autism and traumatic brain injuries, hugged often and exchanged high-fives. At times, they had trouble understanding the teacher's explanations, but they kept trying.

Holden, in particular, seemed to be bursting with things to say. Thin, petite and with an obvious sense of poise, she was eager to participate, whether listing her favorite restaurants or doodling hearts and flowers on a piece of paper. When she is excited, her voice zooms upward in pitch like a slide whistle.

"Awesome!" Holden squeals when she hears a classmate's jazzy cellphone ring tone.

Because of her disability, Holden has to work hard at things that are easy for many others. She did not always understand what the instructors or people outside the class were talking about. Making herself understood can be difficult as well because of a speech impediment and sometimes broken syntax.

Her day began in a literature class with a simplified version of Jules Verne's "20,000 Leagues Under the Sea." Then came an independent-living session that included an explanation of how to prepare a tuna sandwich and use the Metro system.

Waiting on campus for the Green 2 shuttle bus that will drop the students off near Fair City Mall in Fairfax, Holden gets caught up in teasing insults that ping-pong between her and the class cutup.

The group of eight students and two instructors disembarks in front of W.T. Woodson High School. At the crosswalk to the mall, there is a momentary scare when three students step into traffic while the light is green. Fortunately, there are no cars on the three-lane street, and the students scamper back onto the curb.

At Wendy's, Holden is first in line. Clutching her pink wallet, she follows the zigzag maze to the counter and waits for the cashier. The cashier looks at Holden, then past her, with a look of expectation that someone else must be doing the ordering.

"Hi. May I have a cheeseburger, please?" Holden says. "Small fries. And small drink."

"Okay," the cashier says. "$3.26."

Holden hands the cashier a $10 bill and two $5s.

The cashier takes a $5 bill, returns the other bills without comment and tells Holden that the rest of her change is in the chute attached to the register.

Holden lifts her tray and heads for the condiments, then finds a table with friends. She puts the receipt for her meal into her purse.

"For banking," she says.

While Holden is eating, a white-haired woman stops at the table and tells instructor Megan Kime that a nearby church offers a crafts program for "Down syndrome kids."

"That's not me," Holden interjects. Kime listens politely as the woman speaks. After the woman leaves, Kime turns to Holden.

"You're a person with a disability," she says.

"I know," Holden says.

"You're a person first. Remember that."

After lunch, as the Green 2 bus rumbles past the Metro lot, signs of weariness are evident among instructors and students. Holden, her blond hair pressed against the bus window, watches the scenery go by as they head back to campus. Her lips move as she begins muttering something to herself. Suddenly, she looks up.

"Imagination," she says. She explains that she was daydreaming.

"The Three Musketeers wanted to see me," she says.

Chapter Seven

Organizations, Associations, and Government Agencies

NATIONAL CONTACTS

Alexander Graham Bell Association for the Deaf (AG Bell)
3417 Volta Place NW Washington, DC 20007-2778
(202) 337-5220 (Voice)
(202) 337-5221 (TTY)
Fax: (202) 337-8314
Web site: http://www.agbell.org

Founded in 1890 by Alexander Graham Bell as an information provider and support network, AG Bell is the largest organization in the United States focused on the needs of hearing impaired children who use auditory approaches to communicate. AG Bell offers a variety of member-oriented programs, financial aid, publications, software, audiovisual materials, and other information on hearing impairment, with an auditory-oral emphasis.

American Amputee Foundation (AAF)
P.O. Box 250218
Hillcrest Station
Little Rock, AR 72225
(501) 666-2523
Fax: (501) 666-8367
Web site: http://www.americanamputee.org

The American Amputee Foundation (AAF) began in 1975 as a national information clearinghouse and referral center serving primarily amputees and their families. AAF offers a variety of services, including help with insurance claims, financial aid for prosthetic devices, counseling services, and information concerning support groups, and self-help publications.

American Association of People with Disabilities (AAPD)
1819 H Street NW, Suite 330
Washington, DC 20006
(202) 457-0046
(800) 840-8844
Web site: http://www.aapd.com

The AAPS is a nonprofit, nonpartisan membership organization that promotes the goal of full inclusion of people with disabilities in American society. This newly organized association promises to bring about "the next step in the evolution of the disability rights movement"—economic clout and power through numbers, with unity, leadership, and impact.

American Association of the Deaf-Blind (AADB)
814 Thayer Avenue
Silver Spring, MD 20910
(800) 735-2258 (Voice)
(301) 588-6545 (TTY)
Fax: (301) 588-8705
Web site: http://www.aadb.org/

The AADB is a consumer advocacy organization for people who have combined hearing and vision impairments. It is open to all persons who are deaf-blind as well as to individuals directly concerned with their well being, including spouses, children, friends, and health care professionals.

American Association on Mental Retardation (AAMR)
444 North Capitol Street NW, Suite 846
Washington, DC 20001
(202) 387-1968
(800) 424-3688
Fax: (202) 387-2193
Web site: http:www.aamr.org/About_AAIDD/index.shtml

This organization provides leadership in the field of mental retardation. The AAMR is the oldest and largest interdisciplinary organization of professionals (and others) concerned about mental retardation and related disabilities.

American Council of the Blind (ACB)
1155 15th Street NW, Suite 1004
Washington, DC 20005
(202) 467-5081
(800) 424-8666
Fax: (202) 467-5085
Web site: http://www.acb.org

The ACB is the nation's leading membership organization of blind and visually impaired people. It strives to improve the well-being of all blind and visually impaired people and by offering educational and rehabilitation facilities and opportunities, and it cooperates with public and private institutions and organizations concerned with blind services. The organization also publishes *The Braille Forum,* a free monthly magazine.

American Council on Education
One Dupont Circle, NW
Washington, DC 20036
(202) 939-9300
Fax: (202) 833-4760
Web site: http://www.acenet.edu?AM/Template.cfm?Section=Home

This is a national coordinating higher education association dedicated to equal educational opportunities and a strong higher education system.

American Disability Association (ADA)
2201 Sixth Avenue S
Birmingham, AL 35233
(205) 328-9090
Fax: (205) 251-7417
Web site: http://www.ada.gov/

This organization serves as an informational and resource center for Americans with diverse disabilities. It provides an international distributed computer network serving the interests of people with disabilities.

American Epilepsy Society
342 North Main Street
West Hartford, CT 06117-2507
(860) 586-7505
Fax: (860) 586-7550
Web site: http://www.aesnet.org

The society promotes research and education for professionals dedicated to the prevention, treatment, and cure of epilepsy.

American Federation of Teachers
555 New Jersey Avenue NW
Washington, DC 20001
(202) 879-4400
Web site: http://www.aft.org/contact.html

This teachers union strives to attain a quality public education for all citizens and efficient and effective delivery of public services. It also has a goal to secure adequate health care for every American, especially children.

American Foundation for the Blind (AFB)
11 Penn Plaza, Suite 300
New York, NY 10001
(212) 502-7661
(212) 502-7662 (TDD)
(800) 232-5463
Fax: (212) 502-7777
Web site: http://www.afb.org/default.asp

A nonprofit organization founded in 1921, AFB is a resource for people who are blind or visually impaired, the organizations that serve them, and the general public. It publishes books, pamphlets, videos, and periodicals about blindness for professionals and consumers through AFB Press.

American Heart Association (AHA)
National Center
7272 Greenville Avenue
Dallas, TX 75231
(800) 242-8721
Fax: (214) 369-3685
Web site: http://www.americanheart.org

The American Heart Association (AHA) is a not-for-profit, voluntary health organization funded by private contributions. Its mission is to reduce disability and death from cardiovascular diseases and stroke. The AHA provides reliable information to the American public on prevention and treatment of heart disease and stroke.

American Lung Association (ALA)
1740 Broadway
New York, NY 10019
(800) LUNG-USA (586-4872)
Web site: http://www.lungusa.org/

Founded in 1904 to fight tuberculosis, the ALA today fights lung disease in all its forms. It offers a variety of programs and strategies for fighting lung disease as well as a wide variety of printed informational materials, public service announcements, news releases, and conferences.

American Paralysis Association and the Christopher Reeve Paralysis Foundation
500 Morris Avenue
Springfield, NJ 07081
(800) 225-0292
Fax: (973) 912-9433
Web site: http://www.apacure.com

This organization encourages and supports research to develop effective treatments and a cure for paralysis caused by spinal cord injury and other central nervous system disorders. The foundation also allocates a portion of its resources to grants that improve the quality of life for people with disabilities.

American Red Cross
431 18th Street NW
Washington, DC 20006
(202) 639-3520
Web site: http://www.redcross.org

The American Red Cross is a humanitarian organization that provides relief to victims of disasters and helps people prevent, prepare for, and respond to emergencies.

American Society for Deaf Children (ASDC)
National Office
P.O. Box 3355
Gettysburg, PA 17325
(800) 942-2732 (Hotline)
(717) 334-7922 (Business Voice/TTY)
Fax: (717) 334-8808
Web site: http://www.deafchildren.org

The ASDC is an organization of parents and families that advocates for deaf or hard-of-hearing children's total quality participation in education, the family, and the community. Staff handle inquiries on a variety of topics related to raising children who are deaf or hard of hearing.

American Speech-Language-Hearing Foundation
10801 Rockville Pike
Rockville, MD 20852
(301) 897-7341
Web site: http://www.ashfoundation.org/about.htm

The foundation is a charitable research and education organization that helps ensure the gift of communication for 42 million Americans with communication disorders.

American Spinal Injury Association (ASIA)
345 East Superior Street, Room 1436
Chicago, IL 60611
(312) 238-1242
Fax: (312) 238-0869
Web site: http://www.asia-spinalinjury.org

ASIA is composed of professionals who have contributed to the field of spinal cord injury. The group promotes and establishes standards of excellence for all aspects of health care of individuals with spinal cord injury from onset through life and facilitates communication between members and other physicians, other health care professionals, researchers, and consumers.

The Annie E. Casey Foundation
701 Saint Paul Street
Baltimore, MD 21202
(410) 547-6600
Fax: (410) 547-6624
Web site: http://www.aecf.org

The Casey Foundation is a private charitable organization dedicated to helping build better futures for disadvantage children in the United States.

The Arc of the United States
1010 Wayne Avenue, Suite 650
Silver Spring, MD 20910
(301) 565-3842
Fax: (301) 565-5342
Web site: http://www.thearc.org

The nation's leading national organization on mental retardation, the Arc provides organizational support to affiliated chapters and represents its membership on advocacy and programmatic issues pertaining to mental retardation.

Autism Society of America
7910 Woodmont Avenue, Suite 300
Bethesda, MD 20814-3015
(301) 657-0881
(800) 328-8476, ext. 150
Fax: (301) 657-0869
Web site: http://www.autism-society.org

The society serves the needs of individuals with autism and their families through advocacy, education, public awareness, and research.

Autism Speaks Family Services
http://www.autismspeaks.org/community/family_services/index.php

Autism Speaks Family Services is dedicated to empowering individuals and families impacted by autism. They help families maximize their child's developmental potential and improve their quality of life.

Avenues, a National Support Group for Arthrogryposis Multiplex Congenita
P.O. Box 5192
Sonora, CA 95370
(209) 928-3688
Web site: avenuessforamc.com/

Avenues is a nonprofit information and support group for individuals and families affected by arthrogryposis multiplex congenita, a neuromuscular disease leading to multiple joint contractures at birth.

Blind Children's Fund
4740 Okemos Road
Okemos, MI 48864
(517) 347-1357
Fax: (517) 347-1459
Web site: http://www.blindchildrensfund.org/

The fund is a nonprofit organization providing parents and professionals with information, materials, and resources that help them successfully teach and nurture infants and children who are blind or visually or multi-impaired.

Centers for Disease Control (CDC) National AIDS Hotline
American Society Health Association
P.O. Box 13827
Research Triangle Park, NC 27709
(800) 342-2437
Web site: http://www.ashastd.org

The National AIDS Hotline operates under contract with the Centers for Disease Control and Prevention. Information concerning prevention, risk, testing, treatment, and other HIV/AIDS-related concerns is available.

Center for Study of Autism
P.O. Box 4538
Salem, OR 97302
Web site: http://www.autism.org

The center provides information about autism to parents and professionals, and conducts research on the efficacy of various therapeutic interventions.

CHADD: Children and Adults with Attention-Deficit/Hyperactivity Disorder
8181 Professional Place, Suite 201
Landover, MD 20785
(301) 306-7070
(800) 233-4050
Fax: (301) 306-7070
Web site: http://www.chadd.org

CHADD is an advocacy group dedicated to improving the lives of people with attention-deficit/hyperactivity disorder through education, advocacy, and support. Information concerning AD/HD, conferences, and educational materials is available.

Child Welfare League of America (CWLA)
440 First Street NW, Third Floor
Washington, DC 20001-2085
(202) 638-2952
Fax: (202) 638-4004
Web site: http://www.cwla.org

The CWLA is the oldest and largest nonprofit organization dedicated to developing and promoting policies and programs to protect America's children and strengthen America's families.

Children's Brain Tumor Foundation
20312 Watkins Meadow Drive
Germantown, MD 20876
(301) 515-2900
Web site: http://www.childhoodbraintumor.org

The foundation raises funds for scientific research on brain tumors and provides public awareness of this most devastating disease; it seeks to improve prognosis and the quality of life for those that are affected.

Clearinghouse on Disability Information
Office of Special Education and Rehabilitation Services
U.S. Department of Education
Switzer Building, Room 3132
330 C Street SW
Washington, DC 20202
(202) 205-8241
Fax: (202) 401-2608
Web site: http://www.ed.gov/about/offices/list/osers/index.html

The clearinghouse provides information, research, and documents in response to inquiries concerning disabilities. The data is used by disabled individuals and their families, schools and universities, teachers and school administrators, and organizations that have persons with disabilities as clients.

Compassionate Friends
P.O. Box 3696
Oak Brook, IL 60522
(630) 990-0010
Fax: (630) 990-0246
Web site: http://www.compassionatefriends.org

Compassionate Friends is a nonprofit, self-help support organization that assists families in the positive resolution of grief following the death of a child.

The Council for Exceptional Children (CEC), Division of Learning Disabilities (DLD)
1110 N. Glebe Road
Reston, VA 22201–5704
(703) -620-3660
888-CEC-SPED
Fax: (703) 264-9494
Web site: http://www.cec.sped.org

CEC is the largest international professional organization dedicated to improving educational outcomes for individuals with exceptionalities, students with disabilities, and the gifted. The council advocates for governmental policies, sets professional standards, provides professional development, and helps professionals obtain conditions and resources necessary for effective professional practice.

Council for Learning Disabilities (CLD)
www.cldinternational.org

The CLD is an international professional organization that promotes strategies for research and practice through collaboration and advocacy.

Council of Parent Attorneys and Advocates
http://www.copaa.net/

The Council of Parent Attorney and Advocates (COPAA) is the national organization of attorneys, education advocates and parents. COPAA focuses on special education rights and excellence in advocacy. Membership to COPAA allows one to acess discussion groups (listservs), databanks of legal documents, and materials by leading special education attorney and advocates.

Division of Mental Retardation and Developmental Disabilities
105 Fairgrounds Road, P.O. Box 1098
Rolla, MO 65402
(573) 368-2200
Fax: (573) 368-2206
Web site: dmh.missouri.gov/mrdd/mrddindex.htm

Serving a population that has developmental disabilities such as mental retardation, cerebral palsy, head injuries, autism, epilepsy, and certain learning disabilities, the division works to improve their lives through programs and services to enable them to live independently and productively.

Education Commission of the States
707 17th Street, #2700
Denver, CO 80202-3427
(303) 299-3600
Fax: (303) 296-8332
Web site: http://www.ecs.org

This organization provides information concerning early childhood education. It provides helpful information about educational initiatives and direction as to other policy and informational sites.

Education Research Information Center (ERIC EC)
The Council for Exceptional Children (CEC)
1920 Association Drive
Reston, VA 20191
(800) 328-0272
Web site: http://ericec.org/abouterc.htm

The ERIC Clearinghouse on Disabilities and Gifted Education (ERIC EC) is a nationwide information network sponsored by the U.S. Department of Education. The center gathers and provides professional literature, information, and resources on the education and development of individuals of all ages who have disabilities and/or who are gifted.

Epilepsy Foundation of America
4351 Garden City Drive
Landover, MD 20785
(800) 332-1000
(301) 459-3700
Fax: (301) 577-4941
Web site: epilepsyfoundation.org/

The Epilepsy Foundation is a charitable organization dedicated to the welfare of individuals with epilepsy and their families. It works with children and adults who are affected by seizures and provides education, advocacy, and service.

Equal Employment Opportunity Commission (EEOC)
1801 L Street NW
Washington, DC 20507
(202) 663-4900
(800) 669-4000
Web site: http://www.eeoc.gov

The EEOC enforces the principal federal statutes prohibiting employment discrimination.

Federal Communications Commission (FCC)
445 12th Street SW
Washington, DC 20554
(202) 418-0190
Web site: http://www.fcc.gov/cib/dro

The FCC maintains a Disabilities Rights Office, which has an obligation to ensure that telecommunications are accessible and usable to the 54 million Americans with disabilities. Information concerning closed captioning and video description, hearing aid compatibility, and general answers to questions that the public may have about the FCC Disabilities Issues Task Force (DITF) are provided.

Federal Resource Center (FRC) for Special Education
Academy for Educational Development
1825 Connecticut Avenue NW
Washington, DC 20009

(202) 884-8215
Fax: (202) 884-8443
Web site: http://www.dssc.org/frc/about.htm

The FRC supports a nationwide technical assistance network to respond to the needs of students with disabilities, especially students from underrepresented populations.

Federation for Children with Special Needs
1135 Tremont Street, Suite 420
Boston, MA 02120
(617) 236-7210
(800) 331-0688
Fax: (617) 572-2094
Web site: http://www.fcsn.org

The federation is a center for parents and parent organizations to work together on behalf of children with special needs and their families.

Institute on Community Integration
102 Pattee Hall
150 Pillsbury Drive SE
Minneapolis, MN 55455
(612) 624-9344
Fax: (612) 624-9344
Web site: http://ici.umn.edu/default.html

The Institute on Community Integration is a University Affiliated Program committed to improving the quality and community orientation of professional services and social supports available to individuals with disabilities and their families. It publishes numerous newsletters, resource guides, technical reports, and brochures.

International Dyslexia Association (IDA)
www.interdysorg

The IDA is an international, nonprofit, scientific, and educational organization dedicated to the study and treatment of dyslexia. The IDA provides information on assistive technology, medical and educational research, conferences and seminars, and teaching methods.

Learning Disabilities Association of America
4156 Library Road
Pittsburgh, PA 15234
(412) 341-1515
Fax: (412) 344-0224
Web site: http://www.ldanatl.org

This nonprofit organization works to advance the education and general welfare of children and adults of normal or potentially normal intelligence who manifest disabilities of a perceptual, conceptual, or coordinative nature. LDA is dedicated to enhancing the quality of life for all individuals with learning disabilities and their families, to alleviating the restricting effects of learning disabilities, and to supporting endeavors to determine the causes of learning disabilities. The IDA Web site provides information about state chapters and recent publications.

Muscular Dystrophy Association—USA
3300 East Sunrise Drive
Tucson, AZ 85718
(800) 572-1717
Fax: (602) 529-5300
Web site: http://www.mdausa.org

This association is a source for news and information about neuromuscular disease, research, and services for adults and children with neuromuscular diseases and their families. Publications are available on issues such as treatments, therapies, diagnosis, and daily living.

National Amputation Foundation (NAF)
38-40 Church Street
Malverne, NY 11565
(516) 887-3600
Fax: (516) 887-3667
Web site: http://www.nationalamputation.org

This organization's membership is made of amputee volunteers who offer their support to fellow amputees and their families. The NAF provides legal counsel, vocational guidance and placement, psychological aid, and training in the use of prosthetic devices. It publishes a bimonthly newsletter and a variety of pamphlets.

National Association for Gifted Children (NAGC)
1707 L Street NW, Suite 550
Washington, DC 20036
(202) 785-4268
Web site: http://www.nagc.org/

The NAGC is an organization of parents, educators, other professionals, and community leaders to address the unique needs of children and youth with demonstrated gifts and talents. It also supports children who may be able to develop their talent potential with appropriate educational experiences. NAGC engages in research and development, staff development, advocacy, communication, and collaboration with other organizations and agencies that strive to improve the quality of education for all students.

National Association for the Education of Young Children (NAEYC)
1509 16th Street NW
Washington, DC 20036
(202) 232-877
(800) 424-2460
Fax: (202) 328-1846
Web site: http://www.naeyc.org

The NAEYC consolidates the efforts of individuals and groups working to achieve healthy development and constructive education for all young children. It devotes primary attention to assuring the provision of high-quality early childhood programs for young children.

National Association for Visually Handicapped
22 West 21st Street, Sixth Floor
New York, NY 10010
(212) 889-3141
Fax: (212) 727-2931
Web site: http://www.navh.org/faq.html

This association works with millions of people worldwide dealing with difficulties of vision impairment. Its goal is to provide the finest nonprofit independent health agency solely dedicated to serving the visually impaired.

National Association of Developmental Disabilities Council
1234 Massachusetts Avenue NW, Suite 103
Washington, DC 20005
(202) 347-1234
Fax: (202) 347-4023
Web site: http:www.nacdd.org/

The council promotes national policies that enable individuals with developmental disabilities the opportunity to make choices regarding the quality of their lives and to be included in the community.

National Association of Private Schools for Exceptional Children (NAPSEC)
1522 K Street, NW, Suite 1032
Washington, DC 20005
(202) 408-3338
Fax: (202) 408-3340
Email: http://www.napsec.org/contact.html
Web site: http://www.napsec.org?

NAPSEC is a nonprofit association whose mission is to ensure access for individuals to private special education as a vital component of the continuum of appropriate placement and services in American education. The association consists solely of private special education schools that serve both privately and publicly placed individuals with disabilities. Their web site advertises a free referral service.

National Association of Secondary School Principals
www.nassp.org

The NASSP is a source where middle and high school educators and administrators can find news, services, resources, and an online community of principals, assistant principals, and aspiring school leaders.

National Association of State Directors of Special Education (NASDSE)
1800 Diagonal Road Suite 320
Alexandria, VA 22314
(703) 519-3800
Fax: (703) 519-3808

Email: http://www.nasdese.org/contactus.cfm
Web site: http://www.nasdse.org/home.htm

National Brain Tumor Foundation
c/o Michael McKechnie
785 Market Street, Suite 1600
San Francisco, CA 94102
(800) 934-2873
Fax: (415) 284-0209
Web site: http://www.braintumor.org/GeneralMenu/

This not-for-profit health organization is dedicated to providing information and support for brain tumor patients, family members, and healthcare professionals while supporting innovative research into better treatment options and a cure for brain tumors.

National Center for Learning Disabilities (NCLD)
381 Park Avenue South, Suite 1420
New York, NY 10016
(212) 545-7510
(888) 575-7373 (Referral Service)
Fax: (212) 545-9665
Web site: http://www.ncld.org

The NCLD provides advocacy, resources, and referral services for children and adults with learning disabilities. The center develops and supports innovative educational programs, seminars, and workshops; conducts public awareness campaigns; and works for more effective policies and legislation to help individuals with learning disabilities. The NCLD Web site provides a database of state resources, educational programs, legislative advocacy, and public policy.

National Clearing House for Professions in Special Education
1110 N. Glebe Road
Arlington, VA 22201—5704
(800) 641-7824
Fax: (703) 264-1637
Email: ncpse@cec.sped.org
Web site: http://www.specialedcareers.org/

National Down Syndrome Congress
7000 Peachtree-Dunwoody Road NE
Lake Ridge 400 Office Park Building #5, Suite 100
Atlanta, GA 30328
(770) 604-9500
(800) 232-NDSC
Web site: http://www.ndsccenter.org/

This organization provides leadership in all areas of concern related to persons with Down Syndrome and their families.

National Early Childhood Technical Assistance System (NECTAS)
Frank Porter Graham Child Development Center
University of North Carolina at Chapel Hill
137 East Franklin Street, Suite 500
Chapel Hill, NC 27514
(919) 962-2001
Web site: http://www.uri.edu/frp/frplink20.html

NECTAS provides information and resources about the Individuals with Disabilities Education Act (IDEA) and programs and projects funded under IDEA.

National Education Association
www.nea.org

The National Education Association provides classroom tips, information on higher education, and current news in education.

National Educational Service
1252 Loesch Road
Bloomington, IN 47401
(812) 336-7700
(800) 733-6786
Fax: (812) 336-7790
Web site: http://cecp.air.org/teams/stratpart/nes.asp

The National Educational Service provides tested and proven resources to help those who work with youth create safe and caring schools, agencies, and communities.

National Head Start Association
1651 Prince Street
Alexandria, VA 22314
(703) 739-0875
Fax: (703) 739-0878
Web site: http://www.nhsa.org

This is a private, not-for-profit membership organization representing the Head Start programs. It works to improve the quality of Head Start's comprehensive services for America's children and families.

National Hydrocephalus Foundation (NHF)
1670 Green Oak Circle
Lawrenceville, GA 30243
(770) 995-9570
Fax: (770) 995-8982
Web site: http://www.nhfonline.org/aboutus.php?id=news_view

The NHF seeks to remove stigma from individuals with hydrocephalus and improve their lives. To that end, it collects and disseminates information about hydrocephalus, counsels parents on specific problems encountered as a result of hydrocephalus in their children, and works to obtain health insurance covering this disease. It also has created a consumer pressure group to get government funding for research.

National Information Clearinghouse on Children Who Are Deaf-Blind
U.S. Department of Education
400 Maryland Avenue SW
Washington, DC 20202
(800) USA-LEARN
(800) 438-9376
Web site: http://www.tr.wou.edu/dblink

This information center is supported by the U.S. Department of Education, Office of Special Education Programs. The center provides links to publications as well as state resources concerning children who are deaf-blind.

National Organization for Rare Disorders (NORD)
P.O. Box 8923
New Fairfield, CT 06812
(800) 999-6673
Fax: (203) 746-6927
Web site: http://www.rarediseases.org

NORD offers programs and services for the patient community, the public, physicians, support groups, researchers, and medically related companies. The organization also offers programs that provide assistance to people who need specific prescription drugs but cannot afford them.

National Organization of Parents of Blind Children
1800 Johnson Street
Baltimore, MD 21230
(410) 659-9314
Fax: (410) 685-5653
Web site: http://www.nfb.org/nfb/Parents_and_Teachers.asp

This is a support group of parents and friends of blind children who wish to reach out to each other to give vital encouragement and share information.

National Organization on Fetal Alcohol Syndrome
216 G Street NE
Washington, DC 20002
(202) 785-4585
Fax: (202) 466-6456
Web site: http://www.nofas.org/

This nonprofit organization is dedicated to eliminating birth defects caused by alcohol consumption during pregnancy and improving the quality of life for those individuals and families affected by fetal alcohol syndrome.

National Parent Information Network (NPIN)
ERIC Clearinghouse on Elementary and Early Childhood Education
University of Illinois at Urbana-Champaign
Children's Research Center
51 Gerty Drive
Champaign, IL 61820

(800) 583-4135
Fax: (217) 333-3767
Web site: http://npin.org

NPIN is a project of the ERIC system, which is administered by the National Library of Education in the U.S. Department of Education. Its goal is to provide access to research-based information about the process of parenting and about family involvement in education.

The Future of Children
http://www.futureofchildren.org/pubs-info2825/pubs-info_show.htm?doc_id=72440

The Future of Children is an organization supported through The David and Lucile Packard Foundation. The purpose of the Future of Children is to disseminate timely information on major issues related to children's well-being, with special emphasis on providng objective analysis and evaluation, translating existing knowledge into effective programs and policies, and promoting constructive institutional change. Products such as a bi-annual journal, issue guides and summaries of critical topics and issues are available on the website.

The National Parent Network on Disabilities (NPND)
1130 17th Street NW, Suite 400
Washington, DC 20036
(202) 463-2299
Fax: (202) 463-9403
Web site: http://www.npnd.org

The NPND is a parent network dedicated to providing a national voice for families of children, youth, and adults with disabilities.

National Pediatric and Family HIV Resource Center
University of Medicine and Dentistry of New Jersey
30 Bergen Street ADMC #4
Newark, NJ 07103
(973) 972-0410
(800) 362-0071
Fax: (973) 0399
Web site: http://www.pedhivaids.org

This nonprofit center serves professionals who care for children, adolescents, and families with HIV infections and AIDS. It offers education, consultation, technical assistance, and training for health and social service professionals.

National School Age Alliance (NSACA)
1137 Washington Street
Boston, MA 02124
(617) 298-5012
Fax: (617) 298-5022
Web site: http://www.nsaca.org

Representing an array of public, private, and community-based providers of after-school programs, the NSACA promotes national standards of quality school-age care for children and youth 5–14 years old, grants accreditation to programs meeting the standards, and connects people who work with school-age children and youth in a variety of agencies and settings.

Tuberous Sclerosis Alliance (TS Alliance)
8181 Professional Place, Suite 110
Landover, MD 20785
(301) 459-9888
(800) 225-6872
Fax: (301) 459-0394
Web site: http://www.tsalliance.org/

The TS Alliance provides support to people with tuberous sclerosis and their families, awards grants to researchers, and offers education to the public and professional communities.

Office of Special Education Programs
U. S. Department of Education
400 Maryland Avenue SW
Washington, DC 20202
(800) USA-LEARN
Web site: http://www.ed.gov/about/offices/list/osers/osep/index.html

The Office of Special Education Programs is a component of the Office of Special Education and Rehabilitative Services, which is one of the principal components of the U.S. Department of Education. This organization focuses on the free, appropriate public education of children and youth with disabilities from birth through age twenty-one.

Office of Special Education and Rehabilitative Services
http://www.ed.gov/about/offices/list/osers/news.html

The Office of Special Eucation and Rehabilitative Services offers information, publications, teaching resources and online services.

Osteogenesis Imperfecta Foundation
804 West Diamond Avenue, Suite 210
Gaithersburg, MD 20878
(301) 947-0083
(800) 981-2663
Fax: (301) 947-0456
Web site: http://www.oif.org/tier1/contact.htm

This organization is dedicated to helping people cope with problems associated with osteogenesis imperfecta (OI) and to improve the quality of life for individuals affected by OI through research to find a cure, education, awareness, and mutual support. It provides funding for research and hosts support groups in twenty-one states.

Phoenix Society for Burn Survivors
2153 Wealthy Street SE, #215
East Grand Rapids, MI 49506
(800) 888-BURN (2876)
Web site: http://www.phoenix-society.org

This nonprofit organization provides peer support, education, collaboration, and advocacy for individuals affected by burn injuries.

Spina Bifida Association of America
4590 MacArthur Boulevard NW, Suite 250
Washington, DC 20007
(800) 621-3141
Fax: (202) 944-3285
Web site: http://www.sbaa.org

This association is charged with promoting the prevention of spina bifida and is dedicated to enhancing the lives of all affected. It serves as the national representative of more than seventy chapters.

United Cerebral Palsy Association
1522 K Street NW, #1112
Washington, DC 20005
(800) 872-5827
Web site: http://www.ucpa.org

A national organization whose mission is to serve people with cerebral palsy through programs and research.

U.S. Department of Education
400 Maryland Avenue SW
Washington, DC 20202
(202) 205-9021 (Assistance to States)
(202) 205-9084 (Early Childhood Branch)
(800) USA-LEARN
Web site: http://www.ed.gov

The administration's priorities include national efforts to improve reading and math, reduce class size, strengthen school construction, and promote major initiatives and partnerships for family involvement in education.

U.S. Department of Transportation (DOT)
400 Seventh Street SW
Washington, DC 20590
(202) 366-9305
Web site: http://www.dot.gov

The DOT is charged with providing safe, efficient, accessible, and convenient transportation for all persons within the United States.

World Council for Gifted and Talented Children
Lamar University
P.O. Box 10034
Beaumont, TX 77710
Web site: http://www.worldgifted.org

The purpose of this group is to promote worldwide communication related to gifted and talented children.

ADVOCACY AND LEGAL ASSISTANCE

Association for Retarded Citizens
2709 Avenue E East
Arlington, TX 76011
Web site: http://www.thearc.org

This organization advocates for parents and professionals of children with mental retardation and has local chapters in each state.

Association for the Care of Children's Health (ACCH)
7910 Woodmont Avenue, Suite 300
Bethesda, MD 20814-9635
(301) 654-6549

Advocates for the improvement of child development skills.

Children's Defense Fund (CDF)
25 E Street NW
Washington, DC 20001
(202) 628-8787
Web site: http://www.cdinfo@childrensdefense.org

The CDF's online Parent Resource Network provides access to a variety of national Web sites offering parents information on caring for their children and on getting involved in group efforts to help children in their own communities or states.

Children's Institute International
711 South New Hampshire Avenue
Los Angeles, CA 90005
Web site: http://www.childrensinstitute.org

This private, nonprofit organization works to protect, preserve, and strengthen the family through child abuse prevention and treatment services for high-need, low-resource families, as well as through professional training, research, and advocacy.

Consortium for Citizens with Disabilities
1730 K Street NW, Suite 1212
Washington, DC 20006
(202) 785-3388
Fax: (202) 467-4179
Web site: http://www.c-c-d.org/

This is a coalition of national consumer, advocacy, provider, and professional organizations that advocates on behalf of people of all ages with physical and mental disabilities and their families.

Consumer Information Bureau
445 12th Street SW
Washington, DC 20554
(888) CALL FCC (225-5322)
Web site: http://www.fcc.gov/cib

The bureau provides consumers with disabilities information regarding resolution of their complaints and rights concerning telecommunications.

Council for Exceptional Children (CEC)
Division for Early Childhood
1920 Association Drive
Reston, VA 22091
(703) 620-3660
Web site: http://www.dec-sped.org

The CEC is a nonprofit organization advocating for individuals who work with or on behalf of special-needs children from birth through age eight and their families. It promotes policies and practices that support families and enhance the optimal development of children.

Disabilities Rights Office
Federal Communications Commission (FCC)
445 12th Street SW
Washington, DC 20554
(888) CALLFCC (225-5322)
Web site: http://www.fcc.gov/cib/dro

The FCC's Disabilities Rights Office provides information and technical assistance to consumers, business, and other entities on their rights and responsibilities to provide disability access and to protect consumers with disabilities.

Disability Government
U.S. Department of Justice
P.O. Box 66118
Washington, DC 20035
(800) 514-0301
Web site: http://www.disability.gov

This is a new site created by the Presidential Task Force on Employment of Adults with Disabilities in honor of the tenth anniversary of the signing of the Americans with Disabilities Act. It provides access to resources, services, and information available throughout the federal government.

The National Association of Developmental Disabilities Councils (NADDC)
1234 Massachusetts Ave NW, Suite 103
Washington, DC 20005

(202) 347-1234
Fax: (202) 347-4023
Web site: http://www.nacdd.org/

NADDC advocates and works for change on behalf of people with developmental and other disabilities and their families. It promotes national policy to enhance the quality of life for all people with developmental disabilities.

National Association of Protection and Advocacy Systems (NAPAS)
900 Second Street NE, Suite 211
Washington, DC 20002
(202) 408-9514
Fax: (202) 408-9520
Web site: http://www.iser.com/NAPAS.html

NAPAS works to promote and strengthen the role and performance of its members in providing quality legally based advocacy services.

National Council on Disability
1331 F Street NW, Suite 1050
Washington, DC 20004
(202) 272-2004
Fax: (202) 272-2022
Web site: http://www.ncd.gov

The council is an independent federal agency making recommendation to the president and Congress on issues affecting 54 million Americans with disabilities. Its purpose is to promote policies, programs, practices, and procedures that guarantee equal opportunity for all individuals with disabilities, regardless of the nature of severity of the disability; and to empower individuals with disabilities to achieve economic self-sufficiency, independent living, and inclusion and integration into all aspects of society.

National Information Center for Children and Youth with Disabilities
P.O. Box 1492
Washington, DC 20013-1492
(800) 695-0285
Web site: http://nichcy.org/index.html

This center provides information on disabilities and disability-related issues for families, educators, and other professionals, as well as referrals. Its focus is on children and youth from birth to age twenty-two.

National Maternal and Child Health Clearinghouse (NMCHC)
2070 Chain Bridge Road, Suite 450
Vienna, VA 22182
(703) 821-8955, ext. 254
Web site: web site under construction

The NMCHC produces and disseminates educational materials to the public.

Office for Dispute Resolution
6340 Flank Drive
Harrisburg, PA 17112
Web site: http://odr.pattan.net/about/default.aspx

The Office for Dispute Resolution (ODR) is funded through the Pennsylvania Department of Education. It is responsible for the operation and management of Pennsylvania's Education and Gifted Education Dispute Resolution System. The ODR provides to parents of gifted children, children with special needs, and the agencies which serve them, opportunities to resolve educational disputes

Office of Program Compliance and Disability Rights
Office of Fair Housing and Equal Opportunity
U.S. Department of Housing and Urban Development
451 7th Street S.W. Room 5242
Washington, DC 20410
800-669-9777 (voice)
800-927-9275 (TTY)
www.fairhousingfirst.org

Complaints, violations and questions regarding the Fair Housing Act may be reported to this office. Additionally, the Department of Justice can file cases involving a pattern or practice of discrimination. The Fair Housing Act may also be enforced through private lawsuits.

Stand For Children
1834 Connecticut Avenue NW
Washington, DC 20009
(800) 663-4032
Fax: (202) 234-0217
Web site: http://www.stand.org

Stand For Children identifies, trains, and connects local children's activists engaging in advocacy, awareness-raising, and service initiatives on an ongoing basis.

U.S. Department of Health and Human Services
Administration of Children, Youth, and Families
Child Care Bureau
330 C Street SW
Washington, DC 20447
(202) 690-6782
Web site: http://www.hhs.gov/

The Child Care Bureau examines child care as an essential support to low-income families in achieving economic self-sufficiency while balancing work and family life. It has funded two waves of research partnerships with state child care agencies; university research teams; national, state, and local child care resource and referral networks; providers and parents; professional organizations; and businesses.

U.S. Department of Health and Human Services
Health Finder Information Center
PO Box 1133
Washington, DC 20012
Web site: http://www.healthfinder.gov
The Health Finder Information Center provides information on a topic from an alphabetized list. It provides a guide for each topic regarding health information. This site is sponsored by the Office of Disease Prevention and Health Promotion.

U.S. Department of Justice
Civil Rights Division
Office of the Americans with Disabilities Act
P.O. Box 66118
Washington, DC 20035-6118
(800) 514-0301 (Voice)
(800) 514-0383 (TDD)
Web site: http://www.usdoj.gov

The Department of Justice has an office to provide information about the Americans with Disabilities Act (ADA) to businesses, state and local governments, and individuals. It answers questions concerning specific ADA requirements, including questions about the ADA Standards for Accessible Design, provides free ADA materials, and explains how to file a complaint.

U.S. Equal Employment Opportunity Commission (EEOC)
1801 L Street NW
Washington, DC 20507
(202) 663-4900
(202) 663-4494) (TTY)
(800) 669-4000
Web site: http://www.eeoc.gov

The EEOC is an independent federal agency originally created by Congress in 1964 to enforce Title VII of the Civil Rights Act of 1964. It provides informational materials and assistance to individuals and entities concerning rights and responsibilities under EEOC enforced laws. Most materials and assistance are provided to the public at no cost.

Zero to Three
National Center for Infants, Toddlers, and Families
734 15th Street NW, Suite 1000
Washington, DC 20005
(202) 638-1144
Web site: http://www.zerotothree.org

This national nonprofit organization was founded by pediatricians, child development specialists, and researchers in 1977 to promote the healthy social, emotional, and intellectual development of babies and toddlers by supporting and strengthening families, communities, and those who work on their behalf.

FREE MEDICAL SERVICES

Alexander Graham Bell Association for the Deaf
3417 Volta Place NW
Washington, DC 20007
(202) 337-5220
Web site: http://www.agbell.org

Provides financial aid to the parents of severely to profoundly hearing-impaired infants enrolled in preschool.

American Amputee Foundation—Give a Limb Program
P.O. Box 250218, Hillcrest Station
Little Rock, AR 72225
(501) 666-2523)

Prostheses available.

Children's Hope Foundation: Childcare Necessities Program
295 Lafayette, Suite 801
New York, NY 10012
(212) 941-7432

Provides vital equipment such as strollers, cribs, diapers, and beds to children who are infected with HIV or have AIDS.

Deborah Heart and Lung Association
Department of Pediatric Cardiology
200 Trenton Road
Brown Mills, NJ 08015
(609) 735-2923

Cardiac surgery.

Disabled Children's Relief Fund
50 Harrison Avenue
Freeport, NY 11520
(516) 377-1605

Assistive devices/equipment and rehabilitative services.

Gift of Life
P.O. Box 776
Middle Island, NY 11953
(516) 924-4434

Cardiac surgery.

Hear Now
9745 East Hampden Avenue, Suite 300
Denver, CO 80231
(800) 648-4327

Provides hearing aids to doctors, who will prescribe and fit them to needy patients.

Hearing Aid Foundation
c/o National Hearing Aid Society
20361 Middlebelt Road
Livonia, MI 48152
(313) 478-2610

Hearing aids.

Miracle Ear Children's Foundation
P.O. Box 59261
Minneapolis, MN 55459
(800) 234-5422

Hearing aids. Money is sent directly to vendor.

Operation Smile
717 Boush Street
Norfolk, VA 23510
(804) 625-0375

For children with craniofacial abnormalities, burns, and orthopedic impairments.

Pharmaceutical Manufacturers Association
(800) 762-4636

Free medications.

Shriners Hospitals for Crippled Children
P.O. Box 31356
Tampa, FL 33631
(800) 237-5055

For children with burns or orthopedic impairments.

St. Jude Children's Research Hospital
332 North Lauderdale
Memphis, TN 38105
(901) 495-3300

Cancer treatment for children (birth–18 years of age) who are newly diagnosed. Referring physician should call.

FEDERAL ASSISTANCE

Medicaid
800-MEDICARE
www.cms.hhs.gov

Medicaid is a government assistance program that pays for a range of medical services for persons with low income and resources. There are income and other eligibility requirements.

Supplemental Security Income (SSI)
800-772-1213
www.ssa.gov

SSI consists of monthly cash benefits to low-income families having a child with a disability. Not all children with disabilities will qualify. You should obtain as much detailed medical and social/emotional documentation as possible before applying. If denied, file for a hearing. With the denial letter, information will be provided about the hearing process. Legal Aid can assist the family with this process.

FRATERNAL ORGANIZATIONS

The following charitable organizations maintain local chapters throughout the nation. They often will consider assisting families in need who live in their geographic area. It is always best to contact your local branch, which can be accessed through the national office.

Elks
2750 North Lakeview Avenue
Chicago, IL 60614
(312) 477-2750

Kiwanis International
3636 Woodview Trace
Indianapolis, IL 46268
(317) 875-8755

Lions Club
300 22nd Street
Oakbrook, IL 60521
(708) 571-5466

Rotary Club
1560 Sherman Avenue
Evanston, IL 60201
(708) 866-3000

WISH ORGANIZATIONS

Wish granting organizations most often only consider children who have life-threatening conditions, but not always! It never hurts to contact them.

A Special Wish Foundation
2244 South Hamilton Road, Suite 202
Columbus, OH 43232
(614) 575-9474

A Wish With Wings
P.O. Box 3479
Arlington, TX 76007
(817) 469-9474

Children's Hopes and Dreams Foundation
280 Route 46
Dover, NJ 07801
(201) 361-7348

Children's Wish Foundation International
7840 Roswell Road, Suite 301
Atlanta, GA 30350
(800) 323-9474

Dream Factory
315 Guthrie Green
Louisville, KY 40202
(800) 456-7556

Friends of Karen
P.O. Box 190, 118 Titicus Road
Purdys, NY 10578
(914) 277-4547

Give Kids the World
210 South Bass Road
Kissimmee, FL 34746
(407) 396-1114

Make a Wish Foundation
85 Old Shore Road
Port Washington, NY 11050
(212) 505-9474

The Marty Lyons Foundation, Inc.
333 Earle Ovington Boulevard, Suite 600
Mitchel Field, NY
(516) 745-8966

Rainbows Hope, Inc./Wish Is Granted Foundation
48 Heinz Avenue
Staten Island, NY 10308
(718) 317-9078

Starlight Foundation
1560 Broadway, Suite 402
New York, NY 10036
(212) 354-2878

Sunshine Foundation
P.O. Box 255
Loughman, FL 33858
(800) 457-1976

Wish Is Granted
43 West Main Street
Smithtown, NY 11787
(800) 357-9229

FREE MEDICAL AIR TRANSPORTATION

The following organizations provide free air transportation for appointments with medical specialists. Call for details. You can also contact the National Patient Air Transport Hotline at (800) 296-1217, which will refer you to the best type of transportation for your need.

Air Care Alliance
P.O. Box 1940
Manassas, VA 22110
(800) 296-1217

Air Life Line
6133 Freeport Boulevard
Sacramento, Ca 95822
(800) 446-1231

American Airlines—Miles for Kids
P.O. Box 619688, Mail Drop 1396
Dallas–Fort Worth, TX 75261
(817) 963-8118

Angel Planes
2756 North Green Valley Parkway, #115
Green Valley, NV 89014
(800) 359-1711

Care Force
P.O. Box 3816
Humble, TX 77347
(713) 438-0376

Corporate Angel Network
Westchester City Airport, Building 1
Westchester, NY 10604
(914) 328-1313

TRANSPORTATION FOR CANCER PATIENTS AND DONORS

Lifeline Pilots
1028 East Avenue South
Oak Park, IL 60304
(217) 373-4195

Roads to Recovery
2516 Wilkins Avenue
Baltimore, MD 21223
(410) 945-6761

Volunteer Pilots Association
P.O. Box 95, 100 Main Street
Hickory, PA 15340
(412) 356-4007

Wings for Children
20th and Smallman Street, Second Floor
Pittsburgh, PA 15222

Wings of Mercy
A-5006 146 Avenue
Holland, MI 49423
(616) 396-1077

Chapter Eight
Selected Print and Nonprint Resources

BOOKS AND CD-ROMS

Adapting Instruction to Accommodate Students in Inclusive Settings by Judy W. Wood

Adaptive Play for Special Needs Children: Strategies to Enhance Communication and Learning, by C. R. Musselwhite (Borgo Press, 1991)
Order from:
Exceptional Parent Magazine
555 Kinderkamack Road
Aradell, NJ 07649
(201) 634-6550

Provides ideas for adaptive play activities for special needs children to reinforce communication and learning.

ADD/Adhd Behavior-Change Resource Kit: Ready-To-Use Strategies and Activities for Helping Children with Attention Deficit Disorder by Grad L. Flick

ADHD Handbook for Families: A Guide to Communicating with Professionals, by Paul L. Weingartner (Child Welfare League of America, 1999)

Offers families who have a child with ADHD real-life strategies and techniques that can be useful to their everyday existence.

Alternative Approaches to the Definition and Identification of Learning Disabilities: Some Questions and Answers by Jack Fletcher, Alan Coulter, Daniel Reschly and Sharon Vaughn. Published in Annals of Dyslexia.

Provides information regarding adequate instruction for students with LD, identification, and assessments that are directly related to instruction.

A Survival Kit for the Special Education Teacher by Roger Pierangelo.

A Parent's Guide to Response to Intervention by National Center for Learning Disabilities.

A Parent's guide to Response to Intervention describes the response to intervention process and answers questions parents and teachers may have about it.

Asperger Syndrome, by Ami Klin, Fred R. Volkmar, and Sara S. Sparrow, eds. (Guilford Press, 2000)

Discusses Asperger Syndrome and brings together scholars and practitioners to offer current research and information significant in this new field regarding Asperger Syndrome. It provides additional information with regard to clinical practice.

Assessing Students with Special Needs, by John J. Venn (Prentice-Hall, 1999)

Provides comprehensive coverage of assessment principles and practices for understanding how to work with individuals who have mild, moderate, and severe disabilities.

Assistive Technology in Special Education: Policy and Practice, by Diane Golden (Council for Exceptional Children, Council of Administrators of Special Education, Technology and Media Division, 1998)

Provides an overview of the critical policy and practice issues facing education in the area of assistive technology (AT) and discusses the emerging policy directives and best practices for service delivery in a way that is supportive of quality AT programs in schools.

Behavioral Intervention for Young Children with Autism: A Manual for Parents and Professionals, by Catherine Maurice, Stephen C. Luce, and Gina Green, eds. (PRO-ED International Publisher, 1996)

Provides information concerning effective treatment strategies for young children with autism.

Characteristics of and Strategies for Teaching Students with Mild Disabilities, by Martin Henley, Roberta S. Ramsey, and Robert F. Algozzine (Allyn and Bacon, 1998)

Written by experts in the field who have produced other important works regarding children with disabilities, this is intended for undergraduate and graduate students majoring in either general or special education. The authors provide a comprehensive overview of educational practices influencing the identification, placement, and teaching of students with mild disabilities.

The Child with Special Needs: Encouraging Intellectual and Emotional Growth, by Stanley I. Greenspan, Robin Siomon, and Serena Wieder (Addison Wesley Longman, 1997)

Provides information to parents concerning ways of helping special needs children.

The Classroom Observer: Developing Observation Skills in Early Childhood Settings, by Ann E. Boehm and Richard A. Weinberg (Teachers College Press, 1996)

Emphasizes early childhood and focuses on those skills that will enable the observer to make appropriate, valid inferences and to arrive at decisions based on objective observational data gathering in natural learning environments and diverse educational settings.

Collaboration: A Success Strategy for Special Educators, by Sharon F. Cramer (Allyn and Bacon, 1998)

A book for educators who would like to improve their skills by collaborating with other educators.

Collaboration for Inclusive Education: Developing Successful Programs, by Chriss Walther-Thomas, Lori Korinek, Virginia L. McLaughlin, and Brenda Toler Williams (Allyn and Bacon, 2000)

Teaches professionals how to work with others to develop education programs for students with special learning needs.

Complete Guide to Special Education Transition Services: Ready-to-Use Help and Materials for Succcessful Transitions from School to Adulthood by Roger Peirangelo, and Rochelle Crane.

The Complete Learning Disabilities Handbook: Ready-To-UseTechniques for Teaching Learning-Handicapped Students by Joan M. Harwell.

The Complete IEP Guide: How to Advocate for Your Special Ed Child, by Lawrence M. Siegel; edited by Marcia Stewart (Nolo Press, 1997)

A research book for learning how to advocate for children with special needs.

Consultation, Collaboration, and Teamwork for Students with Special Needs, by Peggy Dettmer, Norma Dyck, and Linda P. Thurston (Allyn and Bacon, 1999)

Explains the roles and responsibilities of collaborative school consultants in providing for the needs of students with special needs.

Controversial Issues Confronting Special Education: Divergent Perspectives, by William Stainback and Susan Stainback (Allyn and Bacon, 1995)

Perspectives on hot issues in special education.

Creative Play Activities for Children with Disabilities, by Lisa Rappaport Morris and Linda Schulz (Redleaf Press, 1989)

Order from:
Redleaf Press
450 North Syndicate, Suite 5
St. Paul, MN 55104
(800) 423-8309

The authors suggest a variety of activities and include directions, a list of equipment needed, an explanation of the benefits of the activity, and possible adaptations for children with particular disabilities

The Child with Special Needs: Encouraging Intellectural and Emotional Growth by Stanley I. Greenspan, Serena Weider, and Robin Simon (Contributor).

The Demise of IQ Testing for Children with Learning Disabilities (2002) by Robert Pasternak.

The author describes the "fallacies of the IQ-Achievent Discrepancy Model and explains that this is not a valied way to identify individuals with LD. He reports that eliminating IQ tests may shift the emphasis away from eligibility and toward interventions that children need.

Developing and Implementing Individualized Education Programs by Bonnie B. Strickland, Ann P. Turnbull, and Bonnie R. Strickland.

Different Road to Learning

Online catalog and store offering more than 300 books, flashcards, videos and more, including ABA and Verbal Behavior materials. www.difflearn.com

The Survival Guide for Parents of Gifted Kids: How to Understand, Live With, and Stick Up for Your Gifted Child by Sally Yahnke Walker and Susan K. Perry.

Driven to Distaction: Recognizing and Coping with Attention Deficit Disorder from Childhood Through Adulthood by Edward M. Hallowell & John J. Ratey

Early Warning System (2001) by G. R. Lyon and Jack Fletcher.

The authors describe three factors that led to a dramatic increase in children identified with LD. The make a case for implementing effective early intervention programs.

Education Week

Digital Directions Trends and Advice for K-12 Technology Leaders www.digitaldirections.org

Educational Care: A System for Understanding and Helping Children with Learning Problems at Home and in School, by Melvin D. Levine (Educators Publishing Service, 1998)

Topics regarding curriculum and testing tools to assist teachers who serve special needs children.

Emotional and Behavioral Disorders: Theory and Practice by Margaret Cecil Coleman, and David S. Coleman

Exceptional Children and Youth by Norris G. Haring, Linda McCormick, and Thomas G. Haring.

Exceptional Learners: Introduction to Special Education, by Daniel P. Hallahan and James M. Kauffman (Allyn and Bacon, 1999)

Written by authors with great experience in the publication of special education texts, this is a general introduction to the characteristics of exceptional persons and their education.

Final Gifts: Understanding the Special Awareness, Needs, and Communications of the Dying, by Maggie Callanan and Patricia Kelly (Bantam Doubleday Dell Publishing Group, 1997)

Advice for family members and professionals regarding death awareness.

Financial Aid for the Disabled and Their Families, by Gail Ann Schlachter and R. David Weber (Reference Service Press, 1998)
Order from:
Reference Service Press
1100 Industrial Road, Suite 9
San Carlos, CA 94070
(415) 594-0411

A reference book that provides information concerning foundations, scholarships, and assistance for the disabled and their families.

The Gift of Dyslexia: Why Some of the Smartest People Can't Read and How They Can Learn, by Ronald D. Davis, with Eldon M. Braun (Berkley Publishing Group, 1997)

The author discusses his own experience with dyslexia and provides a plan as to how readers can help themselves overcome the disability.

The Gifted Kids' Survival Guide: For Ages 10 and Under, by Judy Galbraith, Pamela Espeland, and Albert Molnar (Free Spirit Publishing, 1998)

Designed for young children, this book explains giftedness and provides encouragement.

Guide to Writing Quality Individualized Education Programs: What's Best for Students with Disabilities, by Gordon S. Gibb and Tina Taylor Dyches (Allyn and Bacon, 1999)

A guide for professionals that provides information for enhancing IEP writing skills.

Guiding the Gifted Child: A Practical Source for Parents and Teachers by James T. Webb, Elizabeth A. Meckstroth, and Stephanie S. Tolan (Contributor).

Holler if You Hear Me: The Education of a Teacher and His Students, by Gregory Michie (Teachers College Press, Teachers College, Columbia University, 1999)

Provides information concerning different teaching styles and stresses teacher/student involvement.

How Students Learn: Reforming Schools through Learner-Centered Education, by Nadine M. Lambert and Barbara L. McCombs, eds. (American Psychological Association, 1997)

Examines current research on how students learn and presents the theoretical perspectives and research findings of leading authors in educational psychology.

How to Get Services by Being Assertive, by Charlotte Des Jardins (1998)

Order from:
Family Resource Center on Disabilities
20 East Jackson Boulevard, Room 900
Chicago, IL 60604
(313) 939-3513

A handbook on assertive communication techniques for parents and professionals.

How to Reach and Teach ADD/ADHD Children: Practical Techniques, Strategies, and Interventions for Helping Children with Attention Problems and Hyperactivity, by Sandra Rief (Center for Applied Research in Education, 1995)

Provides information for professionals concerning techniques, strategies, and interventions for reaching and teaching children with attention problems and hyperactivity.

Human Exceptionality: Society, School, and Family, by Michael L. Hardman, Clifford J. Drew, and M. Winston Egan (Allyn and Bacon, 1999)

Focuses on the challenges that individuals with exceptionalities face on a daily basis.

The Inclusive Classroom: Strategies for Effective Instruction, by Margo A. Mastropierie and Thomas E. Scruggs (Prentice-Hall, 1999)

Focuses on inclusive teaching ideas and lessons with curriculum and instructional strategy implications in content areas for children in the K–12 teaching experience.

Inclusive High Schools: Learning from Contemporary Classrooms, by Douglas Fisher, Caren Sax, and Ian Pumpian (Paul H. Brooks Publishing, 1999)

This text provides a framework for developing inclusive high schools and addresses processes and outcomes. Issues include building school-based relationships, developing support strategies, communicating responsibilities, preparing for the classroom, establishing continuity, planning lessons and adapting curricula, and redistributing school resources.

Infant Development and Risk: An Introduction, by Anne H. Widerstrom, Barbara A. Mowder, and Susan R. Sandall (Paul H. Brookes Publishing, 1997)

This book provides a comprehensive overview of typical and atypical infant development while explaining key assessment issues and intervention programs.

Interprofessional Collaboration in Schools: Practical Action in the Classroom, by Mark P. Mostert (Allyn and Bacon, 1998)

Practical information for teachers to use in the classroom. Teaching collaboration between students is stressed.

Introduction to Learning Disabilities by Daniel P. Hallahan, James M. Kauffman, and John Lloyd

Introduction to Special Education: Teaching in an Age of Challenge, by Deborah Deutsch Smith (Prentice Hall, 1997)

Discusses insight to important issues in special education.

The K & W Guide to Colleges for Students with Learning Disabilities or Attention Deficit Disorders: A Resource Book for Students, Parents, and Professionals, by Marybeth Kravets (Random House, 1999)

A resource book that provides information concerning college-level programs and services for the learning disabled.

The Language of Toys: Teaching Communication Skills to Special Needs Children, by S. Schwartz and J. E. Heller Miller (1998)
Order from:
Exceptional Parent Magazine
Dept. EPCAT2, P.O. Box 8045
Brick, NJ 08723
(800) 535-1910

Teaches parents how to improve their child's communication skills at home with fun exercises.

Learning to Read and Write: Developmentally Appropriate Practices for Young Children, by Susan B. Neuman, Carol Copple, and Sue Bredekamp (National Association for Education, 2000)

Focuses on research-based strategies for children's learning in elementary and infant and toddler classrooms. Classroom photos and children's work accompany innovative ideas for teachers to help young children progress in their reading and writing competence.

Life Skills Activities for Special Children by Darlene Mannix

Making a Difference: Advocacy Competencies for Special Education Professionals, by Craig R. Fiedler (Allyn and Bacon, 2000)

A source on the role and responsibilities of special education professionals as advocates for children with disabilities.

Meeting the Needs of Students with Special Physical and Health Care Needs by Jennifere Leigh Hill, and Ann Castel Davis.

Models of Collaboration, by Mary E. Fishbaugh (Allyn and Bacon, 1997)

Collaboration models such as consulting, coaching, and teaming are discussed.

Mrs. Jeepers in Outer Space (Adventures of the Bailey School Kids Series), by Debbie Dadey and John Steven Gurney (Scholastic, 1999)

A children's book that focuses on how children can deal with fear and insecurities through the use of an interesting and easy-to-read narrative.

On Babies and Bathwater: Addressing the Problems of Identification of Learning Disabilities (2002) by Thomas E. Scruggs, and Margo A. Mastropieri.

This article reviews problems in identifying learning disabilities and proposed alternatives to current procedures. The authors argue that the proposed alternatives do not meet all necessary criteria for identifying LD.

Peterson's Colleges: With Programs for Students with Learning Disabilities or Attention Deficit Disorders, by Charles T. Mangrum and Stephen Strichart, eds. (Peterson's, 1997)

A directory that provides information about programs and services for college students with learning disabilities.

Physical, Sensory, and Health Disabilities: An Introduction, by Frank G. Bowe (Prentice-Hall, 1999)

This text covers all major disability areas and presents material on barriers that can hinder a full and rewarding life. It focuses on the delivery of services to children and individuals with disabilities.

Response to Intervention: Guidelines for Parents and Practitioners, by James Hale, (n.d.)

This publication presents guidelines for parents and practitioners who would like to know more about identifying intervention for children with disabilities.

Response to Intervention (RTI): A Primer for Parents, by Mary Beth Klotz and Andrea Canter.

Response to Instruction in the Identification of Learning Disabilities: A Guide for School Teams. (2004) by Joseph Kovaleski and David Prasse. Published in NASP Communique, 32 (5).

The authors explain why response to intervention is a promising alternative to the traditional IQ- achievement discrepancy model for identifying students with learning disabilities and improving classroom instruction in general education.

Responsiveness to Intervention: A Blueprint for Practitioners, Policymakers, and Parents in Teaching Exceptional Children by Douglas Fuchs and Lynn S. Fuchs (2001).

Describes a "three-tier" system (beginning in general education and ending in special education) that serves the early intervention and disability identification objectives of RBI. The focus is on standard tutoring protocols, not "problem solving model," because available scientific research supports this approach.

Responsiveness to Intervention: A New Method of Identifying Students with Disabilities by Douglas Fuchs, Lynn Fuchs, Donald Compton, Joan Bryant and National Research Center on Learning Disabilities (2005).

Responsiveness to Intervention & Learning Disabilities (2005) by National Joint Committee on Learning Disabilities.

Examines concepts, potential benefits, practical issues, and questions about responsiveness to intervention (RTI) and learning disabilities (LD). Includes questions about implementation, eligibility, parent participation, structure and components, professional roles and competencies, and needed research.

Restructuring for Caring and Effective Education: Piecing the Puzzle Together, by Richard A. Villa and Jacqueline S. Thousand, eds. (Paul H. Brookes Publishing, 1999)

Reexamines the purposes of schooling and the rationalities for inclusive schooling.

Rethinking Learning Disabilities (2001) by G. R. Lyon, J. M. Fletcher, S. E. Shaywitz, B. A. Shaywitz, J. K. Torgesen, F. B. Wood, et al. Washington, DC: Thomas Fordham Founation.

Describes reasons to reject the IQ-achievement discrepancy models. Discrepancy models delay classification until the child is in 3rd or 4th grade when academic achievement problems are more difficult to resolve. The IQ-achievement discrepancy is not related to decisions about intervention methods, goals, or results.

Savage Inequalities: Children in America's Schools, by Jonathan Kozol (Harper Trade, 1992)

Describes and provides insight into the classrooms of the minority poor.

The Learning Mystique: A Critical Look at "Learning Disabilities by Gerald Coles.

In this book Gerald Coles asserts that there are partisan agendas behind the educational policy-makers and that the scientific research that they use to support their arguments regarding the teaching of literacy are flawed. These include the idea that there are neurological exp;anations for learning disabilities.

The Self-Help Sourcebook: Finding and Forming Mutual Aid Self Help Groups, by Barbara White (1995)
Order from:
American Self-Help Clearinghouse
Northwest Covenant Medical Center
Denville, NJ 07834
(201) 625-7101

A directory of over 700 groups that offer support and information about particular issues and concerns.

Skills for Success: A Career Education Handbook for Children and Adolescents with Visual Impairments, by Karen E. Wolffee, ed. (American Foundation for the Blind, 1999)

Written to establish a foundation that will enable children with visual impairments to compete and cooperate with sighted children, this book provides practical learning experiences in the environments that children frequent: school, home, and community. Topics include career education, high expectations, socialization, compensatory skills, and realistic feedback.

Social Skills Activities for Special Children by Darlene Mannix

Songs in Sign, by S. Harold Collins; illustrated by Kathy Kifer and Dahna Sola (Garlic Press, 1995)

Provides six songs in signed English with easy-to-follow illustrations.

Special Education Resources on the Internet (SERI)
http://www.seriweb.com/

Special Education Resources on the Internet (SERI) is a collection of Internet accessible information resources of interest to those involved in the fields related to Special Education.

The Special Education Yellow Pages, by Roger Pierangelo and Rochelle Crane (Prentice-Hall, 1999)

A resource guide for finding information on organizations, specific disabilities, web sites, professional organizations, books, materials, laws and legal issues, federal agencies, university libraries, transportation issues, computer and technology resources, free materials, employment issues, and much more.

Staff Development: The Key to Effective Gifted Education Programs, by Peggy Dettmer, and Mary Landrum, eds. (Kentucky Department of Education Middle School Initiative, 1998)

Guides the reader through the process of staff development—from organizing, planning, and conducting to following up. By learning skills as staff developers, education professionals can help teachers adopt more accepting and facilitative attitudes toward highly able students.

Supporting Children with Communication Difficulties in Inclusive Settings: School-Based Language Intervention by Linda McCormick, Diane Frome Loeb (Contributor), and Richard L. Schiefelbusch (Contributor).

The Survival Guide for Parents of Gifted Kids: How to Understand, Live with, and Stick up for Your Gifted Child, by Sally Yahnke Walker (Free Spirit Publishing, 1991)

An easy-to-understand approach to some of the problems faced by parents of gifted children.

Tax Guide for Parents, by Family Resource Center on Disabilities (1999)
Order from:
The Connecticut Association for Children with Learning Disabilities
18 Marshall Street
South Norwalk, CT 06854
(203) 838-5010

Provides information and helpful tips as to accounting for purchases and expenses related to special-needs children.

Teacher Unions and TQE (Total Quality Education): Building Quality Labor Relations, by William A. Streshly and Todd A. DeMitchell (Corwin Press, 1994)

An overview of the educational labor movement, principles in union relations, the ins and outs of collective bargaining, and the transition of unionism.

Teaching Gifted Kids in the Regular Classroom: Strategies and Techniques Every Teacher Can Use to Meet the Academic Needs of the Gifted and Talented, by Susan Winebrenner and Pamela Espeland, eds. (Free Spirit Publishing, 2000)

A resource book for parents and teachers of gifted children who are in the regular classroom.

Teaching Kids with Learning Difficulties in the Regular Classroom: Strategies and Techniques Every Teacher Can use to Challenge and Motivate Struggling Students by Susan Winebrenner, and Pamela Espeland (Editor).

Teaching Study Skills and Strategies to Students with learning Disabilities, Attention Deficit Disorders, or Special Needs by Stephen S. Strichart, Patricia Iannuzzi, and Charles T. Mangrum,

The ABCs of Learning Disabilities by Bernice y. L. Wong

The Exceptional Student in the Regular Classroom by Bill R. Gearheart, Mel W. Weishahn and Carol J. Gearheart.

The Tool Kit on Teaching and Assessing Students with Disabilities

Provides up-to-date guidance on assessing the achievement and progress of special education students. It also includes a series of technical assistance products that offer practical, research-based approaches to the challenges schools are facing in instruction, assessment, accommodations and behavioral interventions. This colorful publication is complete with charts, tables and illustrations . The Tool Kit on Teaching and Assessing Students with Disabilities is a joint effort of the Office of Elementary and Secondary Education and the Office of Special Education and Rehabilitative Services. Free copies may be downloaded at www.osepideasthatwork.org and ordered on CD-ROM by calling 1-877—4ED-PUBS wutg udebtufucatuib bynber EH/e0110C, while supplies last.

Technology Cooperation Vital in Special Education by Michell R. Davis (2008)
Education Week's Digital Directions
Assistive Technology—Helping Students with Disabilities, Winter 2008
www.digitaldirections.org

Toy Resource List, by Colleen Roth (Toledo Association for the Blind, 1993)
Order from:
Network on the Blind Multiple-Handicapped Child/Adult
1912 Tracy Road
Northwood, OH 43619
(419) 666-6212

Toys are listed by developmental age and are chosen for durability.

Toys "R" Us Toy Guide for Differently Abled Kids! (1999; updated regularly)
Order from:
Toys "R" Us
P.O. Box 8501
Nevada, IA 50201

Toys are categorized by skill (gross motor, fine motor, tactile, visual, language, social, etc.).

Transdisciplinary Play-Based Intervention (TPBI) Guidelines for Developing a Meaningful Curriculum for Young Children, by Toni W. Linder (Paul H. Brookes Publishing, 1993)

This guide offers individualized play-based intervention activities for young children in home-and center-based environments.

Understanding Responsiveness to Intervention in Learning Disabilities Determination by Daryl Mellard and the National Research Center on Learning Disabilities.

An excellent article that describes core features of RTI including the use of assessment to match students with appropriate instruction.

What's Best for Matthew? Interactive CD-ROM Case Study for Learning to Develop Individualized Education Programs, by M. Winston Egan (Allyn and Bacon, 2001)
Helps preservice and inservice teachers develop IEP writing skills.

A Work in Progress: Behavior Management Strategies and a Curriculum for Intensive Behavioral Treatment of Autism, by John McEachin, Ron Leaf, Marlene Boehm, and Jamison Day Harsh (Different Roads to Learning, 1999)
The authors use applied behavioral analysis (ABA) to suggest individualized programs and curricula for teaching skills to autistic children.

Young Children with Special Needs by Warren Umansky, Stephen R. Hooper and Nancy H. Young.

GUIDES AND REFERENCE MATERIALS

The Americans with Disabilities Act: A Guide for People with Disabilities, Their Families, and Advocates (1993)
Order from:
Pacer Center
4826 Chicago Avenue South
Minneapolis, MN 55417
(612) 827-2966

Drugs, Alcohol, and Other Addictions: A Directory of Treatment Centers and Prevention Programs Nationwide
Order from:
The Oryx Press
2214 North Central at Encanto
Phoenix, AZ 85004

Early Warning, Timely Response: A Guide to Safe Schools
To order, call:
(800) 279-6799
Published by the Office of Special Education and Rehabilitative Services, this guide helps school personnel, parents, community members, and others identify early indicators of problems within the school setting.

Financial Aid for the Disabled and Their Families by Gail Ann Schlachter and R. David Weber (1995)
Order from:
Reference Service Press
1100 Industrial Road, Suite 9
San Carlos, CA 94070

How to Get Services by Being Assertive by Charlotte Des Jardins (1993)
Order from:
Family Resource Center on Disabilities

20 East Jackson Boulevard, Room 900
Chicago, IL 60604

A handbook on assertive communication techniques for parents and professionals.

Parents Guide to the Internet
Order from:
U.S. Department of Education
Office of Educational Research and Improvement
Media and Information Services
555 New Jersey Avenue NW
Washington, DC 20208
(800) USA-Learn

The full text of this publication also is available on-line at the department's home page (see Web Directories in this chapter).

The Self-Help Sourcebook: Finding and Forming Mutual Aid Self-Help Groups (1995)
Order from:
American Self-Help Clearinghouse
Northwest Covenant Medical Center
Denville, NJ 07834
(201) 625-7101

JOURNALS AND MAGAZINES

American Journal on Mental Retardation
1719 Kalorama Road NW
Washington, DC 20009

A bimonthly publication by the AAMR, this journal publishes studies and discussions dealing with behavioral and biological aspects of mental retardation.

Behavioral Residential Treatment
605 Third Avenue
New York, NY 10158

Quarterly reports of behavioral treatment programs.

British Journal of Learning Disabilities
http://www.blackwellpublishing.com/journal.asp?ref=1354-4187&site=1 (electronic

British Journal of Special Education
http://www.blackwellpublishing.com/submit.asp?ref=0952-3383&site=1 (electronic

Career Development for Exceptional Individuals
Division on Career Development, CEC
1920 Association Drive
Reston, VA 22091

Published semi-annually with a focus in vocational, residential, and leisure activities for children and adults with disabilities.

Child Abuse & Neglect, The International Journal
Elsevier, Inc.
655 Avenue of the Americas
New York, NY 10011
(212) 633-3950

Published monthly.

Childhood Education
Association for Childhood Education International
17904 Georgia Avenue, Suite 215
Olney, MD 20832
(301) 570-2111

Published six times a year. Articles related to infancy through early adolescence.

Clinical Child Psychology and Psychiatry
http://ccp.sagepub.com/ (electronic)

Day Care and Early Education
Behavioral Publications
72 Fifth Avenue
New York, NY 10016

Published bimonthly, directed at day care personnel focusing on new ideas for educating preschool children.

Developmental Neurorehabilitation
http://www.informaworld.com/smpp/title-content=t713695358-db=all (electronic)

Disability & Society
http://www.informaworld.com/smpp/title-content=t713393838-db=all (electronic)

eSchool News
7920 Norfolk Avenue
Suite 900
Bethesda, MD 20814
1-800-394-0115
http://www.eschoolnews.com/

eSchool News Online connects you to all the latest news, information, and resources on how today's K-20 educators are using technology to improve management and student learning.

Early Childhood Education Journal
Human Sciences Press, Inc.
233 Spring Street
New York, NY 10013

Published quarterly. A professional publication of original peer-reviewed articles, both invited and unsolicited, that reflect exemplary practices in the rapidly changing field of contemporary early childhood education.

Early Childhood Research & Practice
Web site: http://ecrp.uiuc.edu/

An Internet journal on the development, care, and education of young children.

Early Childhood Research Quarterly
Ablex Publishing Corporation
55 Old Post Road #2
P.O. Box 5297
Greenwich, CT 06831
(203) 661-7602

Quarterly publication. Includes articles presenting significant research and scholarship on all topics related to the care and education of children from birth through eight years.

Education and Training of the Mentally Retarded
Division of Mental Retardation of CEC
1920 Association Drive
Reston, VA 22091

Published four times annually, this journal publishes experimental studies and articles dealing with mental retardation.

Exceptional Parent
Order from:
Council for Exceptional Children
1920 Association Drive
Reston, VA 22091

A monthly magazine for families and professionals.

Gifted Child Quarterly
National Association for Gifted Children
1155 15th Street NW, #1002
Washington, DC 20005

Articles are by both parents and teachers of gifted children.

Gifted Child Today
350 Weinacker Avenue
Mobile, AL 36604

Published six times annually. Ideas and information aimed at parents and teachers of gifted, talented, and creative youngsters.

Gifted International
World Council for Gifted and Talented Children
Dr. Dorothy Sisk, Secretariat

Lamar University
College of Education
P.O. Box 10034
Beaumont, TX 77710

Published semiannually. Devoted to international communication among educators, researchers, and parents.

Holistic Special Education: Camphill Principles and Practice
Robin Jackson, Edinburgh: Florida Books.

Infant Toddler Intervention
Singular Thomson Learning
7625 Empire Drive
Florence, KY 41042

A journal that focuses on the delivery of effective intervention services for children under three years of age.

International Journal of Rehabilitative Research Quarterly
International Society for Rehabilitation of the Disabled
432 Park Avenue South
New York, NY 10016

A quarterly publication that focuses on rehabilitation of the disabled.

Journal of Applied Research in Intellectual Disabilties
http://www.blackwellpublishing.com/submit.asp?ref=1360-2322&site=1 (electronic)
ISSN:1360-2322 (paper) Blackwell Publishing.

Journal of Intellectual Disability Reserch
http://www.blackwellpublishing.com/journal.asp?ref=0964-2633&site=1 (electronic)

Journal of Policy and Practice in Intellectual Disabilities
http://www.blackwellpublishing.com/journal.asp?ref=1741-1122&site=1 (electronic)

Journal for the Education of the Gifted
Association for the Gifted, CEC
1920 Association Drive
Reston, VA 22091

Published quarterly. Presents theoretical, descriptive, and research articles of diverse ideas and points of view on the education of the gifted and talented.

Journal of Creative Behavior
Creative Educational Foundation, Inc.
State University College
1300 Elmwood Avenue
Buffalo, NY 14222

Contains research reports and suggestions to encourage creative behavior in children and adults. Published annually.

Journal of Early Intervention
Division of Early Childhood Education, CEC
1920 Association Drive
Reston, VA 22091

Provides information and research regarding early childhood intervention, education, and strategies.

Journal of Educational Research
Heldref Publications
1319 18th Street NW
Washington, DC 20036
(202) 296-6267

This quarterly publishes articles that describe or synthesize research of direct relevance to educational practice in elementary and secondary schools.

Journal of Special Education
Pro-Ed
8700 Shoal Creek Boulevard
Austin, TX 78757

Published quarterly.

Journal of the International Association of Special Education
IASE, c/o Dr. Ann Wilson
Box 2950
Storm Lake, IA 50588

Published two times a year.

Journal of the National Center for Clinical Infant Programs
P.O. Box 25494
Richmond, VA 23260
(800) 899-4301

Focuses on the first three years of life and of the importance of early intervention and prevention to healthy growth and development.

Journal of Vocational Rehabilitation
Andover Medical Publishers, Inc.
80 Montvale Avenue
Stoneham, MA 02180

This publication concerns itself with vocational rehabilitation issues.

Remedial and Special Education
Pro-Ed
8700 Shoal Creek Boulevard
Austin, TX 78757

Published bimonthly.

Research in Developmental Disabilities
Maxwell House, Fairview Park
Elmsford, NY 10523

Published six times a year by ProgMan Press, this journal focuses on research in developmental disabilities.

Roeper Review
Roeper City and County Schools
2190 North Woodward
Broomfield Hills, MI 48013

Published quarterly. contains articles by teachers, researchers, and students in gifted education.

Topics in Early Childhood Special Education
Pro-Ed
8700 Shoal Creek Boulevard
Austin, TX 78757

Quarterly publication.

The Transdisciplinary Journal
Singular Publishing Group
4284 41st Street
San Diego, CA 92105

Quarterly publication. Provides members of the early intervention team with information that will enhance the clinical services they provide to infants and toddlers who are at-risk or have disabilities, and their families

Young Children
National Association for the Education of Young Children
1834 Connecticut Avenue NW
Washington, DC 20001

Published bimonthly. Focuses on projects and research in early childhood education.

Young Exceptional Children
Division for Early Childhood, CEC
Executive Office
1444 Wazee Street, Suite 230
Denver, CO 80202
(303) 620-4579

Quarterly publication.

WEB DIRECTORIES

Whenever possible, the following Web sites have been listed according to official site name. A listing of sites specifically helpful for children's advocates can be found at the section's end.

Abcteach:
http://www.abcteach.com
More than 5,000 reproducible pages and worksheets organized by subject area; formats for reports, awards, portfolios, flashcards, thematic units and games.

All Kinds of Minds:
www.allkindsofminds.org
A non profit institute for the understanding of differences in learning. Each month the All Kinds of Minds Web site explores different areas of importance to students with learning differences.

American Academy of child and Adolescent Psychiatry:
http://www.aacap.org
Facts for families—information sheets on specific emotional and behavioral challenges (e.g., bipolar disorder, depression, lying, stealing, substance abuse); reviews of popular culture media events (music, books, movies) in light of behavioral and emotional development; related links.

Americans with Disabilities Act (ADA) Technical Assistance Programs Centers:
http://www.ncddr.org/relativeact/adatech/index.html
This page within the National Center for the Dissemination of Disabilities Research (NCDDR) Web site lists centers that provide technical assistance, training, and resource referral on all aspects of the ADA.

AskERIC Virtual Library:
http://ericir.syr.edu
Educational Resources Information Center (ERIC), a federally-funded national information system that provides a variety of services and products on a broad range of education-related issues for teachers, librarians, counselors, administrators, parents, and others throughout the US and the world.

Association on Higher Education and Disability:
http://www.ahead.org
Committed to full participation of persons with disabilities in postsecondary education; information for students on such topics as financial aid and assistive technology; and resources for postsecondary institutions.

Attention Deficit Disorder Resources
http://www.addresources.org/
Add/ADHD Education Resources website offers Articles, Links, National Directory, Podcasts, eNews and more.

Autism Society of America:
http://www.autism-society.org
Information and research related to diagnosis, treatment, education, inclusion, and planning for the future of individuals with autism.

Best Buddies International:
http://www.bestbuddies.org

An international nonprofit organizationdedicated to providing opportunities for one-to-one friendships and integrated employment; locations found in public schools and colleges around the world.

Center for Effective Collaboration and Practice:
http://cecp.air.org/

Resources and Web links related to emotional and behavioral problems; covers such areas as education, families, mental health, juvenile justice, child welfare, early intervention, school safety, and legislation; downloadable strategies for early intervention, functional assessment, and other topics.

Council for Children with Behavior Disorders (Council for Exceptional Children):
http://www.ccbd.net

Resources and advocacy information for those working with students who have emotional and/or behavioral disorders; links to other resources.

Council for Learning Disabilities:
http://www.cldinternational.org

Information sheets on topics related to learning disabilities; Web links to further resources.

Curriculum Based Measurement (CMB) Websites

Dynamic Indicators of Basic Early Literacy Skills (DIBELS)
http://dibels.uoregon.edu

AIMSweb
http://www.aimsweb.com

Monitoring Basic Skills Progess (MBSPP)
http://www.proedinc.com

Yearly Progress Pro
http://www.mhdigitalllearning.com

Additional information on these and other scientifically based progress monitoring tools is available from the National Center on Student Progress Monitoring at www.studentprogress.org

Division for Developmental Disabilities:
http://www.dddcec.org/

Resources and advocacy information for those working with students who have cognitive disabilities, mental retardation, autism, or related disabilities.

Division for Learning Disabilities (Council for Exceptional Children:
http://www.dldcec.org

Discussions; engaging teaching ideas for classroom use; resources; links to research centers; and topics of interest to teachers.

ERIC Clearinghouse on Disabilities and Gifted Education (ERIC_EC):
www.ericec.org
ERIC EC is part of the US Department of Education's information network and can be used as a resource for conducting general information searches. This site publishes free or low-cost information on special-education research, programs, and practices.

Autism Society of America:
http://www.autism-society.org
This web site contains a wide range of information regarding autism, treatments and supports for families.

Awesome Library—K-12 Special Education Lesson Plans:
http://www.awesomelibrary.org/special-ed.html
This site provides projects, discussions, interactions, collaborations, lessons, curriculums, and standards for grades K-12. The site also covers assistive technology, ADD and ADHD, physically handicapped developmental disabilities, gifted, learning disabilities.

Building the Legacy: IDEA 2004
http://idea.ed.gov/
This site is written and maintained by the US Deparment of Education to disseminate the final regulations pertaining to the 2004 reauthorization of IDEA.

Center for Education Reform:
http://www.edreform.com/index.html
This Web site is the home base for the Center for Education Reform (CER), a national independent, nonprofit advocacy organization committed to education reform. The Web site contains information about school choice options and charter schools as well as a range of other efforts for changing schools.

Center for Law and Education:
http://www.cleweb.org
This web site is a source for information about legal access issues for students with disabilities, with a special focus on those who have the added challenge of low income. This site has numerous links to current legal issues, upcoming changes in regulation, and hot issues such as curriculum access, discipline, and testing.

Center for Special Education Finance:
http://csef.air.org
The Center for Special Education Finance (CSEF) addresses fiscal and policy questions related to the delivery and and support of special education services in the United States. This site provides access to CSEF publications, studies, and research activities.

Child Care Bureau:
http://www.acf.dhhs.gov/programs/ccb/index.htm
Research, data and systems information.

Children and Adults with Attention-Deficit/Hyperactivity Disoreder
http://www.chadd.org

The CHADD web site contains extensive information on ADHD and ADD which is helpful to anyone who wants to learn more about these conditions.

Children's Defense Fund:
http://www.childrensdefense.org

Provides information regarding advocacy for children.

Circle of Inclusion:
http://circleofinclusion.org/

Materials for use by practitioners in inclusive preschool or early childhood settings. Links to additional resources and videoclips can be found on this web site.

Consumer Information Bureau:
http://www.fcc.gov/cib/

The FCC's page for its Consumer Information Bureau provides useful links to sites concerning communications and consumer rights.

Department of Defense Education Activity (DODEA) Special Education Resource Directory for Special Educators:
http://www.brus-dso.odedodea.edu/special/home.html

This exhaustive guide to education and technology resources includes a list of professional associations and related organizations, education and federal government sites, teacher resources, recommended software, and a special education parent guide.

Disability Resources:
http://www.disabilityresources.org/DRMabout.html

Organized and maintained by volunteers who work in disability-related fields.

Disabilities Rights Office:
http://www.fcc.gov/cib/dro/

This government-run site provides information specific to the FCC's Disabilities Rights Office.

DIBELS—the Dynamic Indicators of Basic Early Literacy Skills:
www.dibels.uoregon.edu/

A web site designed to provide information regarding individually administered measures of early literacy development used to monitor the development of pre-reading and early rading skills.

Early Head Start National Resource Center (EHS NRC):
http://www.ehsnrc.org/

Provides training and technical assistance for the Early Head Start program. The site is operated by Zero to Three: National Center for Infants, Toddlers, and Families and West End's Center for Child and Family Studies.

Education Place:
http://www.eduplace.com
Online support for reading series; online leveled books; forms for downloadable graphic organizers; classroom games for practice in various subject areas for pre-K to Grade 8.

Enchanted Learning Software:
http://www.enchantedlearning.com
Resources for the elementary classroom, including printable books and other resources on topics such as foreign languages, diversity, science, and mathematics.

Federation for Children with Special Needs:
http://www.fcsn.org/
Useful for families of children with special needs, this site will keep them informed of their rights in the areas of education, health care, and many other topics of concern.

Florida Center for Reading Research (FCRR):
www.fcrr.org/
The FCRR established a review process to analyze reading curricula and materials. The website provides reports about reading programs.

FunBrain.com:
http://www.funbrain.com
Free games, quizzes, and teaching tools for K through Grade 8, linked to McREL subject standards; site sponsored by Pearson Education.

Helloriend/Ennis William Cosby Foundation:
www.hellofriend.org
This web site is dedicated to helping you learn about Ennis William Cosby and the foundation established in his memory, and about learning and learning differences. The site offers resources and information on how parents an teachers can help individuals with learning differences.

IDEAdata:
http://www.ideadata.org
State reported data collected by the US Department of Education as required uner Section 618 of IDEA

IDEA Partnership:
http://www.ideapartnership.org
This site is funded through the Research to Practice Division of OSEO and is part of the National Technical Assistance and Dissemination Network. The site provides documentation and information regarding provisions and changes in laws affecting special education practice, with a growing library of annotated resources, including curricula, strategies, tools and products available for instruction and assessment in general and special education.

IDEA Practices—ideaLINKS:
http://www.ideapractices.org/links/index.php

A sige designed to assist teachers, school administrators and related service professionals implement recent changes to the nation's primary special education law, IDEA'97.

Ideal Lines:
http://www.emtech.net/

Maintained by Lisa Simmons, a certified education advocate, teacher, and music therapist, this site provides links to other sites related to disabilities and is divided into categories such as education and associations, legal, disabilities and exceptionalities, medical, and assistive technology

IDEAs That Work:
http://www.osepideasthatwork.org/toolkit/index.asp

A web site provided by the U.S. Office of Special Education Programs that provides a Tool Kit on teaching and assessing students with disabilities.

Inclusion and Parent Advocacy: A Resource Guide:
http://www.disabilityresources.org/DRMincl.html

An on-line guide to multicultural multimedia materials about inclusion and parent advocacy.

Inclusive Education Web Site:
http://www.uni.edu/coe/inclusion/index.html

This web site includes links to resources that have an emphasis on teacher education and training as related to inclusion.

Inclusive Learning Environments for Students with Special Needs
http://www.newhorizons.org/spneeds/inclusion/front_inclusion.htm

A web site with resources on inclusive learning environments for students with special needs. This website has been developed to provide information on successful programs, practices, and research-based strategies in Washington State. The information on this site is in the public domain and can be freely copied and used in trainings as handouts at parent and community meetings, and in creating your school or district programs, as long as proper credit is given to the source.

Inside HealthCare:
http://www.insidehealthcare.com

An information service offering news, directories, search engines, business research tools, funding sources, organizations, and publications related to health care.

Institute on disability/UAP:
http://www.iod.unh.edu

This site details the actions of the Institute on Disability/University Affiliated Program, located at the University of New Hampshire in durham, New Hampshire. The institute has a wide scope of activities designed to promote active and effective inclusion of individuals with disabilities in school and work settings.

International Dyslexia Association:
http://www.interdys.org
Information; research; publications on reading disabilities for parents, teachers, and professionals.

Internet Special Education Resources (ISER):
http://www.iser.com/index.shtml
A nationwide directory of professionals who serve the learning disabilities and special education communities. Helps parents and caregivers find local special education professionals to help with learning disabilities and attention deficit disorder assessment, therapy, advocacy, and other special needs.

Intervention Cenral:
http://www.interventioncentral.org/
A collection of freely available tools and resources for differentiating classroom instruction, as well as providing effective behavioral intervention and academic assessment, to meet the needs of all students in incusive settings.

LD OnLine:
www.ldonline.org
An online guide to learning disabilities for parents, teachers, and children. Resources about learning disabilities; articles from leading researchers; yellow pages of topics important to families and professionals; guide to products.

LD Resources:
www.ldresources.com
This site provides a collection of articles, links, and organization contacts for people with learning disabilities. Nearly 1,000 entries on aspects of learning disabilities, including software, educational issues and ideas, electronic text collections, supports, learning materials, and legal resources.

LearningPage.com:
http://www.learningpage.com
Free instructional materials that can be downloaded and printed, including e-books, lesson plans, worksheets and clip art.

LessonPlanZ.com:
http://www.lessonplanz.com
Directory of lesson plans and lesson plan resources for all grades and subjects; games, music, learning center, and thematic unit ideas; links to free resources, worksheets, clip art, and Web sites of interest to teachers.

National Dissemination Center for Children and Youth with Disabilities:
http://www.nichcy.org

State resources; research; free publications; and student guides (information in English and Spanish).

New Circle of Inclusion:
http://circleofinclusion.org/
A web site for early childhood service providers and families of young children. The web site offers demonstrations of and information about the effective practices of inclusive educational programs for children from birth through age eight.

Prevent Child Abuse America:
http://www.preventchildabuse.org/
Outreach to children, families, and communities; resources; fact sheet on maltreatment of children with disabilities; links to further information.

ProTeacher:
http://www.proteacher.com
Successful teaching ideas and resources reviewed and rated for pre-K through Grade8; topics pertain to education, child development, classroom management, collaboration, content instruction, and external supports.

Reading Rockets:
http://www.readingrockets.org
Based at public television station WETA; teaching techniques, strategies, and resources for families and professionals working with struggling readers; downloadable print guides.

Resources for Special Education and Learning Disabilities Professionals:
http://www.iser.com/proresources.html

Special Education Nonprofit Resources:
http://www.iser.com/nps.html

Response to Intervention: a primer:
www/mc;d/prgomdex/[j[?option=content&task=view&id=598

Response to Intervention: Tiers without Tears
http://www.ncld.org/index.php?option=content&task=view&id=549

SchwabLearning.org:
www.schwablearning.org
A parent's guide to learning differences, providing a road map to understanding the language and landscape of learning differences and disabilities.

SchwabLearning.org: Basic Principles of the Responsiveness-to-Intervention Approach
www.schwablearning.org/articles.asp?r=1056

SchwabLearning.org:Responsiveness to Intervention: Implementation in Schools
www.schwablearning.org/articles.asp?r=1057

SpeakingofSpeech.com:
http://www.speakingofspeech.com
An interactive forum to improve communication skills in the school; includes ideas, lessons, materials, and links to resources.

Stop Bullying Now:
http://www.stopbullyingnow.com
Research-based strategies to reduce bullying in schools that consider the target, the bullies, the bystanders, and the staff; articles; reference to books, videos, and CDs.

The George Washington University HEATH Resource Center:
http://www.heath.gwu.edu
Postsecondary educational opportunities and related issues for students with disabilities.

National Advisory Panel (NAP) on the Education of Dependents with Disabilities:
http://www.brus-dso.odedodea.edu/special/charter.htm
The NAP advises the DODEA on matters affecting the education of children with disabilities.

National Association for the Education of Young Children (NAEYC):
http://www.naeyc.org/
Provides numerous links to key sources of information for children's advocates.

National Association of Developmental Disabilities Councils Home Page:
http://www.igc.apc.org/NADDC/
Provides links to information concerning public policy and resources.

National Association of the Deaf:
http://nad.org
The NAD site provides extensive information and links regarding the array of issues pertinent to those who are Deaf and those who are deaf/hard of hearing.

National Association for Rights Protection and Advocacy (NARPA):
http://www.connix.com/-narpa/
Represents protection and advocacy systems.

National Center on Educational Outcomes:
http://education.umn.edu/nceo/
This site produces and disseminates information on the participation and performance of students with disabilities in statewide assessment program.

National Center for Learning Disabilities:
www.ncld.org/
This site provides information to parents, professionals and individuals with learning disabilities, promotes research and programs to foster effective learning, and advocates for policies to protect and strengthen educational rights and opportunities.

National Center on Response to Intervention:
www.rti4success.org/

Through funding from the U.S. Department of Education's Office of Special Education Programs (OSEP have established the National Center on response to intervention. The Center's mission is to provide technical assistance to states and districts and building the capacity of states to assist districts in implementing proven models for RTI/EIS.

National Center on Student Progress Monitoring:
http://www.studentprogress.org/

This site is sponsored by the National Center on Student Progress Monitoring. It provides information on monitoring and measurement of the effectiveness of instruction for individual student, class, or schools.

National Information Center for Children and Youth with Disabilities (NICHCY)
www.nichey.org

NICHCY is an information and referral center that provides free information on disabilities and related issues for families, educators, and other professionals.

National Institute of Mental Health:
http://www.nimh.nih.gov

This web site is focused on generating and disseminating information regarding mental heal conditions. The site contains information regarding the full range of behavioral disorders and conditions as well as up-to-date research information related to their existence, causes, and treatment.

National Reading Panel:
www.nationalreading panel.org/

The National Reading Panel published their findings on research based reading in two reports. They also identified effective instructional strategies for teaching students with reading difficulties.

National Research Center on Learning Disabilities (NRCLD):
www.nrcled.org/

Responsiveness to intervention (RTI) has gained momentum as a means of determing learning disabilities in school-age students. NRCLD has undertaken a number of activities examining RTI best practices and offer the results on their website.

National Resource Center for Paraprofessionals in Education and Related Services
http://www.nrcpara.org

This site addresses questions of policy and practice regarding the work done by paraprofessionals. Bibliography entries on paraprofessionals, articles and research updates enhance knowledge about this growing group of educatiors.

Netscape

Netscape is a leading provider of open software that links people and information over the Internet.

Resources and Guides:
http://directory.netscape.c.on/Special_Education/Resources_and_Guide

Special Education Institutes:
http://directory.netscape.c.nce/Education/Special_Education/Institute

Special Education Materials:
http://directory.netscape.c.nce/Education/Special_Education/Material

Special Education Resources on Inclusion:
http://directory.netscape.c.nce/Education/Special_Education/Inclusion

National Technical Assistance Center of Positive Behavioral Interventions and Supports
http://www.pbis.org

This web site is dedicated to informing educatiors and school systems about an array of school-wide behavioral interventions. Examples of positive practice are available for use with families, entire schoos, classrooms and individuals. The web site also offers links to practicing schools, a newsletter and online information and supports.

Special Connections:
http://www.special connections.ku.edu/cgi-bin/cgiwrap/specconn/index.php

This site offers ideas and materials and is funded through the federal Office of Special Education Programs. Ideas, information and tools fouces on instruction, Assessment, Behvior Plans and Collaboration.

Special Education and the Individuals with Disabilities Education Act:
http://www.nea.org/specialed/index.html

Links to research and other publications about special education and IDEA.

Special Education Expenditure Project:
http://csef.air.org

Funded by the Office of Special Education Programs (OSEP) at the U.S. Department of Education, this is the first national study of special education expenditures in 15 years.

Special Education News Lesson Plans:
http://www.specialednews.com/eductors/lessonplans/lessons.htl

This site provides lesson plans submitted by special education teaches, as well as links to other lesson plan websites.

Special Education Resources on the Internet (SERI):
www.seriweb.com

This is a collection of Internet-accessible information resources of interest to those involved in the fields related to special education

Special Education Schools:
http://directory.netscape.c.rence/Education/Special_Education/School

Special Education Support:
http://directory.netscape.c.rence/Education/Special_Education/Support

TeachingLD:
http://www.didcec.org
A service of the Division for Learning Disabilities (DLD) of the council for Exceptional Children (CEC). An international professional organization which focuses on learning disabilities provides information for teachers and administrators working with exceptional children.

The Educator's Reference Desk:
http://www.eduref.org
Lesson plans by subject for pre-K to Grade 12; links to national education standards by subject area; information on special education, including Individuals with Disabilities Education Improvement Act of 2004; information on vocational, adults, and higher education.

The New York Institute for Special Education:
http://www.nyise.org/
A private, nonprofit, nonsectarian educational facility, which provides quality programs for children who are blind or visually disabled, emotionally and learning disabled and preschoolers who are developmentally delayed.

Toolkit on Teaching and Assessing Students with Disabilities:
http://www.osepideasthatwork.org/toolkit/index.asp
The US Deparment of Education has developed this site, which offers a compilation of current information designed to assist states in educating students with disabilities. The Tool Kit will be added to over time to communicate the results of research on teaching, learning and assessment.

Office of Special Education and Rehabilitative Services (OSERS):
http://www.ed.gov/offices/OSERS/OSEP/links.html

The following OSERS-sponsored Web sites can be accessed from this site:

- The National Information Clearinghouse on Children Who Are Deaf-Blind (DB-Link),
- The National Technical Assistance Consortium for Children and Young Adults Who Are Deaf-Blind (NTAC),
- Center for Appropriate Dispute Resolution in Special Education (CADRE),
- The National Early Childhood Technical Assistance System (NEC*TAS),
- National Center on Educational Outcomes (NCEO),
- Center for Effective Collaboration and Practice,
- Center for Special Education Finance,
- National Information Center for Children and Youth with Disabilities (NICHCY),
- ERIC Clearinghouse on Disabilities and Gifted Education,
- Heath Resource Center,

- IDEA 1997,
- Association of Service Providers Implementing IDEA Reforms in Education (ASPIIRE) (or http://www.ideapractices.org),
- Families and Advocates Partnerships for Education (FAPE) (or http://www.fape.org),
- IDEA Local Implementations by Local Administrators (ILIAD) (or http://www.ideapractices.org),
- The Policy Maker Partnership for Implementing IDEA 97 (or http://www.ideapolicy.org/pmp.htm),
- Consortium on Inclusive Schooling Practices,
- Center of Minority Research in Special Education (COMRISE),
- Technical Assistance Alliance for Parent Center,
- Parents Engaged in Education Reform,
- OSEP Center on Positive Behavioral Interventions and Supports,
- Federal Resource Center for Special Education (FRC),
- OSERS Regional Resource and Federal Centers Network

Office of Special Education and Rehabilitative Services (OSERS):
www.ed.gov/parents/needs/speced/learning

Learning Opportunities for Your Child Through Alternate Assessments. (2007). Office of Special Education and Rehavilitative Services.

A publication booklet designed to introduce parents to the "big ideas" contained in school improvement efforts uner the the No Child Left Behind Act of 2001.

Office of Special Education and Rehabilitative Services (OSERS)
www.ed.gov/about/offices/list/osers/products/opening_doors

Opening Doors: Technology and Communication Options for Children with Hearing Loss, and New Spanish Version, Que se abran las puertas: Opciones de technolgia y communicacion para los ninos con perdida auditiva (2007).

These publications provide background on early intervention, the use of technology and other support available to children with hearing loss and their families.

Office of Special Education and Rehabilitative Services (OSERS), Teachers Guide:
http://www.ed.gov/pubs/TeachersGuide/osers.html

The new teacher's guide to the U.S. Department of Education.

Reading Rockets:
www.readingrockets.org/

A national multimedia project offering information and resources on how young children learn to read, why so many struggle, and how caring adults can help.

Special Education Books:
http://www.respond.com

After a search, can provide a list of suggested books along with news, information, and ideas.

Special Education Network:
http://www.specialednet.com/

Provides information and resources on the education of children with special needs.

Special Education Resources on the Internet (SERI):
http://seriweb.com/

A collection of Internet-accessible information resources of interest to those involved in fields related to special education.

U.S. Department of Justice Americans with Disabilities Act Home Page
http://www.usdoj.gov/crt/ada/adahom1.htm

What Works Clearinghouse:
http://www.w-w-c.org/

This web site provides educators, policymakers, researchers, and the public with a source of scientific evidence of what works in education.

World Wide Web of Private Special Education Schools:
http://www.spedschools.com/

A database of schools searchable by state, name or population served. Also includes related resources and organizations.

Wrightslaw: Individuals with Disabilities Education Act of 2004:
http://www.wrightslaw.com/idea/index.htm

This site provides information of interest to parents, teachers, and school administrators regarding the 2004 reauthorization of IDEA. The author is Pete Wright, an attorney who represents children with special needs.

STARTING POINTS FOR ADVOCACY OF SPECIAL EDUCATION AND CHILDREN'S SERVICES

Each of the following sites contains a vast array of information relevant to professionals, parents, policymakers, and the general public. Search them for publications, news, federal regulations, and links to related sites.

About Autism law
www.AboutAutismLaw.com and www.Special Education.ws

Law Firm of Sherman and Ziegler web sites with updated information regarding law, form letters, resource information about autism.

The Arc:
http://www.thearc.org

Information about the inclusion of people with mental retardation and developmental disabilities; links to estate planning, education, assistive technology, and advocacy information.

Autism and Pervasive Developmental Disabilities Support Network:
http://www.autism-pdd.net
Educational, financial, legal, and employment information; current topics; extensive listing of Web links to services by state.

The Beach Center on Disability (University of Kansas):
http://www.beachcenter.org
Promoting the highest quality of living for individuals and families, includes IDEA/IEP resources and information on many topics, including self-determination, family control, education, and health care.

Child Care Bureau:
http://www.acf.dhhs.gov/programs/ccb
Community Grants
familyservicesgrants@autismspeak.org

DisabilityInfo.gov:
http://www.disabilityinfo.gov
Online connection to the federal government's disability-related information and resources; topics covered include employment, education, housing, transportation, healthe benefits, technology, community life, and civil rights.

ERIC Clearinghouse on Elementary and Early Childhood Education:
http://ericeece.org

Head Start Bureau:
http://www.acf.dhhs.gov/programs/hsb
Interventions and Strategies for Success by Susan Stokes
www.cesa7.k12.wi.us/sped/autism/index2.htm

Learning Disabilities Association of America:
http://www.ldaamerica.org or http://www.ldanatl.org
Information for parents, teachers, and individuals with learning disabilities; news; current topics, Web links, and resources on teaching and learning.

LD Pride:
http://www.ldpride.net
Interactive resource for individuals with learning disabilities and/or attention-deficit disorders sponsored by the Vancouver Island Invisible Disability Association, British Columbia, Canada.

Learning Disabilities Worldwide:
http//www.ldworldwide.org
Information on learning disabilities for individuals with learning disabilities, parents and professionals; includes articles, publications and conferences.

National Autism Websites
gfcf-diet.talkaboutcuringautism.org

Talk About Curing Autism. Information about understanding the gluten-free diet and tips for making it more affordable.

National Center for Learning Disabilities:
http://www.ld.org

Resources, information, fact sheets, advocacy support, and support fo living with a learning disability.

National Child Care Information Center:
http://www.nccic.org
100 Day Kit
100daykit@autismspeaks.org

Parent Advocacy Coalition for Educational Rights:
http://www.pacer.org

Nationally recognized resource where parents of children with disabilities assist each other with access to resources and information.

Parents Helping Parents:
http://www.php.com

A resource for families of children with special needs containing information on services, emotional support, and living with dignity.

Recommended Competencies for Persons Delivering Assistive Technology
www.cde.ca.gov/spbranc/sed/atstaff.htm

Schwab Learning Center:
http://www.schwablearning.org

Free publications, newsletters, personal inspirational stories, and information summer camps, legal rights and responsibilities, teaching and learning strategies.

Special Education Web Sites with Loads of Information about Autism and Special Education
http://www.aboutautismlaw.com/autism_sites.html

A website that provides a listing of important web sites regarding Special Education and Autism.

U.S. Department of Education:
www.ed.gov

Welfare Information Network:
http://www.welfareinfo.org

Wrighslaw:
http://www.wrightslaw.org

A law library rlated to special education; access to many topics, yellow pages for children, resources for advocates.

ON-LINE LEGISLATIVE RESOURCES

The following Web sites provide detailed information about legislative proposals, congressional committee membership, and congressional activity. You can also link to your representative's home pages and send them e-mail messages.

Daily Digest of the House of Representatives and the Senate:
http://www.access.gpo.gov/su_docs/aces/digest001.shtml

House of Representatives:
http://www.house.gov

Senate:
http://www.senate.gov

Thomas Legislative Information on the Internet:
http://thomas.loc.gov

White House:
http://www.whitehouse.gov

COMMUNITY OUTREACH

The organizations listed here offer children's advocates useful information, on-line tools, and networking opportunities to stimulate community involvement.

America Reads Challenge Resource Kit:
pubaff@naeyc.org

Children's Defense Fund:
http://www.childrensdefense.org

Families and Work Institute:
http://www.familiesandworkinst.org

I Am Your Child:
http://www.iamyourchild.org

Stand for Children:
pubaff@naeyc.org

TOYS

Abledata
(800) 346-2742
This is the National Rehabilitation Center's computer database of products. They will do a search for any product.

A.D.D. WareHouse
300 NW 70th Avenue, Suite 102
Plantation, FL 33317
(800) 233-9273

Specializes in products for attention deficit disorder/hyperactivity and related problems. Includes books and videos.

Childcraft Education Corporation
20 Kilmer Road
Edison, NJ 08817
(800) 631-5652

Educational materials for early childhood professionals, including storage cabinets, shelving and unit blocks, arts and crafts, and literature.

Childswork/Childsplay
Genesis Direct
P.O. Box 1600
Secaucus, NJ 07096
(800) 962-1141
Fax: (201) 583-3644

Play equipment, board games, and literature.

Constructive Playthings
1227 East 119th Street
Grandview, MO 64030
(800) 832-0224

Toys designed for early childhood education and first learning.

Educational Toys & Products
www.beevisual.com

Choiceworks Visual Support System

A visual system for supporting children, their parents and professionals in daily routines and activities.

Educational DVD/CD
http://www.trpyoga.com

Occupational Therapy for Children with Autism Special Needs and Typical

An instructional DVD that combines Occupational Therapy exercises with ABA to teach parents and caregivers skills that can assist in sensory integration.

Flaghouse
150 North MacQuesten Parkway
Mount Vernon, NY 10550
(800) 793-7900

Toys and developmental activities for children with special needs.

Funtastic Learning
206 Woodland Road
Hampton, NH 03824
(800) 722-7375

Toys, games, and tools for children with skill-development needs.

Jesana Limited
P.O. Box 17
Irvington, NY 10533
(800) 443-4728

Catalog includes adapted toys and augmentative communication equipment.

Kapable Kids
P.O. Box 250
Bohemia, NY 11716
(800) 356-1564

Catalog is coded to indicate a toy's educational benefit.

Lakeshore Learning Materials
2695 East Dominguez Street
Carson, CA 90749
(800) 421-5354

Educational toys, language materials, and multicultural materials.

National Lekotek Center
2100 Ridge Avenue
Evanston, IL 60201
(847) 328-0001)
(800) 366-PLAY (7529; Helpline)
Web site: www.lekotek.org

This nonprofit organization with a national network of fifty affiliates promotes access to play for children with special needs and provides supportive services for their families.

Network on the Blind Multiple-Handicapped
1912 Tracy Road
Northwood, OH 43619
(419) 666-6212

Toys are listed by developmental age and chosen for durability.

Sportime Abilitations
One Sportime Way
Atlanta, GA 30340
(800) 444-5700

Equipment for development of physical and mental ability through movement.

TFH Limited
4537 Gibsonia Road
Gibsonia, PA 15044
(412) 444-6400

Distributes outdoor play equipment, toys that help with dexterity and speech, toys that are sensitive to sound, and more.

Therapeutic Toys
P.O. Box 418
Moodus, CT 06469
(800) 638-0676

Toys and playground equipment for physically challenged children.

Therapro
225 Arlington Street
Framingham, MA 01702
(800) 257-5376

Developmental devices, products, and toys that address the needs of children with special needs.

Toys for Special Children
385 Warburton Avenue
Hastings-on-Hudson, NY 10706
(800) 832-8697

Toys, games, and tools designed to improve the skills of special needs children.

Toys "R" Us Toy Guide for Differently Abled Kids!
Toys "R" Us
P.O. Box 8501
Nevada, IA 50201

Toys are categorized by skill (gross motor, fine motor, tactile, visual, language, social, etc.).

VIDEOS

A Is for Autism (1992)

This video examines people who lack a small piece of their frontal cortex and suffer from a mild form of autism. 30 minutes. Produced by the BBC.

Augmentative and Alternative Communication (1998)

This video program provides an overview of augmentative and alternative communication (AAC) and the considerations that should be made in choosing an AAC system for individuals. 22 minutes. Produced and distributed by Assistive Technology Programs, Center for Development and Disability, University of New Mexico.

"But He Knows His Colors": Characteristics of Autism in Children Birth to Three

In this video four children with a diagnosis of autism demonstrate some of the characteristic behaviors. It helps in teaching families, educators, early interventionists, occupational therapists, speech and language pathologists, and physicians about the spectrum of behavioral characteristics seen in children with autism who are under the age of three. It speaks to the importance of early diagnosis and intervention for children and their families. 28 minutes. Produced by the New Mexico Autism Program. Order from Child Development Media, Inc., (800) 405-8942.

Child Care and Children with Special Needs (2001)

This is a training tool for program directors who wish to meet the needs of children with disabilities. Produced by Video Active Productions. To order, log on to http://www.naeyc.org/resources/catalog.

Classroom Interventions for ADHD (1999)

This video program is designed specifically to help teachers with students who have ADHD and to help them provide a better learning environment for the entire class. 35 minutes. Produced and distributed by National Professional Resources, Inc., (800) 453-7461.

Curriculum

In this video you will observe toddlers, preschoolers, and kindergarten-aged children in three classrooms. Their teachers each provide a learning environment with a wide variety of hands-on activities and open-ended materials. 35 minutes. Produced by Magna Systems, Inc. Order from Child Development Media, Inc., (800) 405-8942.

A Day at a Time

Filmed over a period of four years, this unforgettable story will inspire everyone concerned with the challenges of family life and the place of disabled children in our society. 58 minutes. Produced by William Garcia and Charles Schultz. Order from Child Development Media, Inc., (800) 405-8942.

Developing the Young Bilingual Learner (2000)

Today many children enter early childhood programs with home languages other than English. This video explores the importance of supporting children's home language while helping them learn English, and it gives strategies for helping children become bilingual learners. 21 minutes. Produced for NAEYC by Resources and Instruction in Staff Excellence in Cincinnati, Ohio. To order, log on to http://www.naeyc.org/resources/catalog/default.asp.

Effective Education: Adapting to Include All Students (1998)

Shows how to adapt regular education classrooms to include students with several disabilities. 19 minutes. Produced by the South Dakota Department of Education and Cultural Affairs, and the Indiana Deafblind Project, the Blumberg Center.

Including Samuel (2007)

Dan Habib's documentary film "Including Samuel" examines the educational and social inclusion of youth with disabilities as a civil rights issue.

Intervention Central

Films from Intervention Central to help school staff and parents to promote positive classroom behaviors and foster effective learning for all children and youth. Information regarding "Movies: such as Academic Intervention Ideas That Any Teacher Can Use and Defiant Kids: Communication Tools for Teachers can be requested by going to the Intervention Central Website: http://www.interventioncentral.org/

The Exceptional Child I: Building Understanding (1999)

Defines the educationally exceptional child by using scenes of children and interviews to help viewers develop an understanding of a wide span of exceptionalities. 30 minutes. Produced and distributed by Magna Systems, Inc.

The Exceptional Child II: Focusing on Nurturing and Learning (1999)

Explores how families feel and change in response to having children with exceptional needs. 30 minutes. Produced and distributed by Magna Systems, Inc.

A Family's Guide to the Individualized Family Service Plan (1999)

Tells families what the IFSP process is all about. It shows parents how an IFSP is developed and implemented. 17 minutes. Produced by Juliann J. Woods Cripe. Distributed by Child Development Media, Inc., (800) 405-8942.

The IEP: A Tool for Realizing Possibilities (1998)

Produced by parents for parents, this video gives an overview of the individual educational plan (IEP) process from referral for assessment to the IEP meeting. Included are interviews with parents, teachers, paraprofessionals, principals, and peers. 20 minutes. To order, contact Howard George, georgeh@mail.doe.state.fl.us.

Learning and Communication: Functional Learning Programs for Young Children (1998)

Shows brief, longitudinal studies of three children and their parents involved together in functional learning activities. 18 minutes. Produced by Katrin Stroh and Thelma Robinson, Highgate, London, England.

A New I.D.E.A. for Special Education (1998)

Seeks to help educators and parents better understand the 1997 changes to the Individual with Disabilities in Education Act. 45 minutes. Produced and distributed by Edvantage Media, Inc.

RTI Toolkit: A Practical Guide for Schools (2007)

This book provides school administrators, teachers, and support staff with essential techniques, resources, and guidelines to bring "Response to Intervention" to their schools. By Jim Wright.

Shining Bright: Head Start Inclusion (1998)

Presents the experiences of a Head Start and local education agency's collaborative effort to include children with severe disabilities in a Head Start program. 23 minutes. Produced and distributed by the Kansas University Affiliated Program.

Standards and Inclusion: Can We Have Both? (1999)

Addresses the issue of inclusion for educators in both pre-service and in-service training. 40 minutes. Produced by Dorothy Kerzner Lipsky and Alan Gartner for the National Center on Educational Restructuring and Inclusion.

Success with Technology: Practices and Programs for Students with Special Needs (1999)

Vignettes that demonstrate successful applications of technology in educational programs that include students with disabilities are the focus of this video. 50 minutes. Produced and distributed by MACRO International, Inc.

Three R's for Special Education: Rights, Resources, and Results. A Guide for Parents, a Tool for Educators (1999)

A practical step-by-step guide that enables parents to be effective managers on behalf of their special-needs child. It shows parents how to work with the system, what resources are available, and how to plan for the disabled person's future. 48 minutes. Produced and distributed by Edvantage Media, Inc.

Transition: A Time for Growth (1998)

This short video was developed from numerous interviews with families in transition. 12 minutes. Produced and distributed by Bridging Early Services Transition Project. Close captioned.

EDUCATIONAL SOFTWARE

American Education Corporation
7506 North Broadway Extension
Oklahoma City, OK 73116
(800) 342-7587
Web site: www.amered.com

Advanced Learning System—Reading, writing, language arts, math, science, and social studies software with on-line capabilities featuring more than 4,000 lessons for grade levels K–12.

ABLEDATA:
http://www.abledata.com

Comprehensive, extensive, and descriptive listing and reviews of assistive technology producs.

Alliance for Technology Access:
http://www.ataccess.org

Network for developers and vendors of low-cost or no-cost online tools for individuals, families, and professionals; online articles; locations of technology centers nationwide; and frequently asked questions.

Attainment Company, Inc.
P.O. Box 930160
Verona, WI 53593
(800) 327-4269
Web site: http://www.attainmentcompany.com

Academic and Life Skills Software, First Money, Time Scales.

Broderbund Software, Inc.
500 Redwood Boulevard
P.O. Box 6125
Novato, CA 94948
(800) 521-6263
Web site: http://www.broderbund.com

Living Books Series CD-ROMs—twelve titles, including *Just Grandma and Me, Arthur's Birthday,* and *The Cat in the Hat.*

Linda Burkhart
6201 Candle Court
Eldersburg, MD 21780
(410) 795-4561
Web site: http://www./burkhart.com

Early Play Activities (contains activities authored in IntelliPix), switches, devices, and books regarding software use.

CactusKids.com:
http://www.cactuskids.com/

Special Needs Software and Products. Fun and educational software for students with disabilities from birth all the way to adulthood.

Center for Accessible Technology:
http:www.cforat.org

Resources to help persons with disabilities be fully included in all aspects of life, especially school, employment, and recreation.

Closing the Gap:
http://www.closingthegap.com

Computer-related and technology resources for persons with disabilities; annual conference information; publications; and forums.

Cognitive Concepts, Inc.
(888) 328-8199
Web site: http://www.cogcon.com

Earobics Step 1 for ages 4–7, Earobics Step 2 for ages 7–11.

Computer Curriculum Corporation
1287 Lawrence Station Road
Sunnyvale, CA 94088
(800) 227-8324
Web site: http://www.ccclearn.com

CCC Successmaker—Multidiscipline software with an Internet subscription service that provides on-line activities in math, reading, language arts, science, and social studies.

Davidson and Associates, Inc.
19840 Pioneer Avenue
Torrance, CA 90503
(310) 793-0600

Games and entertainment software designed for children.

Don Johnston, Inc.
1000 North Rand Road, Building 115
P.O. Box 639
Wauconda, IL 60084
Web site: http://www.donjohnston.com

Co:Writer and Write:Outland (revised version contains Franklin speller),Simon Spells, Simon Sound It Out, Story Time Tales and Circle Time Tales Deluxe, Ensy and Friends, Blocks in Motion, Press-to-Play Series, UkanDu Little Books (primary), Start to Finish Books (middle/high school).

Edmark Corporation
P.O. Box 3218
Redmond, WA 98073
(800) 362-2890
Web site: http://www.edmark.com

Millie's Math House, Bailey's Book House, Stanley Sticker Stories, Sammy's Science House, Trudy's Time and Place, Let's Go Read, Mighty Math Series, Imagination Express.

Heartsoft
P.O. Box 691381
Tulsa, OK 74169
(800) 285-3475

Software designed to teach basic skills, thinking, and learning.

Inspiration Software, Inc.
7412 SW Beaverton Hillsdale Highway, Suite 102
Portland, OR 97225
(800) 877-4292
Web site: http://www.inspiration.com

Visual thinking and learning software.

Intelligent Peripherals
20380 Town Center Lane, Suite 270
Cupertino, CA 95014
(408) 252-9400
Web site: http://www.alphasmart.com

Turbo Charger, Get Utility, Writing Activity CD-ROM, Keywords to be used with AlphaSmart 2000.

Intellitools
5221 Central Avenue, Suite 205
Richmond, CA 94804
(800) 899-6687
Web site: http://www.intellitools.com

IntelliPics, IntelliTalk, Overlay Maker, Click It.

Knowledge Adventure
19840 Pioneer Avenue
Torrance, CA 90503
(800) 545-7677
Web site: www.KnowledgeAdventure.com

Classworks Gold—Curriculum management software for math and language arts in K–8 with more than 8,000 activities. Hyper Studio, Jump Start series.

Laureate Learning Systems
110 East Spring Street
Winsooski, VT 05404
(800) 562-6801
Web site: http://www.LLSys.com

First Words; Talking Nouns I, II; Talking Verbs I, II; Tiger's Tale; Creature Chorus; Creature Magic.

The Learning Company (TLC)
One Anthenaeum Street
Cambridge, MA 09214
(800) 685-6322
Web site: http://www.learningcompanyschool.com/school/

Instructional software titles featuring Broderbund, Creative Wonders, Mindscape, The Learning Company, MECC, and Compton's plus Resource Center and Free demos.

The Lightspan Partnership, Inc.
10140 Campus Point Drive
San Diego, CA 92121
(888) 425-5543
Web site: www.lightspan.com

Lightspan Achieve Now—Interactive software for reading, math, and language arts for grades K–8. Includes school and home learning activities, teacher materials, interactive software, student assessment, professional development, and Internet resources.

Macmillan/McGraw-Hill
10 Union Square East
New York, NY 10003-3384
(212) 353-5676

An array of software designed to teach skills, teaching ideas, and curriculum.

Marblesoft
12301 Central Avenue NE, Suite 205
Blaine, MN 55434
(612) 755-1402
Web site: http://www.marblesoft.com

Early Learning (I, II, III), Functional Life Skills, Money Skills, Overlays for IntelliKeys.

Mayer-Johnson Company
P.O. Box 1579
Solana Beach, CA 92075
(619) 550-0449
Web site: http://www.mayerjohnson.com

Boardmaker, Communication Board-Builder, HyperSign-Interactive ASL Dictionary, Picture Communications Symbols (PCS), Writing with Symbols 2000.

McGraw-Hill Learning Technologies
8787 Orion Place
Columbus, OH 43240
(800) 598-4077
Web site: www.passkeylearning.com

Passkey, a Prescriptive Learning System—A networkable CD-ROM program for basic skills and test preparation in math, reading, writing, and science.

National Computer Systems, Inc.
3450 East Sunrise Drive, Suite 140
Tucson, AZ 85718
(800) 937-6682
Web site: www.novanet.com

The Novanet System—An on-line standards-based curriculum for children ages 3–12+ featuring more than 600 new lessons, multimedia resources, and a management system.

Psychological Corporation
555 Academic Court
San Antonio, TX 78204
(800) 232-1223
Web site: http://www.hbtpc.com

CELF-3, clinical assistant-scoring software for the CELF-3 test.

R. J. Cooper and Associates
24843 Del Prado, Suite 283
Dana Point, CA 92629
(800) 752-6673
Web site: http://rjcooper.com

Early and Advanced Switch Games, Point to Pictures, Turn-Taking.

Recording for the Blind and Dyslexic:
http://www.rfbd.org

Recordings and computer-compatible resources to promote learning through listening for all ages.

Scholastic, Inc.
730 Broadway
New York, NY 10003
(212) 353-8219
Web site: http://www.scholastic.com

Wiggleworks Plus (K–2), Smart Place (3–6) CD-ROMs.

Simtech Publications
134 East Street
Litchfield, CT 06759
Web site: http://www.hsj.com

Single-switch software called Switch Kids, New Frog, and Flyk; Scan and Match series (for preschoolers and teens).

Soft Touch Software
4300 Stine Road, Suite 401
Bakersfield, CA 93309
(877) 763-8868
Web site: http://www.funsoftware.com

Teach Me to Talk, Songs I Sing at Preschool, Old MacDonald's Farm Delux, Monkeys Jumping on the Bed, Switch Basics Software, IntelliKeys Overlays.

Sunburst
101 Castleton Street
Pleasantville, NY 10570
(800) 321-7511
Web site: http://www.sunburst.com

Write On! Plus (middle/high school series).

Tom Snyder Productions
80 Coolidge Hill Road
Watertown, MA 02172
(617) 926-6000
Web site: http://www.tomsnyder.com/index.shtml

Educational software designed to enhance the teaching process and improve performance and understanding.

UCLA Microcomputer Project
1000 Veteran Avenue, Room 23-10
Los Angeles, CA 90095
(310) 825-4821

Wheels on the Bus (for Mac and old Apple computers only).

ADAPTIVE DEVICES

Ability Research
P.O. Box 1791
Minnetonka, MN 55345
(612) 939-0121

Products and devices that make computer access easier for individuals with special needs, including switches and Dynamic Delivery Talk Back.

AbleNet, Inc.
1081 10th Avenue SE
Minneapolis, MN 55414
(800) 322-0956
Web site: http://www.ablenetinc.com

BIGmack Single Message One Step Communicator, Step-by-Step Communicator 75, Speak Easy Communication Device, Big Red and Jellybean Switches.

Adaptive Communication Systems, Inc.
P.O. Box 12440
Pittsburg, PA 15231
(800) 247-3433

The Great Talking Box, alternative keyboards such as the Fixed-Split Keyboard, AdapTek, and Mouse Emulator.

Adaptive Consulting Services
253 Merritt Square Mall, Suite 642
Merritt Island, FL 32952
(407) 639-7116

Communication devices such as DynaVox and DynaMyte, and Dectalk voice synthesis.

Adaptive Devices Group
1278 North Farris Avenue
Fresno, CA 93728
(800) 766-4234

Vocalize, Double Talk Switch.

Attainment Company, Inc.
P.O. Box 930160
Verona, WI 53593
(800) 327-4269
Web site: http://www.attainmentcompany.com
15 Talker, 5 Talker, Memory Pad, Talking Picture Frame.

Crestwood Company
6625 North Sidney Place
Milwaukee, WI 53209
(414) 352-5678
Web site: http://www.communicationaids.com
Adapted toys: Fireman, Cutie Penguin, Leo The Lion, Baby Brontosaurus, and more (work with switches like the Big Red and Jelly Bean from AbleNet).

COMMUNICATION DEVICES

Dynamic Delux Talk Back 24, Mini Talk Back I and II, Talk Back III.

Dragon Sysems, Inc.
320 Nevada Street
Newton, MA 02160
(617) 965-2374
Web site: http://www.dragonsys.com
Dragon Naturally Speaking for Teens (for ages 11 and up).

ENABLING DEVICES

Edmark Corporation
P.O. Box 3218
Redmond, WA 98073
(800) 362-2890
Web site: http://www.edmark.com
Touch Window (touchscreen).

Flaghouse Special Populations
601 Flaghouse Drive
Hasbrouck Heights, NJ 07604
(800) 793-7900
Web site: http://www.flaghouse.com
Super Sensitive switch.

Intelligent Peripherals
20380 Town Center Lane, Suite 270
Cupertino, CA 95014

(408) 252-9400
Web site: http://www.alphasmart.com
AlphaSmart 2000.

Intellitools
5221 Central Avenue, Suite 205
Richmond, CA 94804
(800) 899-6687
Web site: http://www.intellitools.com
IntelliKeys.

Mayer-Johnson Company
P.O. Box 1579
Solana Beach, CA 92075
(619) 550-0084
Web site: http://www.mayerjohnson.com
Tech/Speak, Tech/TALK, Tech/Four, Magic Touch (touchscreen).

R. J. Cooper and Associates
24843 Del Prado, Suite 283
Dana Point, CA 92629
(949) 661-6904
(800) 752-6673
Web site: http://rjcooper.com
Magic Touch screens, Switch-Adapted Mouse devices/interfaces.

Toys for Special Children
385 Warburton Avenue
Hastings-on-Hudson, NY 10706
(914) 478-0960
Web site: http://www.enablingdevices.com
Cheap Talk, Cheap Talk 4 Inline, Cheap Talk 8, Talking Switch Plate, Twin Talk, Step Talk Switch Plate, Hip-Step Talker, Specially-Adapted Toys, Sensory Devices.

ON-LINE RESOURCES FOR ASSISTIVE TECHNOLOGY

Abledata
http://www.abledata.com

Access Unlimited (numerous links to other disability sites)
http://www.accessunlimited.com

Apple Computer's Disability Home Page
http://www.apple.com/education/k12/disability/

Archimedes Project (Design Issues for Tomorrow's Technology)
http://archimedes.stanford.edu//arch.html

DDInsite (Developmental Disabilities/Assistive Technology)
http://ddinsite.gatech.edu/

disABILITY Resource on the Internet
http://www.dinf.org/disability_resources/

DO-IT
http://www.washington.edu/doit/

DREAMMS for Kids, Inc.
http://www.dreamms.org/

EASI, Access to Information for Persons with Disabilities
http://www.rit.edu/~easi/

Information Technology and Disabilities (a refereed journal)
http://www.rit.edu/~easi/itd.html

Job Accommodation Network (JAN)
http://janweb.icdi.wvu.edu

Microsoft's Accessibility and Disability Home Page
http://www.microsoft.com/enable

National Rehabilitation Information Center (NARIC)
http://www.naric.com/naric

NCSA Mosaic Disability Access Page
http://bucky.aa.uic.edu/

Project Link
http://cosmos.buffalo.edu/t2rerc/

RESNA Technical Assistance Project
http://www.resna.org

SuperKids Educational Software Review
http://www.superkids.com/

Trace Research and Development Center
http://www.trace.wisc.edu

Way Cool Software Reviews by Students
http://www.ucc.uconn.edu/~wwwpcse/wcool.html

WebABLE
http://www.webable.com

Glossary

The following terms and concepts are defined as they relate to special education.

ABC model—A framework for analyzing behavior that takes into account both the events that precede the behavior and the events that are subsequent to it; A = antecedent, B = behavior, C = consequence.

Ability grouping—Placement of students with comparable achievement and skill levels in the same classes or courses, an arrangement often used in the education of students who are gifted.

Academic—Having to do with subjects such as reading, writing, math, social studies, and science.

Academic achievement—The grade level at which a student functions in specific academic areas such as reading and mathematics, typically determined through standardized achievement tests.

Acceleration—More-rapid-than-usual passage by a student through a curriculum or grades in school.

Accommodation—Learning to do things differently from other students because of a handicap, impairment, or disability; the tendency to change one's way of thinking to fit a new objective or stimulus. Changes in the administration of an assessment (such as setting, scheduling, timing, presentation format, response mode, or others), including any combination of these that does not change the construct intended to be measured by the assessment or the meaning of the resulting scores. Assessment accommodations must be identified in the student's Individualized Education Program (IEP) or Section 504 plan and used regularly during instruction and classroom assessment.

Achievement—The quality and quantity of a student's work.

Achievement levels/proficiency levels—Descriptions of a test taker's compentence in a particular area of knowledge or skill, usually defined as ordered categories on a continuum, often labeled from "basic" to "advanced," or "novice" to "expert," that constitute broad ranges for classifying performance.

Achievement Test—A test to evaluate the extent of knowledge and skills attained by a test taker in a content domain in which he or she has received instruction.

Acquired disability—A disability occurring after birth.

Acquired handicap—A disabling condition having onset after birth.

Adaptive behavior—Individual behavior that meets the standards of personal independence and social responsibility expected for age and culture group; an essential component in the diagnosis of mental retardation.

Adaptive instruction—Instructional practice by which materials are modified to accommodate the unique characteristics of the learner.

Advance organizers—Written materials or statements made by a teacher to focus students' attention on the upcoming lesson by previewing the material to be covered and providing a rationale for the importance of the information to be presented.

Adventitious hearing loss—A hearing loss that was acquired after the development of speech.

Adversarial bargaining—A situation that is created when both parties continually attempt to gain power over each other.

Advocacy—An advanced stage of collective bargaining in which the two sides respect and accept the rights and roles of the other and do not challenge or threaten each other's leadership.

Advocate—An individual, parent, or professional who promotes the interests of persons with disabilities.

Age-appropriate and functional curricula—Real-life materials, activities, and teaching methods.

Age of onset—The age at which a handicap begins.

Aggression—Hostile and attacking behavior—which can include verbal communication—directed toward self, others, or the physical environment.

AIDS—Acquired immune deficiency syndrome.

Alternate Assessment- An assessment designed for the small number of students with disabilities who are unable to participate in the regular state assessment, even with appropriate accommodations.

American Association on Mental Deficiency (AAMD)—An earlier name for the American Association on Mental Retardation.

American Association on Mental Retardation (AAMR)—The oldest and largest multidisciplinary mental retardation organization. It investigates and promotes the best practices for people with mental retardation.

American Federation of Labor–Congress of Industrial Organizations (AFL-CIO)—The nation's largest private sector union.

American Federation of Teachers (AFT)—An affiliate of the AFL-CIO. It was formed in 1916 out of the belief that the organizing of teachers should follow the model of a labor union rather than that of a professional association. It promotes collective bargaining for teachers and other educational employees; conducts research on teacher stress, special education, and other education-related issues; and lobbies for the passage of legislation of importance to education.

American Sign Language (ASL)—A fully developed natural language, one of the world's many signed languages; the sign language or manual communication system preferred by many adults in the United States who are deaf.

American Speech-LanguageHhearing Association (ASHA)—A professional organization concerned with communication disorders.

Americans with Disabilities Act (ADA)—Federal disability antidiscrimination legislation originally enacted in 1990.

Analytical listening—Hearing, analyzing, and possibly interpreting another person's communication or verbal message.

Anencephaly—A condition in which the brain fails to develop completely or is absent.

Annual appeal—A written request for a court to review or change the decision of a hearing officer.

Annual goal—A statement of an IEP as directed in IDEA of what an exceptional student needs to learn and should be able to learn in his special program over the time period of a year.

Anoxia—Inadequate supply of oxygen to the body and brain, usually at birth.

Anxiety—A state of painful uneasiness, emotional tension, or emotional confusion.

Aphasia—Impaired ability to use language or articulate ideas due to brain injury or stroke.

Appropriate education—A standard, required by IDEA, which guarantees that students with disabilities receive an educational program individually tailored to their abilities and needs.

Aptitude—Capacity for learning.

Array of services—A wide selection of services that are available so that an appropriate education can be provided to each student with special needs.

Articulation—The process of forming speech sounds.

Assessment—A way of collecting information about a student's special learning needs, strengths, and interests. An assessment may include giving individual tests, observing the student, looking at records, and talking with the student and/or parent.

Assessment Approach System – A system for assessing students that uses some combination of selected or constructed responses and includes one of four dominant methods: (a) ratings based on teacher reflections or observations; (b) portfolios that include collections of evidence; (c) performance tasks comprising constructed responses; or (d) performance events that provide more extended complex constructewd responses.

Assimilation—The incorporation of a new object or stimulus into an existing way of thinking.

Assistive technology (AT)—Technological equipment designed to help individuals function in their environment.

Association for Children and Adults with Learning Disabilities (ACALD)—*See* Learning Disability Association of America.

Associative thinking—The ability to see relationships among differing concepts or knowledge bases.

Ataxia—A form of cerebral palsy characterized by poor muscle coordination that negatively influences balance and coordination.

At risk—Children whose history (family, developmental, medical), physical characteristics, life circumstances, or environment suggest that without interventions they will be identified as having disabilities later in life; a category of preschoolers under the age of three who are suspected of having a handicap and are eligible for special services without needing a specific label.

Attentive listening—Focusing on one specific form of heard communication while ignoring others heard simultaneously.

Attention deficit disorder (ADD)—A condition characterized by hyperactivity, inability to control one's own behavior, and constant movement.

Attention deficits—Characteristics often associated with learning disabilities that impair learning; students do not pay attention to the learning task or to the correct features of the task.

Attentional capacity—A limited pool of energy available to receive and process information.

Augmentive communication device—Equipment, such as a microcomputer with synthesized speech, that helps individuals communicate with others.

Autism—A severe disorder of thinking, communication, interpersonal relationships, and behavior; A disturbance of behavior noted in early childhood that may be characterized by self-stimulation, self-injurious behavior, or the absence of speech.

Autistic—A word describing a handicap or exceptionality where the student seems to act, talk, think, or behave differently from other students in that he or she does not want to physically be close to others.

Autistic behavior—A term used in reference to children and youth with autism; a subgroup of pervasive developmental disorder.

Aversive treatment—A noxious and sometimes painful consequence that would usually be avoided, for example electric shock, used for behavior modification.

Behavior modification—Systematic use of the principles of learning, including rewards and punishment, to promote desired behaviors and discourage undesired behaviors in an individual.

Behavior rating instruments—Checklists consisting of a list of behavioral descriptors to which an observer responds by indicating a choice along a positive-negative continuum.

Behavioral approach—A theory that views human behavior as learned.

Behavioral disorders—A condition of disruptive or inappropriate behaviors that interferes with a student's learning, relationships with others, or personal satisfaction to such a degree the intervention is required.

Behavioral goals and objectives—Expected and desired learning outcomes for students; stated in measurable terms so the teaching and learning process can be evaluated.

Behavioral management—Systematic use of behavioral techniques, such as behavior modification, to control or direct responses.

Biochemical disorders—Any number of disorders (such as learning disabilities) that are caused by biological or physiological imbalances or dysfunctions.

Blindisms—Inappropriate social behaviors possibly due to understimulation of infants with low vision.

Braille—A system of reading and writing that uses dot codes that are embossed on paper, developed by Louis Braille around 1829.

Brain damage—An identifiable insult to the structure of the brain.

Brainstem-evoked response—A technique involving electroencephalograph measurement of changes in brainwave activity in response to sound.

Career education—A curriculum designed to teach individuals the skills and knowledge necessary in the world of work.

Cascade of services—A model associating particular special education services and placements with severity of handicap, developed by Deno and his colleagues.

Categorical—A system of labeling using specific classifications such as "learning disabled" or "mentally retarded."

Categorical programs—Classes available only to those students identified as having a specific disability, such as learning disabilities, mental retardation, visual impairments, and hearing impairments.

Center schools—Segregated school settings that typically serve students with a particular type of handicapping condition (for example, visual impairments, hearing impairments); some of these schools are residential.

Central nervous system dysfunction—An improper functioning of a component of the brain, spinal cord, or nervous system.

Cerebral palsy—A nonprogressive disorder due to brain damage that results in lack of control of voluntary muscles, paralysis, weakness, or lack of coordination of certain large and small muscles. Can be very mild or extremely debilitating. Often causes speech problems.

Chaining—A strategy to teach the steps of skills that have been task analyzed; in the chain either the first step can be taught first (*forward chaining*) or the last taught first (*backward chaining*).

Child Find—Child Find is a component of IDEA that requires states to identify, locate, and evaluate all children with disabilities, aged birth to 21, who are in need of early intervention or special education services.

Child study team (CST)—A group of people working within the school and providing help to the teacher. This team tries to help the teacher meet the learning needs of students within the classroom.

Chronologically ill—Long-term illness.

Clinical teaching—An informal strategy involving systematic presentation of curriculum and response requests to children undergoing evaluation.

Cluster programs—A plan where gifted students spend a part of their day in the regular classroom on enriched or accelerated activities.

Cognitive behavior modification (CBM)—Instructional strategies that use internal control methods (such as self-talk) in structured ways to held students learn how to learn; the approach was initially developed by Meichenbaum.

Cognitive development—Learning skills associated with memory, concepts (e.g., color, shape, size), recognition, and attention.

Collaboration—Group effort of special education teachers, regular education teachers, other service providers, and families working together to provide the best possible services and education.

Communication symbols—Spoken words or utterances, letters of the alphabet, pictures, or gestures used to relay a message; these usually refer to a past, present, or future event, person, object, action, or emotion.

Community-based instruction (CBI)—A strategy of teaching functional skill in the environments in which they occur; for example, shopping skills taught in the local market rather than in the classroom.

Compliance training—A method of assessing children and youth with autism by giving simple commands requiring motor and other nonverbal responses.

Computer-assisted instruction (CAI)—Instructional programs focusing on a particular topic that supplement or replace traditional teacher-directed instructional methods and are delivered at least in part by using a computer.

Computer-enhanced instruction—Software programs that supplement traditional instruction, used primarily for drill and practice.

Conceptualize—Generate questions and formulate abstract ideas.

Concrete operational thinking—The first stage of operational thought and the third major stage in cognitive development; extends from ages seven to twelve. Characterized by ability to form mental representations, understanding of relational terms, class inclusion, and serialization.

Conduct disorder—A psychiatric classification found in the *DSM-III-R* that some school districts believe is excluded from the federal definition of seriously emotionally disturbed; a type of behavioral disorder in which persistent, negative, hostile, antisocial behavior impairs daily life functioning.

Confidential school records—Private files of students, which are often not kept at the child's school; they include test scores, observations, family history, and evaluations of social, academic, and other skills.

Conflict resolution curriculum—An educational violence prevention strategy that helps develop empathy, impulse control, and skills in communication, problem solving, and anger management.

Congenital defects—Abnormalities in the child originating before birth.

Congenital onset—The presence of a condition at birth.

Consent—Parents demonstrate that they agree to let the school take an action that affects their child's education. This is usually in the form of a parent signing his or her name to a form or letter describing the action the school wishes to take.

Construct—The concept or the characteristic that a test is designed to measure

Consulting teacher—A specially trained teacher who serves as a resource person to advise and provide instructional support to teachers who have students with disabilities in regular classrooms.

Continuum of services—Full range of educational services arranged in a stair-step fashion, where one level of service leads directly to the next one. *See also* Cascade of services *and* Array of services.

Convergent thinking—The process of reaching conclusions by using known facts; using thinking skills associated with academic learning such as memory, classification, and reasoning.

Cooperative learning—An educational method that emphasizes group cooperation and success through activities rather than individual competition.

Council for Exceptional Children (CEC)—The largest professional organization of special educators concerned with all exceptionality areas, founded by Elizabeth Farrell in 1922.

Creativity—A form of intelligence categorized by advanced divergent thought, the production of many original ideas, and the ability to develop flexible and detailed responses and ideas.

Criterion-referenced test—A measure to ascertain an individual performance compared to a set of criterion. The person is evaluated on his or her own performance and not in comparison to others.

Critical thinking—Evaluative thinking; problem-solving abilities.

Cross-categorical—Classes available to students with a variety of disabilities, usually according to level of severity.

Curriculum—A systematic grouping of content, activities, and instructional materials.

Curriculum-based assessment (CBA)—A method of evaluating children's learning and the instructional procedures by collecting data on students' daily progress on each instructional task.

Curriculum Based Measurement (CBM)—The form of progress monitoring that is scientifically validated is Curriculum Based Measurement (CBM)—CBM is one way of tracking and recording a child's progress in specific learning areas. Using CBM, teachers regularly assess students' performance (e.g., each week) using bery brief, simple tests. The results help teachers determine whether students are learning well from their instructional program. CBM results also provide the teacher with the information needed to tailor instruction for a particular student. CBM practices, supported by a great deal of research, are available in pre-reading, reading, spelling, mathematics and written expression for grades 1-6. CBM procedures have also been developed for kindergarten and middle school.

Cystic fibrosis—A disorder of chronic lung infections and malabsorption of food.

Deaf—A profound hearing disability; a person who is deaf cannot understand sounds in the environment, such as speech and language of others, with or without the use of a hearing aid; hearing cannot be used as the primary way to gain information.

Deducing—A thinking skill where a person comes to a conclusion from known facts or general principles; a type of convergent thinking.

Deinstitutionalization—Decreasing the number of individuals with disabilities living in large congregate facilities.

Delayed development—Development along the normal sequence of developmental milestones but at a slower than normal rate.

Delinquency—Illegal behavior, which may or may not be the result of a behavioral disorder, committed by juveniles.

Developing Understanding of Self and Others (DUSO)—A commercially available instructional program designed to increase language, cognitive, and social skills for students in the primary grades.

Development—Changes in functioning through the acquisition of knowledge, skills, and behavior.

Developmental delay—A lag in child development in any one or more of the five domains, which are cognitive, communication, physical, adaptive, and social or emotional.

Developmental disability—A condition that originates in childhood and results in a significant handicap for the individual, such as mental retardation, cerebral palsy, epilepsy, and conditions associated with neurological damage.

Developmental domains—An educational philosophy and approach for organizing educational objectives and classifying children's problems according to four domains: cognitive, motor, social, and communication.

Diagnosis—Process of identifying an individual as having a disability by using a series of standardized tests and observational procedures. *See also* Assessment.

Dignity of risk—Enhancing the human dignity of individuals by enabling them to experience the risk taking of ordinary life that is necessary for normal growth and development.

Direct instruction—A method of teaching academic subjects; involves systematic instruction of the skill to be learned and the collection of data evaluating the effectiveness of the teaching procedure selected.

Direction observation—A direct method of assessing problem behaviors in which the teacher systematically records, by time and condition, the frequency with which identified problem behavior occur.

Disability—A problem or condition that makes it difficult for a student to learn in the same way as most other students. This may be short term or long term.

Disabled—Refers to an objective, measurable organic dysfunction or impairment.

Discipline—Teaching students self-control; fostering self-management of behavior; teaching students to follow the rules of proper conduct.

Discrepancy—A difference or variance; in learning disabilities, the difference between actual achievement and that expected by intellectual functioning. Prior to 2004, IQ scores were compared to achievement scores and if there was a large discrepancy between the two numbers the student was identified as having a learning disability. Through the reauthorization of IDEA 2004, schools can identify or develop alternate systems of identification which can then be applied to all students.

Discrepancy formulas—Formulas developed by state educational agencies or local school districts to determine the difference between a students' actual achievement and expected achievement based on scores from tests of achievement and intelligence.

Discrepancy scores—The scores resulting from the application of a discrepancy formula; used in some states to determine eligibility for programs designed for students with learning disabilities.

Distance education—The use of telecommunications to deliver live instruction by content experts to remote locations.

Distractibility—A measure of an individual's inability to screen out extraneous stimuli.

Divergent thinking—Using creative thinking skills such as fluency, flexibility, originality, and elaboration; usually, conclusions are reached by reorganizing information and developing a variety of responses.

Down's syndrome (also called Down syndrome)—A chromosomal disorder that causes identifiable physical characteristics and usually causes delays in physical and intellectual development and puts individuals at high risk for communicative disorders and mental retardation.

Dual exceptionalities—Two or more noted deviations from the norm in behavioral or learning levels.

Due process—A set of rights having to do with how decisions are made; the act of following legal steps to ensure that employees are treated fairly and according to the law; a constitutional guarantee ensuring that fair laws and fair process will be used before the government can deprive a person of life, liberty, or property.

Due process hearing—A formal meeting held to settle disagreements between parents and schools in a way that is fair to the student, parents, and the school; when the parents and the special services committee cannot reach an agreement on the types of services and the educational program for a student, a third party settles the dispute. This meeting is run by an impartial hearing officer.

Duration—In relation to an IEP, this signifies the length of time an exceptional student will need a special program or service during the school year or extended school year.

Dyscalculia—Impaired ability to calculate or perform mathematical functions.

Dyslexia—Impaired ability to read, often caused by brain damage.

Early childhood special education (ECSE)—Provides meaningful and appropriate childhood experiences for children aged birth to five who because of some handicapping condition are not likely to benefit from regular early childhood and preschool experiences. These children may be at risk of becoming delayed or developmentally handicapped.

Early childhood programs—Preschool, daycare, and early infant school programs that involve students with disabilities and their families, designed to improve the speech, language, social, and cognitive skills of the students attending.

Early intervention—Early intervention is the process of providing services, education and support to young children who are deemed to have an established condition, those who are evaluated and deemed to have a diagnosed physical or mental condition (with a high probability of resulting in a developmental delay or special need that may affect their or impede their education.

Early Intervention Program for Infants and Toddlers with Disabilities—The Program for Infants and Toddlers with Disabilities (Part C of IDEA) is a federal grant program that assists states in operating a comprehensive statewide program of early intervention services for infants and toddlers with disabilities, ages birth through age 2 years and their families.

Echolalia—A stage in language development characterized by repeating (echoing) words or sentences initially spoken by other people.

Ecological assessment—Taking into consideration all dimensions of the individual's environment, including the individual him- or herself.

Educable mentally retarded (EMR)—A term formally used for people with mild mental retardation.

Educational diagnosticians—Professionals trained to test and evaluate individual children and youth to determine whether they are eligible for special education, and, if so, what special services they require.

Educational placement—The location or type of classroom program (for example, resource room) arranged for a child's education; the setting in which a student receives educational services.

Eligibility staffing—A meeting at which a group of school staff members recommend a student's eligibility for special education programs and services. This decision is made on assessment and other information, and parents may be asked to attend.

Emotional disturbance—A term used interchangeably with *behavioral disorder*.

Emotional maturity—The ability to act, think, and feel in ways similar to other students one's age.

Environmental risk factors—A category of at-risk children who are born biologically and genetically normal but whose environment includes poverty, abuse, and neglect or whose parents have mental health problems or are addicted to substances at a young age.

Enrichment—A common approach to teaching gifted students, whereby topics or skills are added to the traditional curriculum or a particular topic is studied more in depth.

Epilepsy—A physical disorder marked by repeated disturbances to the central nervous system, often manifested in recurrent seizures.

Evaluation—A manner of collecting information about special learning needs, strengths, and interests. It is used to help decide if there is a need for special services and programs. It may include giving individual tests, observing the child, reviewing records, and interviewing parents and peers. Assessment or judgment of special characteristics such as intelligence, physical abilities, sensory abilities, learning preferences, and achievement.

Exceptionality—Refers to children and youth who differ sufficiently from the norm to warrant special consideration in housing, schooling, and/or transportation. Includes gifted as well as those with mental, behavioral, sensorial, and physical disabilities.

Exclusion—The denial of educational opportunities to a student; an appropriate term to use when the educational plan is detrimentally inappropriate to the child's needs.

Externalizing behaviors—Behaviors, especially aggressive behaviors, directed toward others.

Fetal alcohol syndrome (FAS)—A condition where a baby is born with mental impairments, behavioral problems, and perhaps some physical disabilities caused by the mother drinking alcohol during the pregnancy.

Flexibility—A characteristic of creative thinking; the variety of ideas produced by an individual.

Fluency—Smoothness and rapidity in skills; this term is associated with quickness in thinking; in speech, in the rate, flow, and pattern of oral speech; in reading, the rate of correct oral reading; also used synonymously with *proficiency* or *mastery* in a variety of academic subjects.

Follow-up—To provide later monitoring, evaluation, diagnosis, or treatment after the initial diagnosis or treatment of a condition.

Follow-up study—A longitudinal research study that usually analyzes the adult outcomes of people who were subjects in a research study when they were children.

Formal operational thinking—The final stage of cognitive development, which extends from age twelve on.

Free appropriate public education (FAPE)—The term used in the Education of the Handicapped Act and the Individuals with Disabilities Act (IDEA) to describe the right of every student to a special education that will meet his or her individual special learning needs, , including supportive services and highly individualized educational programs.

Full continuum of services—With reference to special education, the availability of instructional arrangements appropriate for a full range of disabilities from least severe to most severe.

Full integration—Physical and social participation in a regular program on a full-time basis.

Full-service school—An environment providing programs and services to include all integrated support systems necessary for the education, health, and well-being of a child.

Functional exclusion—The inappropriate placement of a child in an educational program.

Functional skill—A skill or task that will be used in the individual's normal environment.

Future Problem Solving Program—A national competition and instructional program developed by Torrance and his colleagues to teach creative problem solving; students attempt to find positive solutions to real issues such as the nuclear arms race and water conservation.

Generalize—The process of transferring knowledge or skills learned in one situation to untaught situations; the ability to expand upon knowledge by applying it to novel situations; the transfer of learning from particular instances to other environments, people, times, and events.

Genetic factors—Factors affecting an individual's characteristics that are of a hereditary nature.

Gifted—A term describing individuals with high levels of intelligence, outstanding abilities, and capabilities for high performance.

Goals 2000: Education America Act of 1994—Legislation that provides resources to states and communities to develop and implement education reforms that will help students reach academic and occupational standards.

Group homes—Apartments or homes in which a small number of individuals with mental retardation live together as part of their community and receive assistance from service providers.

Habilitation—An individualized program of education, training, and supportive services designed to enhance the abilities of an individual with mental retardation.

Handicap—Environmental or functional demands placed upon a person with a disability as he or she interacts in a given situation; an individual's reaction to his or her disability.

Head Start—Nationally, federally funded early intervention programs designed primarily to help young children who live in poverty; these programs typically assist at-risk preschoolers by providing an accepting and responsive environment that encourages thinking and communicative skills.

Health impairments—Physical health problems limiting strength.

Health-related problems—Problems generated by physical child abuse, AIDS, and other health problems of children and other individuals.

Hearing impaired—A general term that describes both *hard-of-hearing* and *deaf*.

Hemiplegia—Paralysis of one lateral half of the body or part of it resulting from injury to the motor centers of the brain.

High achiever—A student who expects success and views it as incentive to work harder.

High intelligence—A combination of traits such as the ability to understand complex relationships, to think abstractly, and to solve problems; usually demonstrated by achieving scores on intelligence tests that fall two standard deviations above the mean, or approximately 130 and above.

High-stakes test—A test used to provide results that have important, direct consequences for examinees, programs, or institutions involved in the testing.

Home or hospital teacher—A special teacher who teaches in the child's home or hospital when the child must be absent from school due to health problems.

Homogeneous grouping—Placing students together in a class according to their type of disability.

Human immunodeficiency virus (HIV)—A virus that affects the immune system and impairs the individual's ability to fight infections; often develops into AIDS.

Hyperactive—Persistent, excessive movement; overactivity with or without a clearly defined purpose; the individual is unable to sit or concentrate for long periods of time.

Identification—To seek out and identify children with disabilities within special educational categories.

Illinois Test of Psycholinguistic Abilities (ITPA)—A test to identify students as learning disabled, intended to determine strengths and weaknesses of individual students; also thought to identify students' learning styles and preferences to assist in instructional planning.

Inactive learners—Students who do not become involved in learning situations, approach the learning task purposefully, ask questions, seek help, or initiate learning.

Incidental learning—Knowledge gained as a result of other activities and experiences not specifically designed to teach the knowledge learned; learning that takes place spontaneously or nondeliberately; not focused on a specific task.

Inclusion—In a school setting, inclusion involves educating all children in regular classrooms all of the time, regardless of the degree or severity of individual student disabilities. Effective inclusion programs take place in conjunction with a planned system of training and supports. Such programs usually involve the collaboration of a multidisciplinary team that includes regular and special educators (or other personnel) as well as family members and peers.

Independent study—A common approach to the education of the gifted that allows a student to pursue and study a topic in depth on an individual basis.

Individual transition plan (ITP)—A written plan that identifies the skills and supportive services that an individual needs to function in the community after schooling is completed.

Individualized education program (IEP)—An IEP, which is required by the Individuals with Disabilities Education Act, is a plan for an education program specific to an individual. This plan is developed collaboratively by the school and the parents. The regulations require meetings between school personnel, parents, and other individuals as well as written documents.

Individualized family service plan (IFSP)—The IFSP, which is also required by IDEA, is a written plan for infants and toddlers from birth to three years old who receive early intervention services. The regulations require that children receive early intervention services in "natural" environments (settings that are natural and normal for the child's age peers who do not have disabilities) to the maximum extent possible. Like the IEP, the IFSP must be written with the family's involvement and approval.

Individualized habilitation plan (IHP)—A written plan used to provide educational and social services to individuals living in an intermediate care facility.

Individualized instruction—Instruction planned to meet the individual needs of students; they are presented with instructional tasks reflecting their own pace of learning, pinpointing exactly what the student does and does no know and providing instruction based on that information.

Individuals with Disabilities Education Act (IDEA)—Formally referred to as the Education for All Handicapped Children Act (EHA); originally passed as PL 99–142 in 1975; amended in 1986 by PL 99–457 to also provide instruction and services to infants and toddlers; amended and reauthorized again in 1990 under PL 101–476, which strengthened transitional programs for adolescents and young adults with handicaps; ensures a free appropriate public education in the least restrictive environment for all children and youth with disabilities.

Individual written rehabilitation plan (IWRP)—A written plan used to provide vocational rehabilitation for adults with disabilities.

Inference—Decision or opinion based on assumptions; a conclusion drawn by using reason.

Information processing theory—The suggestion that learning disabilities are caused by an inability to organize thinking and to approach learning tasks systematically.

Instructional goals—A statement about learning that includes a result to be achieved after specific instruction.

Instructional objectives—Statements about learning that relate to an overall goal; includes a description of the student's behavior, the conditions under which the behavior is to occur, and the criteria for acceptable performance.

Integrated classes—Regular education classes where students with special needs learn alongside students without disabilities.

Integration—Often used synonymously with *mainstreaming* to encompass efforts to move students from segregated classes into the mainstream. However, it is sometimes used to represent the ultimate objective of inclusion.

Intellectual functioning—The actual performance of tasks believed to represent intelligence, such as observing, problem solving, and communicating.

Intelligence—A person's ability to think, learn, or understand, often measured by standardized tests.

Intelligence quotient (IQ)—The numerical figure, with a score of 100 being average, obtained from a standardized test; often used to express mental development of ability.

Interactional approach—Stresses communication with a highly interactive environment that encourages the acquisition of language.

Interactive video—A computer-controlled educational device students use to view and hear instructional presentations and make choices regarding the pace and order of the presentations.

Interdisciplinary instruction—An educational approach that involves studying a topic and its issues in the context of several different disciplines; sometimes used in the education of the gifted.

Internalizing behaviors—Behavior that is withdrawn into the individual.

Intervention—A change in instructing a student in the area of learning or behavioral difficulty to try to improve performance and achieve adequate progress.

Interviews—A method of gathering information from an individual by asking a set of questions.

Itinerant specialists—Specialists from various disciplines—special education, speech, occupational therapy, physical therapy—who work at different schools across the week; some travel great distances as they go from school to school.

Job coach—An individual who works alongside people with disabilities, helping them to learn all parts of a job.

Joint Committee on Learning Disabilities (JCLD)—A committee representing a number of professional, parent, and consumer organizations concerned with learning disabilities. These organizations include the International Reading Association, Orton Dyslexia Society, American Speech-Language-Hearing Association, Council for Learning Disabilities, Division for Learning Disabilities (a division of the Council for Exceptional Children), Learning Disability Association of America (formerly ACLD), Council for Children with Communication Disorders (a division of the Council for Exceptional Children), and the National Association of School Psychologists.

Labeling—Assigning an individual as belonging to a group; associating an individual with a specific handicapping condition.

Language—The formalized method of communication used by people; includes the signs and symbols by which ideas are represented and the rules that govern them so the intended message has meaning.

Language delay—When children do not develop skills as quickly as their age peers; some children with language delays are language disordered and require the special assistance of a specialist so they can ultimately use language proficiently.

Language disorder—Difficulty of inability to master the various language systems and their rules of application, morphology, phonology, syntax, and pragmatics, which then interferes with communication.

Learning disabilities—A handicapping condition whereby the individual possesses average intelligence but is substantially delayed in academic achievement.

Learning Disability Association of America (LDAA)—An advocacy organization of parents of children with learning disabilities that provides information to the public, schools, and community programs, formerly called Association for Children with Learning Disabilities (ACLD) and Association for Children and Adults with Learning Disabilities (ACALD).

Learning strategies—Instructional methods to help students read, comprehend, and study better by helping them organize and collect information strategically.

Learning styles—The systematic strategies individuals use to gain new skills and information.

Least restrictive environment (LRE)—LRE is an essential principle of IDEA, which states that "to the maximum extent appropriate, children with disabilities, including children in public or private institutions or other care facilities, are educated with children who are nondisabled." The law requires that the least restrictive environment be determined on an individual basis and be based on the child's IEP. The LRE is the legal basis for inclusive programs.

Life skills—Daily living skills used to shop and cook, and to organize, clean, and manage home.

Likert scale—A system used in questionnaires or surveys to provide a forced-choice answer along a scale of some dimension (such as "strongly agree" to "strongly disagree," or "like" to "dislike"); the numbering system used typically ranges from 1 to 5 or from 1 to 7.

Local education agency (LEA)—Typically a local school district, but may be a cooperative district or set of districts that are funded as a single unit.

Low achiever—A student who expects failure and sees no value in expending effort to learn.

Low-incidence disability—A disability that occurs infrequently; the number of new cases is very low.

Magnet school—A center school that serves children who do not live in the immediate neighborhood; some magnet schools are designed to serve children whose parents work in a nearby area; other magnet schools emphasize a particular theme (such as theater arts, math, and science).

Mainstreaming—An older term that may imply a more gradual, partial, or part-time process (e.g., a student who is mainstreamed may attend separate classes within a regular school or may participate in regular gym and lunch programs only). In mainstreamed programs, students are often expected to fit in the regular class in which they want to participate, whereas in an inclusive program the classes are designed to fit all students.

Mean—The sum of all scores divided by the number of scores; the average.

Medically fragile—An individual who requires medical assisted technology for life support and is more acutely involved than those who are described as chronologically ill.

Mental age—An age estimate of an individual's mental ability; expressed as the average chronological age of children who can ordinarily answer the questions in the test correctly; derived from a comparison of the individual's IQ score and chronological age.

Mental retardation—A handicapping condition that affects cognitive functioning and adaptive behavior.

Mentorships—An approach to education of the gifted where a student is paired with an adult in order to learn to apply knowledge in real life situations.

Metacognition—A cognitive behavior modification strategy in which students use self-management techniques to help them remember what they are taught by taking themselves through systematic problem-solving steps.

Mild mental retardation—The level of mental retardation that usually includes individuals with IQs from approximately 50–55 to 70–75.

Minimal brain dysfunction—A condition associated with learning disabilities; a result of functional problems of the central nervous system or brain damage that can impair individuals' ability to learn or succeed at academic tasks.

Mobility—The ability to travel safely and efficiently from one place to another.

Modeling—An instructional tactic where one person demonstrates how to do a task or solve a problem while another person observes and copies those steps. The expert or teacher will demonstrate the particular skill that's being taught to address a situation (i.e., failure, teasing, accusing, and peer-pressure).

Moderate mental retardation—The level of mental retardation that usually includes individuals with IQs from approximately 35–40 to 50–55.

Morphology—Rules that govern the structure and form of the words; the basic meaning of words.

Motivation—The presence of internal incentives to learn or perform, influenced by previous success or failure.

Motor development—An area in which young children are assessed that includes gross motor (large movements such as walking, jumping, rolling over) and fine motor (smaller movements such as grasping, touching, reaching).

Multicultural—Reflecting more than one culture.

Multidisciplinary team—A group of professionals responsible for evaluating a child and making decisions about the child's educational program. The team must include at least one teacher or other specialist with knowledge in the area of suspected disability.

Multihandicapped—Having more than one handicapping condition; the combination causes severe educational problems. Also called *multiply handicapped.*

Muscular dystrophy—A progressive and pervasive weakness of all muscle groups characterized by a degeneration of muscle cells and their replacement with fatty and fibrous tissue.

National Education Association (NEA)—One of the largest organizations of professional educators.

Natural Environments—The settings are natural or normal for the child's age peers who have no disabilities. Part C of IDEA requires "to the maximum extent appropriate to the needs of the child, early intervention services must be provided in natural environments, including the home and community settings in which children without disabilities participate. By definition, natural environments mean "settings that are natural or normal for the child's age peers who have no disabilities. The provision of early intervention services taking place in a natural environment is not just a guiding principle or suggestion, it is a legal requirement.

Neurological system—Having to do with the central nervous system; the brain, spinal cord, and systems of neural pathways.

Noncategorical—An approach to special education that does not classify or differentiate among disabilities or exceptionalities in providing services.

Noncategorical classes—Classes that are available to students with a variety of handicaps, usually according to the levels of severity (mild, moderate, severe, profound) of individuals' handicaps.

Nondiscriminatory testing—Assessment that properly takes into account a child's cultural and linguistic diversity.

Nonverbal behavior—Physical or gestural communication or actions, like raising your hand for teacher attention, or smiling; body language; communications that do not use oral language.

Norm-reference tests—Instruments used to ascertain an individual's performance compared to others' performance on the same instrument.

Normal curve—A bell-shaped curve plotting the normal distribution of human traits such as intelligence in a population.

Normalization—Making available to people with mental disabilities patterns of life and conditions of everyday living that are as close as possible to or indeed the same as the regular circumstances and ways of life of society.

Objective permanence—The knowledge that objects exist even if they are hidden from view.

Observation systems—Systematic ways to observe and record the functioning of an individual's behavior; usually made for assessment purposes.

Occupational therapist (OT)—A professional who directs activities designed to improve muscular control as well as develop self-help skills; a medical professional who provides treatment from a physician's prescription that enhances daily living and personal care activity skills through the development of fine and gross-motor activities relating to the upper extremities.

Ophthalmologist—A medical doctor specializing in disease processes of the eye.

Oral approach or method—One method of instruction advocated for students who are deaf where they learn to communicate (both receiving and sending information) orally without using sign language.

Orthopedic impairment—A physical impairment that adversely affects academic performance, including impairments caused by congenital anomaly, disease, and trauma.

Osteogenesis imperfecta—A musculoskeletal disorder characterized by brittle bones, especially early in life.

Other health impaired—Having impaired strength, vitality, or alertness as a result of chronic or acute health problems that may require modification in the educational setting; a category in IDEA of children who have limited strength due to health problems.

Outreach programs—Specialized programs offered in local communities by residential schools or centralized agencies serving students with special needs.

Overlearning—More or longer practice than necessary for the immediate recall of a task.

Paraplegia—Paralysis of both legs.

Partial seizure—A seizure beginning in a localized area and affecting only a small part of the brain.

Peabody Language Development Kits (PLDK)—A commercially available series of instructional programs that include prepared lessons aimed at improving language and cognitive skills.

Peabody Picture Collection (PPC)—A set of picture cards that can be used to improve individuals' vocabulary and expressive language skills in teacher-prepared activities.

Peace education curriculum—An educational violence prevention strategy that looks at violence prevention interpersonally and within and among societies as a whole.

Peer coaching—A staff development process that allows fellow teachers to observe each other conducting their classes for the purpose of providing constructive, nonthreatening feedback.

Peer mediation programs—Programs that train students and teachers to identify and mediate conflicts that occur in the school.

Perceptual—Refers to selecting, organizing, and interpreting environmental stimuli.

Perceptual motor process—A basic process involved in learning (along with memory and attention);a deficit may affect the way information is perceived.

Perceptual motor training activities—The training of motor, visual, or auditory skills in an effort to improve academic performance.

Perceptual skills—Ability to decode stimuli and act accordingly.

Performance feedback—Reviewing the situation and identifying the positive and negative consequences of behaviors.

Pervasive developmental disorder (PDD)—A term used in reference to children and youth who are affected in many basic areas of psychological development at the same time and to a severe degree. This classification has only one subgroup: autistic disorder; almost always diagnosed in infancy or early childhood.

Pervasive development disorder, not otherwise specified—Same as pervasive developmental disorder but does not fit the autistic disorder criteria.

Phenylketonuria (PKU)—A metabolic disorder present at birth in which certain proteins are not absorbed by the body, causing damage to the central nervous system and leading to mental retardation; can be prevented by a special diet.

Physical disabilities—Problems with the body that interfere with functioning.

Physical integration—The actual physical placement of a handicapped student into an environment with nonhandicapped students.

Physical therapist (PT)—A professional trained to treat physical disabilities through nonmedical means such as exercise, massage, heat, and water therapy.

Physically challenged—A term sometimes used to describe persons with physical disabilities.

PL 94–142—*See* Individuals with Disabilities Education Act.

Portfolio—In assessment, a systematic collection of educational or work products that hve been compiled or accumulated over time according to a specific set of principles.

Postlingual—Refers to the period after the acquisition of speech.

Postnatal—After birth.

Prelingual—Refers to the period before the acquisition of speech; specifically, before the echolalic stage of speech development.

Prelingually deaf—Individuals who lost their ability to hear before they developed language.

Prenatal—Before birth.

Preoperational thinking—The second stage of cognitive development, which extends from eighteen months or two years to age six or seven. At this stage the child goes from egocentric and static thinking to concept formation and ability to classify objects into groups.

President's Committee on Mental Retardation (PCMR)—A committee of citizens appointed by the president of the United States to annually report to the president on issues related to mental retardation.

Presumed central nervous dysfunction—A medical term referring to the cause of some learning disabilities; thought by some special educators to be misleading because it gives the impression that nothing can be done about the condition. Indicates some brain or neurological damage that impedes individual's motor and/or learning abilities.

Print Disabilities—An umbrella term for a variety of physical, visual and or learning issues that interfere with the ability to read print.

Problem solving—The process of searching out, analyzing, and evaluating facts using various reasoning and thinking skills in order to develop appropriate and effective solutions.

Procedural safeguards/due process—Procedural safeguards are provided in IDEA to ensure fair procedures in the identification, evaluation, and placement of children with disabilities. For example, the law requires that parents receive written notice if a change is proposed in the child's placement. If conflicts arise between parents and schools, either party may request a due process hearing with the right to be represented by others, to have a written record, and to enter an appeal. In order to advocate for their own children, parents must be familiar with these procedural safeguards.

Proficient—Status of being at a satisfactory level of performance on an achievement standard.

Profound mental retardation—The level of mental retardation that usually includes individuals with IQs below approximately 20 to 25.

Program assessment—The process of gathering data from multiple sources to determine how well the organization is accomplishing its goals.

Program planning—An educational assessment that takes place after determining eligibility to determine the student's specific strengths and weaknesses and conditions under which learning will be most successful.

Progress Monitoring—A scientifically based practice used to assess students' academic performance and evaluate the effectiveness of instruction. Progress monitoring can be implemented with individual students or an entire class.

Protected resources—Those instructional resources that are tagged explicitly to serve low achieving students; that is, they cannot be allocated by the teacher to other students.

Psychoeducational approach—An educational outgrowth of psychodynamic theory and prescriptive approaches; this approach is child-centered and believes that the problem resides in an internal, unconscious state.

Public policy—Guidelines legitimized by government that are implemented by laws and regulations and that reflect current or future perceived needs of society or a segment of society.

Pullout programs for gifted students—The most common educational placement for gifted students; gifted students spend part of the school day in a special class.

Quadriplegia—Paralysis of all four limbs.

Reason abstractly—Ability to think about ideas and concepts; ability to draw inferences or conclusions from known or assumed facts.

Recognition & Response (R&R)—An adaptation of the Response to Intervention (RTI) Model for Pre-K. The Recognition part involves screening all children and monitoring the progress of those "requiring specific interventions." The Response part involves creating content interventions, learning activities, and scaffolding strategies from simplest to most complex which create a framework for teachers when reviewing information in order to organize interventions. Problem solving, a third part of the R&R process, involves shared decisions for planning and evaluation.

Regular class—A typical classroom designed to serve students with disabilities as well as "regular" students.

Regular education initiative (REI)—A position held by some special educators that students with disabilities should be served exclusively in regular education classrooms and should not be "pulled out" to attend special classes; an attempt to reform regular and special education so they are a combined system that maximizes mainstreaming.

Related services—Services that may or may not be part of the classroom curriculum but support classroom instruction, such as transportation, physical therapy, occupational therapy, and speech and language therapy.

Reliable—Refers to the consistency and dependability of the results of information-gathering processes; consistency may be over time, from one observer to another, from one form of a test to another, or within the same observer for different times and different children.

Residential instruction—A facility in which the exceptional person receives 24-hour care.

Resocialization—The process of reestablishing values and standards held in common among the teaching staff. The phenomenon is a result of sustained staff interaction and is essential for meaningful culture changes of the sort necessary for a shift to total quality management.

Resource program—Refers to when students attend a regular class for the majority of the day and go to a special education class several hours per day or for blocks of time each week.

Resource teacher model—Students with physical disabilities who attend regular classes are provided services through a pullout program in a resource room in which a special education teacher is available.

Response to Intervention (RTI) – A framework for providing high-quality instruction for all students so as to provide a sound foundation for quality instruction also creating a systematic, data-driven process to determine students' specific learning needs.RTI is a multi-step approach to providing services and interventions to students who struggle with learning at increasing levels of intensity. Progress students make at each stage of intervention is closely monitored. Results of this monitoring are used to make decisions about the need for further resource based instruction and/or intervention in general education special education or both.

Restructuring—Reform proposals that dramatically change the structure of school districts or the manner in which they operate.

Rett Syndrome—A genetic abnormality affecting one in every 10,000 females. Initially, the infant grows normally but begins to have delays in gross motor skills such as crawling or sitting. Eventually brain and head growth slows followed by fait problems, seizures and loss of purposeful hand movement. Some girls display autistic—like symptoms, such as loss of social interaction and communication. Most individuals with Rett Syndrome live well into middle age, making early intervention highly significant.

Ritalin—A drug sometimes prescribed to help students with ADD focus their attention on assigned tasks and reduce their hyperactivity.

Role-playing—Acting out a situation in an action-oriented manner.

Schizophrenia—A type of psychosis; a severe emotional disorder in which the individual becomes irrational, and often delusional and socially withdrawn.

School nurse—A health care professional available at schools to respond to medical crises, distribute medication, and provide consultation and education.

School psychologists—Professionals trained to test and evaluate individual children to determine whether they are eligible for special education, and, if so, what special services they require.

Screening—An assessment procedure used to detect students who may be at high risk for developing serious learning or behavior problems.

Section 504 of the Vocational Rehabilitation Act—A federal law that forbids discrimination in federally funded programs against people with handicaps.

Selective attention—Ability to attend to the critical features of a task.

Selective listening—Focusing on only one sound in an environment, such as a lecture.

Self-advocacy—A social and political movement started by and for people with disabilities to speak for themselves on important issues such as housing, employment, legal rights, and personal relationships.

Self-concept analysis—A means of gaining insight into how one views self-performance or worth.

Self-contained special education classes—Special classes attended by students for most of the school day; at other times, they are mainstreamed into regular education activities. Special classes that provide intensive, specialized instruction; some of these classes are categorical, for students who have the same handicapping condition (e.g., all having hearing impairments), and some are cross-categorical, where class members have different disabling conditions (e.g., several with mental retardation, several with learning disabilities, etc.).

Self-management techniques—Strategies that assist students in identifying and solving problems independently.

Self-stimulation—Self-initiated behavior that generates a desirable sensation.

Sensorimotor—The first stage of cognitive development, occurring between birth and eighteen months or two years of age.

Sensorineural hearing loss—A hearing loss caused by a malfunction of the inner ear or the eighth cranial nerve.

Sensory development—An assessment area for young children that generally includes assessing the child's ability to see and hear.

Seriously emotionally disturbed—A condition with one or more of the following characteristics that exists over a long period of time and that substantially interferes with normal functioning: (1)an inability to learn that cannot be explained by intellectual, sensory, or other factors, (2) an inability to build or maintain satisfactory interpersonal relationships, (3) inappropriate behavior, a general pervasive mood of unhappiness, or depression, or (4) a tendency to develop physical symptoms or fears associated with problems. The term is referred to in IDEA to categorize students with behavioral disorders and emotional disturbance.

Service manager—The person who oversees the implementation and evaluation of an individualized family service plan.

Severe mental retardation—The level of mental retardation that usually includes individuals with IQs from approximately 20–25 to 30–35.

Sheltered workshops—Special segregated workshops attended by some adults with disabilities.

Sickle-cell anemia—A hereditary blood disease characterized by anemia resulting from insufficiency of red blood cells, impairment of liver function, swelling of limbs and joints, severe pain, loss of appetite, and general weakness.

Social interactions—Skills and behaviors occurring between or among people involving social, rather than academic, relationships.

Socioeconomic status (SES)—The status an individual or family unit holds in society, usually determined by one's job, level of education, and the amount of money available to spend.

Sociometric procedures—A means of assessing social preferences of individuals within a group setting.

SOMPA (System of Multicultural Pluralistic Assessment)—An assessment that is sensitive to the influence of cultural factors on performance.

Spasticity—A form of cerebral palsy characterized by involuntary muscle contractions and inaccurate and difficult voluntary motion.

Special education—Individualized education for children with special needs.

Special services committee—A multidisciplinary team, including school administrators, regular and special education teachers, diagnosticians, related service personnel, and the child's parents, who follow the process of identification, planning, writing the IEP, and evaluating the child's progress in special education.

Speech—The vocal production of language, considered the fastest and most efficient means of communicating.

Speech therapist—Responsible for the diagnosis, prescription, and treatment of a full range of communication problems, including speech and language disorders.

Standard of deviation—A statistical measure that expresses the variability of a set of scores.

Standard score—Numbers converted from raw scores with constant means and standard deviations.

State education agency (SEA)—Typically a state's department of education or division of special education.

Statute—Law passed by a legislature or Congress and signed by a governor or the president.

Strabismus—A lack of coordination of ocular muscles resulting in "cross-eyed" appearance.

Subgroups—The groups of individuals who cluster by various characteristics and are already identified as members of a larger group.

Substance abuse—The deliberate and nontherapeutic use of chemicals such as alcohol, tobacco, drugs, gasoline, cleaning fluids, and glue in ways that contribute to health risks, disruption of psychological functioning, or adverse social consequences.

Supportive services—Auxiliary services—such as adaptive physical education, speech and language, audiology, and physical or occupational therapy—required by many students with handicaps.

Systematic instruction—A data-driven method of instruction in which an instructional program is designed from data gathered from formal and informal assessment procedures, instruction is constantly evaluated, and student performance is measured to gauge the effectiveness of the program.

Task analysis—The act of breaking a task or skill into its component parts for instructional purposes.

Technology Related Assistance for Individuals with Disabilities Act of 1988—A federal act that provides funding and allows for technical assistance to persons with disabilities as they select and use assistive technology.

Telephone Devices for the Deaf (TTDs)—A teletypewriter connected to the phone system that allows people who are deaf to communicate telephonically.

Test standardization—Scores of a large number of individuals are collected and analyzed so that the score of a single individual can be compared to the norm.

Test validity—The extent to which a test actually assesses what it claims to assess.

The Association for Persons with Severe Handicaps (TASH)—A professional organization that promotes educational, policy, vocational, and habilitative research and discussion of people with severe disabilities.

Topological brain mapping—A method of analyzing the structure of the brain; used in research into biological causes of learning disabilities.

Total communication approach or method—The philosophical position regarding the development of communication skills that advocates the use of whatever enables the child who is deaf to communicate with others; also refers to the combined use of speech, signing, gestures, speechreading, fingerspelling, and even reading and writing in an attempt to extend the communication capabilities of the child who is deaf.

Trainable mentally retarded (TMR)—A term formerly used for people with moderate mental retardation.

Transfer training—How to use the skills taught in real life situations.

Transition—A period when a person is making a change; in special education, it refers to the period between one setting to another, such as from preschool to school, from elementary to middle school, and from school to work; the process of moving from adolescence to adulthood, within the context of social, cultural, economic, and legal considerations.

Traumatic brain injury—A category of disability included in IDEA in 1990; an injury to the brain that impairs learning, behavior, or motor functioning.

Triplegia—Paralysis of three limbs.

Trisomy 21—The most common cause of Down's syndrome; this genetic anomaly occurs when a third chromosome attaches to the chromosome 21 pair.

Universal Design for Learning (UDL) – UDL lessons and classroom materials created that are flexible enough to accommodate different learning styles; important in an inclusion setting; rethinking how a lesson is developed in order to customize that lesson for students with different needs and learning styles.

Universal Screening – A step taken by school personnel early in the school year to determine which students are "at risk" for not meeting grade level standards. Universal screening can be accomplished by reviewing a student's recent performance on state or district tests or by administering an academic screening to all students in a given grade. Students whose scores on the screening fall below a certain cutoff point are identified as needing continued progress monitoring and possibly more intensive intervention.

Valid—Refers to the ability of an evaluation to yield results that will serve the purposes they are intended to serve; the "truth" component of an evaluation procedure; the extent to which a test measures what the authors state it will measure.

Visual impairments—An overall term that includes all levels of visual loses.

Written symbols—Graphic means, such as the written alphabet, used to relay messages.

About the Author

Arlene Sacks is the Academic Coordinator of the Ph.D. Program at The Union Institute, Miami, Florida. Previously, she directed graduate programs at Barry University and St. Thomas University, both located in Miami. She received her doctorate at West Virginia University in 1974. Previous publications include "Social and Educational Family Empowerment Program Cooperates to Ensure Academic Success," in *The Developmental Process of Positive Attitudes and Mutual Respect: A Multicultural Approach to Advocating School Safety,* R. Duhon-Sells, S. Cooley, and G. Duhon (eds.), "The Full-Service School: A Holistic Approach to Effectively Serve Children in Poverty," in *Reaching and Teaching Children Who Are Victims of Poverty,* A. Duhon-Ross (ed.), 1999; "Brain Research: Implications for Early Intervention—Theory, Research, and Application," in the *Journal of the International Association of Special Education,* 1998; "Children in Protective Services: The Missing Educational Link for Children in Kinship Networks," in *Multisystem Skills and Interventions in School Social Work Practice,* E. M. Freeman, C. G. Franklin, R. Fong, G. L. Shaffer, and E. M. Timberlake (eds.), 1998; and "Positive Peace Education: From Philosophy to Curriculum," in *Exploring Self Science through Peace Education and Conflict Resolution,* R. Duhon-Sells (ed.), 1997.

Index